NEVADA COUNTY LIBRARY

☑ W9-AZA-361

Best Books
for Kids Who
Think
They
^
Hate to
Read

NEVADA COUNTY LIBRARY - NEVADA CITY

NOV - - 2001

LAURA BACKES

Best Books for Kids Who

Think They ^ Hate to Read

125 BOOKS THAT WILL TURN ANY CHILD INTO A LIFELONG READER

PRIMA PUBLISHING

NEVADA COUNTY LIBRARY - NEVADA CITY

© 2001 by Random House, Inc.

All rights reserved. No part of this book may be reproduced or transmitted in any form or by any means, electronic or mechanical, including photocopying, recording, or by any information storage or retrieval system, without written permission from Random House, Inc., except for the inclusion of brief quotations in a review.

Published by Prima Publishing, Roseville, California. Member of the Crown Publishing Group, a division of Random House, Inc.

All products mentioned in this book are trademarks of their respective companies.

PRIMA PUBLISHING and colophon are trademarks of Random House, Inc., registered with the United States Patent and Trademark Office.

A complete list of credits and permissions begins on page 357.

Library of Congress Cataloging-in-Publication Data
Backes, Laura.
   Best books for kids who (think they) hate to read : 125 books that will turn any child into a lifelong reader / Laura Backes.
      p.   cm.
   Includes bibliographical references and index.
   ISBN 0-7615-2755-9
   1. Children—Books and reading—United States. 2. Reading—Parent participation—United States. 3. Children—Books and reading—United States—Bibliography. 4. Children's literature—Bibliography. I. Title.

Z1037.A1 B17 2001
028.5'5—dc21   2001024658

00 01 02 03 DD 10 9 8 7 6 5 4 3 2 1
Printed in the United States of America

Visit us online at www.primapublishing.com

For Matthew, my all-time favorite reading buddy;
for Dad, who told me my first stories; and for Jon,
who helps me live happily ever after.

Contents

Introduction · viii

1. Where Do I Start? · 1

2. When Bribes Fail: How to Help Your Child
    Learn to Love Reading · 9

3. Finding Your Way: A Road Map to
    the Children's Book Department · 19

4. Taking the First Step · 33

5. Keeping It Simple · 59

6. Making the Transition · 99

7. Stretching It Out · 163

8. Ready for Anything · 263

Further Recommended Reading · 345

Resources for Parents · 353

Credits and Permissions · 357

General Index · 363

Author Index · 381

Index of Book Titles · 385

Introduction

’VE ALWAYS had a passion for children's books, and since 1986 I've been lucky enough to turn that passion into a means for earning a living. As an editor, writing instructor, and publisher of a newsletter for children's book authors, I've studied countless books for children and edited hundreds of manuscripts for aspiring writers. And I learned that, though styles and trends come and go, the elements that make a book appealing to a child are timeless and constant. I truly believed that children's books were better written than books for adults and that the most magical, brilliant children's books would always rise to the top where anyone who so desired could easily discover them.

And then I became a parent.

When I introduced my son to books, my first surprise was that he wasn't always taken with the books I love. My second surprise came when, at about a year of age, he had already developed preferences for certain styles of artwork and types of stories. I had to retrain myself to look at books through his eyes.

When I met other parents of young children, their first question was always "Can you give me a list of books my child would like?" Most of these parents understood the value of reading to their children and were eager to nurture a love of books, but they were lost when they entered a bookstore or library. They didn't know where to begin. As my son grew older, I met parents of young reluctant readers. Their question was more desperate: "Can you recommend some books that will help my child want to read?" The answer, I realized, was not as simple as handing over a list of titles.

If you're the parent of a child who doesn't like to read, you've probably felt the same frustration when faced with a wall of children's books at the store or library. This book is created for you, to help you navigate through the ocean of available titles and choose what's right for your child. I'll show you how to recognize a good book for reluctant readers and how to match a book to your child. Because every child is different, there is no one-size-fits-all answer to which books are best, but this guide will help you develop a library your own child can love.

The titles I recommend in the second part of this book are meant to be a starting point. I've given you a mixture of genres and writing styles that I feel best embody those qualities that entice reluctant readers to open a book. Those books that appeal to your child now can be stepping-stones to other works by the same author or to similar books. I've also provided lists for further reading to help you along. My recommendations are by no means a final tabulation of everything wonderful that's ever been published, but I believe that handing you specific, well-chosen information is better than bombarding you with every choice available.

> Those books that appeal to your child now can be stepping-stones to other works by the same author or to similar books.

Above all, remember this: Your child may acquire the skills necessary to read the printed word, but if he or she doesn't develop a love of reading and an emotional connection to books and ideas, reading will never become a big part of his or her life.

So keep it fun. There are worlds waiting to be explored between the covers of books. Provide a gentle nudge, but allow your child to run in whatever direction he or she chooses. That's the only way children ever find the books that really speak to them.

Good luck, and happy reading!

P.S. I have a special gift for you: a free Web site just for readers of *Best Books for Kids Who (Think They) Hate to Read*. At www.best books4kids.com, you'll find useful articles, links to all the Internet resources mentioned in this book, a discount bookshop (featuring all the titles reviewed in this book), and much more. Stop by for a visit.

Chapter One

Where Do I Start?

"It is only in childhood that books have any deep influence on our lives." —GRAHAM GREENE

I HAD MY FIRST literary epiphany when I was six years old. I had mastered *Green Eggs and Ham* by Dr. Seuss and was reading to myself. Suddenly it occurred to me that this book was about more than a pesky guy named Sam who was using his favorite meal to coerce a finicky eater. It was about not jumping to conclusions before you had all the facts. It was about taking risks, trying new things. Even though Dr. Seuss didn't directly express these ideas in the text, I got it. And I never looked at books the same way again.

You may have similar memories of childhood books that left a profound impact on how you viewed the world. Or perhaps you didn't read much as a child and now realize what you missed. Either way, as a parent you want your child to joyfully explore the world of books, experience the excitement of reading, and marvel at discovering new ideas.

But what if your child doesn't like to read?

Some children don't take easily to reading. They may have difficulty learning to read, they may naturally gravitate toward other activities like watching television or playing sports, or they may never have been taught that reading is an activity that can be fun, interesting, or rewarding. In the publishing industry, the term "reluctant reader" is sometimes used to refer to a child who is reading below grade level. Here, I'm using the term to mean a child who would rather do anything but read.

"There seem to be several 'critical junctures' in children's reading patterns," says Nancy Bentley, coordinator for information and technology at Mann Middle School in Colorado Springs, Colorado. "One happens early on—in first grade. If by the end of first grade, a child is having difficulty reading or is a reluctant reader, jump right on that and inquire about testing. Another hurdle seems to be in third and fourth grade. If students are poor readers, they may be able to skate by until the time when content becomes more important. Then reading comprehension will plummet, and they will not understand the science and social studies books. And then, of course, there's middle school—a time when hormones and computers and MTV and peers are much more exciting than reading. Kids who are poor readers will simply stop trying."

If you're the parent of a reluctant reader, words like these can make you panic. Don't. Because you know your child better than anyone else, you're in the perfect position to help nurture the skills—and motivation—your child needs to become a lifelong reader. The earlier you start, the better. But you can help improve your child's reading abilities at any age. You don't need any special training, just some basic knowledge about how children's books are written for different reading levels and where to start looking for the best books for reluctant readers.

What Do the Reading Levels on Books Mean and Should I Pay Attention to Them?

MOST CHILDREN'S BOOKS have a designated reading level printed on the inside jacket flap or the back cover. Sometimes it's an age range (noted as "Reading Level: 6–9" or simply "06–09") and sometimes just a number ("Reading Level 2.3," which means the average student in the third month of second grade can read the book). Reading levels are determined by one of several systems that compute the length and complexity of the words and sentences in a book. Many schools assign reading levels to students on the basis of their performance on standardized tests and use these numbers to match students to appropriate books.

While reading levels can be useful in determining approximately how well your child reads, they should be taken with a grain of salt. "Grade [reading] level is just a statistical formula, and it's different from school to school. It's used mostly for tests and to develop reading series," says Dr. Susan Mandel Glazer, director of the Center for Reading and Writing at Rider University. "Parents shouldn't be worried about what the designated reading level of a book is but whether a child is interested in it and can read some of the words. We let children select books by testing themselves. If they miss five words on a page, the book's too hard. If they don't miss any words, the book's generally too easy. This self-selection device allows the children to feel secure in their abilities."

> Because you know your child better than anyone, you're in the perfect position to help nurture the skills your child needs to become a lifelong reader.

"There is so much emphasis these days on standardized testing; it is difficult not to be acutely aware of your child's reading level," adds Nancy Bentley. "However, kids need the freedom to choose books that are at their personal interest or recreational reading level—which is usually below their instructional [grade] level."

Knowing a book's reading level is useful to you as a parent for two reasons. First, you can find it easier in the bookstore or library. Easy readers are grouped in one place, chapter books and middle-grade novels in another, and nonfiction somewhere else entirely. Second, you know how the book is written in terms of length and content. As I'll explain in chapter 3, books present ideas, plot, and humor differently, depending on the average age and/or reading level of the reader. Match the book to your child, not your child to a book that he or she should supposedly be able to read. And remember that reading is a skill that gets better with practice. The more a child who is below "grade level" reads, the sooner he or she will catch up.

Where Do I Start?

A WELL-MEANING PARENT enters the local Barnes & Noble superstore looking for a book for her 9-year-old son. Ten minutes later, she finally locates the middle-grade fiction aisle, which she knows are books for ages 8 to 12. After staring at shelf after shelf of paperbacks and rows of series that seem to multiply before her eyes (is a series with 50 titles better than one with 20?), she grabs the novelization of her son's favorite television show and heads for the cashier.

> Match the book to your child, not your child to a book that he or she should supposedly be able to read.

If this sounds familiar, don't feel guilty about resorting to mass-market depictions of your child's beloved movies, television shows, or superheroes. As I discuss in chapter 2, reluctant readers are drawn to the familiar, so the novelization of a well-known story from another medium is a perfectly acceptable place to start. But the bigger issue is plowing through the field of available books to find those your child will want to read. Picking a book at random doesn't work; finding one *you* like is just as bad. You need to start by understanding the key elements of books that appeal to reluctant readers, both those with poor reading skills and those who just aren't interested in books.

In chapters 4 through 8, I've used the following eight criteria to choose the books I've recommended for reluctant readers. Each of the books selected must embody at least three of the qualities listed here. Armed with these guidelines, you can scan the first few pages of a promising book or even read book reviews to get a good sense of appropriate titles. Once your child has established a reading habit, he or she can learn to choose books in the same way.

Eight Characteristics That Give Books "Reader Appeal"

Humor Kids love books that stir their emotions. That's why scary stories and suspenseful mysteries are so popular with elementary school readers. But the number one quality that draws reluctant readers to a book over and over is humor. When kids laugh, they're enjoying the reading process, and they'll want to do it again.

The type of humor changes with the age and emotional development of the reader. Books written for children from age 5 to 8 involve wordplay and silly, illogical situations. Jokes can border on the mildly naughty, such as an adult getting a pie in the face or anything including the word "underwear." Once children enter the middle grades (ages 8–12), the humor is more cerebral and subversive. The main character is usually the butt of the joke and often is a willing participant. Situations are more complex and drawn out and thus require a setup and the reader's anticipation of the funny outcome. Jokes contain not only witty dialogue but also broader physical comedy that breaks the rules or results in public embarrassment. The reader understands the possible consequences of such behavior and also appreciates the reactions of the surrounding characters.

Well-Defined Characters Children identify strongly with the characters in their books, be they animals, people, or space aliens. So the characters in books for any age must be three-dimensional beings with strengths and weaknesses. Think of the wildly popular young wizard Harry Potter, the classic Winnie the Pooh, or the Grinch from *How the Grinch Stole Christmas.* Children often imitate characters like these because they're so clearly drawn. In books for younger readers, the characters usually have one or two overriding traits that influence the course of the story. Older readers can handle more complex characters whose personalities slowly unfold along with the plot. In either case, the characters must be believable enough for the child to care about them and want to follow them through the entire book.

Characters are important in nonfiction as well, though these "characters" are real people. In biographies, for example, the author ideally focuses on the aspects of the subject's personality that are relevant to the reader and writes about this person in a way that makes him or her come to life.

Fast-Paced Plot Reluctant readers don't have the patience to wade through long passages describing brilliant sunsets or glistening morning dew on the hillside. They want action. The story should start moving on page one, and soon after the reader should know what problem the main character will be trying to solve. In nonfiction, the author needs to pose interesting questions, reveal astonishing information, or grab the reader with exciting facts right up front. If you as a parent don't feel pulled into a book by the end of the first chapter, your child won't either.

Concise Chapters The way chapters are constructed goes a long way toward pacing a book. Ideally, chapters will contain one clear event (or one specific point in nonfiction) that logically leads to the next event in the following chapter. In good reluctant reader fiction, chapters either are self-contained, sequential episodes in the lives of the main characters or end on an emotional upswing, such as in the middle of a suspenseful scene or at a climactic moment. The former allows the reader to rest between chapters and still feel a sense of fulfillment. The latter makes the reader want to turn the page to see what happens next.

Suitable Text This point has to do with the actual words and sentence structure of the text, not the content. You want your child to be comfortable with the level of writing without becoming bored. So the text has to challenge the reader but not overwhelm him or her. This balance may involve trial and error on your part. But in general, reluctant readers' comprehension is higher than their reading comfort level, so you want to look for books that speak to your child intellectually while conveying the ideas in a simple, straightforward way.

> If you don't feel pulled into a book by the end of the first chapter, your child won't either.

Kid Relevance The issues raised in fiction should be important and relevant to your child's life. Relevance entices your child to become involved with the characters and what happens to them in the story. The conflicts and emotional elements of the plot need to be relevant *to your child and his or her experience and frame of reference.* This is important because adults often fall into the trap of choosing books they think their children *should* be reading or those that teach something they *should* learn. The heroine may be a princess locked in a castle, but she's still trying to convince her overprotective parents to let her stay up past her bedtime. The books must appeal to your child and allow your child to absorb the story through his or her viewpoint.

In nonfiction, look for books that relate the topic directly to the reader, such as a biography that portrays the childhood of a famous person, science that explains how everyday appliances work, or nature books about what lives in the backyard.

Unique Presentation (Nonfiction) Who isn't bored by dry recitations of facts and dates? Nonfiction that appeals to reluctant readers steers away from textbook presentations and finds new, interesting ways to deliver the information. The use of humor, anecdotes, and first-person accounts paired with a lively writing style will hold a reader's attention. Books that take a unique slant on the subject and slip learning in through the back door are also winners. Barbara Seuling, a former editor and author of many children's books, including the Freaky Facts trivia series published by Doubleday (sadly out of print but still available in many libraries), says, "Good nonfiction should make the reader want to know more and inspire the reader's curiosity. Parents can give kids short bursts of interesting information and humor, as in freaky facts, riddles, or pictures with interesting captions, to get them talking. Kids will make the connection between the written source and the discussion."

Visual Appeal (Nonfiction) While appealing illustrations can add to the fiction-reading experience, the look of nonfiction books plays a vital role in how the reader comprehends and processes the information. The design of the book should match the subject, with generous "white space," good leading (the space between the lines of text), and a type style that's easy to read. The illustrations or photographs should be eye-catching and break up the text in a way that allows the reader to absorb the written information while getting visual reinforcement from the pictures.

As you begin to apply these criteria to children's books, planting appealing books in the hands of your reluctant reader will soon become second nature. And then that field of children's books at your local superstore will magically shrink to a nice, manageable garden.

Chapter Two

When Bribes Fail

HOW TO HELP YOUR CHILD
LEARN TO LOVE READING

T HESE DAYS, SCORES on standardized reading tests are being used to judge the performance of students and school districts alike. But, as Betty Carter, a professor at Texas Woman's University's School of Library and Information Studies, points out in her article "Formula for Failure" (*School Library Journal,* July 1, 2000), true reading can't always be tested:

> In fact, for the last several years America's schoolchildren have shown steady growth in reading acuity. But what I call reading behavior—the practice of lifelong readers— extends beyond the ability to pronounce words or select the main idea from a passage. Rather, the desire to read grows from the knowledge that print offers something wonderful and meaningful in a person's life. And only to the extent that one senses this kind of wonder will one continue to read.

As a parent, you understand that no amount of gentle coercion, bribery, or outright threats will make your child care about reading. The love of books must be discovered on your child's own terms. But, like Hansel and Gretel, you can discreetly drop bread crumbs that lead your kid in the right direction. In chapter 1, I outlined the elements of good books for reluctant readers.

Here are 10 tips to help you bring those books and your child together.

1. Play It Cool

IF YOUR CHILD isn't reading as much as—or as well as—you'd like, he probably knows it and is already stressed out about the situation. So don't make it worse by nagging, demanding, or begging that he spend more time with books. Instead, show what an integral and enjoyable role reading plays in everyday life. First, teach by example. Let your child see you reading everything from newspapers to cereal boxes. If you come across information your kid would enjoy, share it: "Look at the caption to this picture. It says this dog rescued her owner from a fire."

Second, subtly rope your child into reading during routine activities. Do this together so your reluctant reader doesn't feel pressure to perform: "Let's look at the TV schedule and pick a movie to watch tonight." The Internet offers a wonderful opportunity to link reading with interesting visual images. You can demonstrate the role that reading plays in cyberspace while you browse for Web sites on your child's favorite subject ("First we type in 'soccer.' Oh look, this site says it covers soccer game rules. Let's try that one.") Your child will learn that reading provides a gateway to all sorts of useful information.

2. Know Your Child

IF YOU HAVEN'T spent much time recently in the children's section of a library or bookstore, you might not realize that children's books are available on virtually any subject for all levels of readers. Is your daughter crazy about horses? There are books about raising and caring for horses, biographies of great equestrians, and fiction series featuring groups of young horse lovers. Does your son collect model trains? You can choose from books that chronicle the history of the railroad, nonfiction accounts of famous train robberies, or adventure stories that take place on cross-country train rides. No matter how broad or obscure, your child's passions can be found in a book. And while you're in the library, don't overlook the children's magazine section. Magazines offer bite-size, high-interest articles and fiction geared to very specific age-groups.

You already know your child; what you might not know is how to connect your child's interests with books. Start with what gets your kid excited. Is your daughter planning her first slumber party? Check out the numerous slumber party guides for adolescents, complete with recipes for snacks and instructions for doing each other's hair. Does your son fancy himself Buzz Lightyear from the *Toy Story* movie? Get the book. While you're at it, pick out a few other books about astronauts and space travel. To find books on any subject, you can start by doing a word search in the children's card catalog at the public library.

Begin with two or three books that are heavily illustrated and appealing to look at. Then simply leave them around the house where your child is sure to find them. And remember: Play it cool. If your kid asks where the book came from, just say, "I saw that at the library and thought it looked interesting." If the subject's important enough to your child, the book will be opened sooner or later.

3. Let Your Child Lead

ACCORDING TO THE Reading Is Fundamental (RIF) organization, kids are more motivated to read if they choose their own books (for more tips from RIF, see its Web site at http://www.rif.org or call 1-877-RIF-READ). This means that if your child prefers comic books over a literary tome, let him read the comics. At this point, you're just opening the door to reading; if your child crosses that threshold with enjoyable reading material, eventually he'll work his way up to the classics. He may also want to read the same book over and over. This is common and nothing to worry about. Reluctant readers are more comfortable with the familiar, and reading a book repeatedly helps them master the text. Once they feel this sense of accomplishment, they'll move on to other books.

Dr. Susan Mandel Glazer, director for the Center of Reading and Writing at Rider University, suggests that parents can help nonreaders pick books by narrowing the choices. Find three or four books on a subject your child loves and say, "Here are some books you might like. Why don't you choose one to take home?" She also advocates asking open-ended questions, such as "Which of these books should we read next?" instead of questions with yes or no answers ("Do you want another book?").

> Kids are more motivated to read if they choose their own books.

Of course, as a parent you have every right to monitor your child's reading and to veto choices in which you feel the content is inappropriate. But try to allow your child as much freedom as possible, especially as he or she gets older. And don't judge your child's personal interests, however narrow they may seem. Children get a sense of power when they become "experts" on a topic, and your daughter's tenth reading of that book on tornadoes may just mean that you have a budding meteorologist on your hands.

4. Don't Give Up "Lap Time"

WHEN YOUR CHILD was younger, you probably spent time with her on your lap as you read picture books. Now that your child is older, this "lap time" doesn't have to end, even if it means reading side by side. Many children in fourth or fifth grade still love being read to. This helps them associate reading with pleasant, shared family time. And since a child's comprehension is often ahead of her reading level, you can read stories aloud that are more complicated than those she can read on her own.

When children are struggling to learn to read, it's helpful if you first read the entire book to them. Have your child sit next to you and watch as you move your finger along the text and read it aloud. Read clearly and slowly, but with a natural rhythm and inflection (don't say each word in a halting monotone). Older children can benefit from having the first chapter of a book read to them. This piques their interest in the story and motivates them to continue on their own.

Keep up the read-aloud routine as long as your child will let you. Even if your child is reading independently, hearing a story helps reinforce the rhythm of the written word, promotes reading comprehension, and exercises the imagination. If your child is still learning to read, he may want to read aloud to you or alternate chapters with you. Reading aloud also lets your child show off his budding reading skills. But if your child suffers from performance anxiety, don't push it. Just gently encourage him to read those familiar stories to himself.

5. Discuss Books with Your Child

ON THE SURFACE, this may smack of testing or homework, so you should approach this tip with caution. However, children—especially those in the middle elementary grades—love giving their opinions on books, and they can be brutally honest. You can start by casually remarking on a book you've read or one you shared with your child: "I thought that joke the boy played on his sister was really funny. How exactly did that go again?" Funny catchphrases or names of characters can become part of the family lexicon. Ask your child which aspects of the story she liked or didn't like. Relate an event in a book to your child's life ("Peter really didn't like his new school. Did you feel like that when we first moved here?"). Give your child a chance to share her knowledge ("Tonight, let's see if we can find the Big Dipper just like in your astronomy book."). Above all, keep it an exchange of ideas, using the book as a springboard for other conversation. Don't turn it into a book report.

Discussing books you've read together shows your child that reading involves ideas and information that are linked to other parts of life. It also shows that you respect his interests and opinions. Be aware, though, that as your child approaches adolescence, he may not want to talk about what he's reading (at least not with his parents). Don't force it. Teens often use books to explore their independence and examine new ideas. They may not want to share this newfound personal connection with reading.

6. Don't Push Your Child to "Read Up"

THINK ABOUT IT: When you choose books for your own reading enjoyment, do you pick genres you're familiar with, subjects that engross you, and writers who have the ability to make the rest of the world disappear? Or do you reach for weighty volumes filled with words you can't pronounce or require a dictionary to understand? Most of us, if we're honest, prefer the lighter side of reading. But many parents sidestep the fun and instead opt for educational enrichment in books for their kids. As Betty Carter cautions in her article "Formula for Failure," "Real readers don't automatically progress to more and more difficult texts. Instead, they move up some levels for some things and down some levels for others. To discourage that movement denies children the very behaviors lifelong readers embrace."

If your child finds the books interesting instead of overwhelming, she'll want more: more information about gymnastics, more names of dinosaurs, more stories about ballerinas. When books satisfy a child's curiosity, she doesn't lock herself into one reading level or worry about moving up. And neither should you. Reading is in itself an educational activity. Also, realize that children's authors strive to present their information in a clear, compelling manner, regardless of the age of their audience. I've learned more about history from editing children's book manuscripts than I ever did from my textbooks in school.

> If your child finds the books interesting instead of overwhelming, she'll want more.

7. Expose Your Child to a Broad Range of Experiences

I'LL NEVER FORGET the first time I took my son, 3 years old, to the natural history museum to see a traveling exhibit of dinosaur fossils. Matthew's face lit up the moment we walked in the door and the huge skeletons of prehistoric beasts came to life in his imagination. Over the next several months, Matthew learned to recognize meat-eating versus plant-eating dinosaurs, assembled his own "paleontologist kit," and correctly pronounced dozens of dinosaur names (much to the surprise of his speech therapist). This intense interest spilled over to insects, spiders, and animals from meerkats to platypuses. He drew pictures of them, pretended to be them, and, of course, read about them.

The more life experiences a child has, the more likely he'll discover passions and interests that connect with books. Those experiences can be as exotic as traveling abroad or as commonplace as baking chocolate chip cookies. The key is in the doing: Coax your child away from the television or computer and actively involve him in the world. Even a half-hour walk through a local park can get the mind moving (What are clouds made of? Why does that flower smell so sweet? Where does that squirrel live?). End your walk at the library and find answers to all those questions.

8. Connect Reading with Other Activities

JUST AS EXPERIENCES can lead to reading, books can be a springboard for activities. After reading about ladybugs, take a magnifying glass out to the backyard and find some live specimens. Read a humorous story about a family camping trip with your child before you go on vacation to Yellowstone National Park. Historical fiction that's set in a nearby city can be especially fun: After your child finishes the book, make a field trip to the story's location and see if any of the places still exist. Many nonfiction books have hands-on activities or experiments for children that demonstrate the scientific principles explained in the text. There are even books for young artists that show (through words and diagrams) how to draw animals and people. Get your child a new set of colored pencils and let her translate those written instructions into pictures.

> The more life experiences a child has, the more likely he'll discover passions and interests that connect with books.

9. Promote Your Child's Oral Language

DR. SUSAN MANDEL GLAZER of the Center for Reading and Writing at Rider University says that among the groups of kids who are most likely to be poor readers are "the ones who don't have the oral vocabulary." This is most crucial in the early elementary grades, when children are learning to read, but even older children who can't adequately express themselves can be at risk.

So talk to your kids. Encourage conversation with open-ended questions ("What did you work on in basketball practice today?") as opposed to simply asking, "How was your day?" ("Fine" will be the likely response.) And actually listen when your children answer. They'll try harder to elaborate or reach to find the right words if they sense you're genuinely interested in what they have to say. Reading, writing, and speaking are different forms of the same thing: communication. As your child gets more adept at expressing herself, she'll become more skilled at understanding what an author wants to express to her through the written word.

10. Give Your Child Time to Read

THE READING IS FUNDAMENTAL organization suggests keeping books in the car or tucking books into your child's sports bag or backpack so he can read between activities. While this works for kids who are already avid readers, reluctant readers might not take the initiative necessary to squeeze in a chapter before baseball practice.

The thing I remember most about my childhood weekends and summers is long hours of unstructured time. My mother limited television to one hour a day during the week and two hours on Saturday mornings, so for the rest of the day my brothers and I had to amuse ourselves. I never remember my mother telling us to pick up a book, but we were all voracious readers because it was something to do. In other words, we had the motive, we had the opportunity, and because we didn't need a day planner to keep our schedules straight, we had the time.

Many well-intentioned parents today feel pressure to involve their children in a huge range of activities from sports to music to Scouting groups. Extracurricular pursuits can certainly enrich a child's life, but it's easy to turn a well-rounded child into an overbooked one. Children today miss out on the "downtime" so prevalent in the past. It's during those quiet, unscheduled hours that kids have the chance to think, daydream, and read.

I've left this tip for last because I feel in many ways it's the most important. Giving your child free time to read means he'll have the opportunity to discover his interests, choose his own books, and absorb what those books mean to him. Making time to talk with your child about books or anything else opens up the connections books have with other parts of life. And if you give your child his own library card and hours to freely roam the stacks, you're saying, "Here's a wonderful world you can explore however you want." To a child, that can be a tremendous gift.

Chapter Three

Finding Your Way

A ROAD MAP TO THE CHILDREN'S BOOK DEPARTMENT

I LEARNED TO READ with Dick and Jane. They lived in a nice, white, suburban neighborhood (along with Mother, Father, baby Sally, and Spot the dog) contained within the pages of a series of basal readers published by Scott, Foresman and Company from the 1930s through the 1960s. Dick and Jane—whose world extended all the way to the edge of their backyard—were supposed to represent Everykid. They spoke in clipped sentences and had a tendency to repeat the same words over and over. They were always polite, cheerful, and boring.

Today, educators know that it makes more sense to teach reading with real books rather than giving children literature after they've learned to read. But the prescribed formula found in the Dick and Jane series did show us that beginning readers have very specific needs when it comes to the structure of the text. As children grow more adept at reading, these needs change. And so, gradually, over the past 40 years, the general category of children's books has expanded and divided into several distinct age-groups. It's helpful that you as a parent understand the differences between these age-groups—not because you want to pigeonhole your reluctant reader into choosing books that are meant for her age but because each type of book speaks to a different level of reading ability and sophistication.

Picture Books

WHEN YOU say "children's books" to most people, they think of picture books. These books are usually 32 pages long, with color illustrations on every page. The text can range from a few words to a paragraph or two per page. Picture book stories rely on strong visual elements (lots of action and concrete descriptions), with the text and illustrations being intricately connected. The average audience for picture books are children ages 3 to 8.

I do not cover picture books in chapters 4 through 8 because these books are designed to be read out loud to a child (some non-fiction presented in the picture book format is intended for children up to age 10, and I have included a few of those titles later in this book). True, many children can read picture books to themselves (and enjoy doing so) once they develop good reading skills, but the language and sentence structure employed in the average picture book is too complex for a beginning reader to master. However, you can certainly reach for some of the many wonderful picture books available when you're reading to your child. Because it's easy to become involved in the story through the illustrations, picture books are a great way to engage your child in literature. You can also get a sense of the kinds of books your child likes (folktales, humorous stories, animal stories, and so on).

> Picture books are a great way to engage your child in literature.

Some picture books tell a story with simple, rhythmic, or repetitive text. If your child is just learning to read and feels intimidated by longer books, these picture books can help boost his confidence. Here are several examples:

Bears on Wheels by Stan and Jan Berenstein (Random House).
Many other Berenstein Bears books also feature simple, rhyming text.

Brown Bear, Brown Bear, What Do You See? by Bill Martin Jr., illustrated by Eric Carle (Henry Holt)

Dinosaurs, Dinosaurs by Byron Barton (HarperCollins). Comes with a pronunciation key at the end of the book for the dinosaurs' names.

Goodnight Moon by Margaret Wise Brown, illustrated by Clement Hurd (HarperCollins)

A House Is a House for Me by Mary Ann Hoberman, illustrated by Betty Fraser (Viking/Puffin)

If You Give a Mouse a Cookie by Laura Joffe Numeroff, illustrated by Felicia Bond (HarperCollins)

I Went Walking by Sue Williams, illustrated by Julie Vivas (Voyager)

Is Your Mama a Llama? by Deborah Guarino, illustrated by Steven Kellogg (Scholastic)

Just My Friend and Me by Mercer Mayer (Golden Books). This is one of a series of many Little Critter books, all of which embody ironic humor in the illustrations.

Mouse Paint by Ellen Stoll Walsh (Harcourt)

Roar and More by Karla Kuskin (HarperCollins)

Picture book fiction has its own section in a bookstore or library, arranged alphabetically by author. Picture book nonfiction is arranged alphabetically by subject on separate shelves (and is often mixed in with older nonfiction).

Easy Readers

EASY READERS—sometimes called early or beginning readers—are designed for children ages 5 to 9 who are learning to read on their own. Though it may look like a picture book (32 pages and color illustrations throughout) with just a few words of text per page, a true easy reader appears more "grown-up." It's smaller in size and sometimes divided into short chapters, and the text is more prominent on each page. Joanne Rocklin, Ph.D., a children's writer, psychologist, and author of *Inside the Mind of a Child: Easy Reader Fiction/Fiction Transition Books* (Children's Book Insider), says that "good easy readers make kids *want* to read." The settings and characters are familiar to a child of this age, and the plots are simple and relevant to a young child's life.

As you examine easy readers in the bookstore or library, you'll notice that most publishers have series divided into different reading levels for preschool through third or fourth grade. Don't worry about the age designation, but do look at the layout of the text. Easy readers tell stories primarily through action and dialogue (which helps break up the text on the page). The earliest easy readers contain sentences of three or four words that embody one clear thought. The typeface is large, and each sentence is given its own line on the page. Full-page color pictures illustrate the text as in picture books. As the reading levels move up, sentences get a bit longer and more complex (you'll see commas linking two thoughts together) and paragraphs expand to four or five sentences. But the emphasis on action, dialogue, and clearly drawn familiar characters remains the same.

One thing that separates easy readers from picture books is the type of humor. Joanne Rocklin explains that once children get to be about 6 years old, they can keep two ideas in their mind simultaneously, and so they love "illogical logic, or logical non-sense," as in wordplay and riddles. Here's an excerpt from her easy reader *Three Smart Pals* (Scholastic):

"I want to race!" said Hal.
"How can I race alone?"
"Race with the clock!" said Sal.
"Silly," said Hal. "Clocks can't swim!"

Humor is the hallmark of easy readers. Whether it's fiction or nonfiction, if kids are laughing, they'll want to read. I do cover some easy readers that will appeal to reluctant readers in third and fourth grades in chapters 4 and 5. Here are some examples for those children who are younger or still learning basic reading skills:

Are You a Ladybug? by Judy Allen and Tudor Humphries (Kingfisher BACKYARD BOOKS series)

Are You My Mother? by P. D. Eastman (Random House BEGINNER BOOKS series)

Astronaut: Living in Space by Kate Hayden (Dorling Kindersley/ DK Readers series)

A Bad, Bad Day by Kirsten Hall, illustrated by Laura Radar (Scholastic HELLO READER! series)

Big Machines by Karen Wallace (Dorling Kindersley EYEWITNESS READERS series)

Frog and Toad Are Friends by Arnold Lobel (Harper I CAN READ series)

> Humor is the hallmark of easy readers.

Froggy Gets Dressed by Jonathan London, illustrated by Frank Remkiewicz (Scholastic). London has written many books featuring the likable Froggy.

The Gym Day Winner by Grace Maccarone, illustrated by Betsy Lewin (FIRST GRADE FRIENDS series, Scholastic HELLO READER! series)

Hooray for Snail! by John Stadler (HarperCollins)

Itchy, Itchy Chicken Pox by Grace Maccarone, illustrated by Betsy Lewin (Scholastic HELLO READER! series)

Little Bear by Else Holmelund Minarik, illustrated by Maurice Sendak (Harper I CAN READ series)

Slower Than a Snail by Anne Schreiber, illustrated by Larry Daste (Scholastic HELLO MATH READER! series)

Wake Up, Sun! by David L. Harrison, illustrated by Hans Wilhelm (Random House STEP INTO READING series)

Who Stole the Cookies? by Judith Moffatt (Grosset ALL ABOARD READING series)

Easy reader fiction has its own shelves in both libraries and bookstores. In libraries, it's arranged alphabetically by author. Bookstores may also arrange it this way, but I've noticed in some large chain stores that easy reader fiction is shelved by publisher. So, if you're looking for a specific book in a big bookstore, it's helpful to know who published it.

You'll have to hunt a little harder for easy reader nonfiction, which is written with the same sentence structure as easy reader fiction but can cover virtually any topic of interest to early elementary school children. Libraries might mix it in with other juvenile nonfiction or keep it next to the easy reader fiction (looking up books in the card catalog is the best way to find them). In bookstores, if the nonfiction is part of an easy reader series (such as Random House's Step Into Reading), then it's probably shelved with the easy reader fiction by the same publisher. However, if it's part of a nonfiction series (such as Dorling Kindersley's EYEWITNESS series), then it's found in the children's nonfiction section arranged by subject. When all else fails, ask a store employee for help.

Chapter Books

CHAPTER BOOKS—or transition books, as they're sometimes called—provide a bridge over that chasm between easy readers and full-length, middle-grade books. Written for kids between ages 7 and 10, chapter books have no illustrations (or just a few black-and-white pictures), smaller typeface, and chapters up to about six pages long. Fiction is under 100 pages; nonfiction is often shorter (nonfiction for this age-group may be more heavily illustrated and might look like a 48-page picture book). The text of chapter books is composed of longer paragraphs (averaging four to seven sentences), more description, and a less controlled vocabulary.

Chapter books begin to move away from relying completely on action and dialogue to tell a story and delve briefly into the inner, emotional lives of the characters. The stories themselves are more complex, sometimes involving subplots. Chapter book fiction looks like novels that have been distilled to their essence and features characters 7 to 11 years old.

Transitional nonfiction can range from a picture book illustrated with photographs but containing two or three paragraphs of information on each page to a 64-page biography broken into short chapters. Anything that's a high-interest topic presented in a lively manner (adding to the reader's knowledge of the subject without burying her under abstract concepts) can qualify. In this book, I discuss chapter books primarily in chapter 6.

> Written for kids between ages 7 and 10, chapter books have no illustrations (or just a few black-and-white pictures), smaller typeface, and chapters up to about six pages long.

Chapter books don't usually have their own place in a bookstore. If the publisher's reading level is listed as ages 6 to 9, they're often mixed in with the easy readers (some easy reader series include chapter books at the higher levels). If the publisher designates the book for ages 7 to 10, then it will probably be found with the middle-grade fiction. Libraries tend to use the same system. Nonfiction is placed with other children's nonfiction (by subject), unless it's part of an easy reader series.

Middle Grade

IN PUBLISHING CIRCLES, the middle grades are known as the golden years of reading. Ideally, the scenario goes like this: between the ages of 8 and 12, children become confident with their reading skills and devour books at a rapid rate, growing into loyal fans of certain authors or series. They can handle novels and nonfiction up to about 150 pages long, complete with complex characters, exotic settings, and compelling subplots. In fact, good middle-grade fiction mirrors the changes children are going through in their own lives as they test their independence and approach adolescence. Author Joanne Rocklin explains it this way in her book *Inside the Mind of a Child: Middle Grade Fiction/Young Adult Fiction:*

> Conflict is always a key in every good story, but in the middle grade novel the conflicts are out in the open. The subversion and war against authority and others aren't only hinted at—the protagonist dares to imagine everything in detail . . . conflict is part of the separation process in the middle years, which involves lots of deep feeling, and often anger.

Children this age will pick up a book with almost any kind of character or setting—from talking animals to fantasy to historic fiction—as long as the characters reflect the thoughts and deep emotions of their readers, who are sorting out their places within their families and peer groups. Middle graders are also developing interests in the world and reading more nonfiction and self-help books (on topics like dating or drugs).

If your reluctant reader isn't relishing books as much as you'd like, I have recommended many great middle-grade titles in chapter 7. When choosing books with your child, be aware that she's probably ready for the more realistic, complex issues addressed in middle-grade fiction and nonfiction. One mistake many parents make is underestimating their children's maturity and giving them books that will feel "babyish" to the reader. This can be easily remedied by keeping informed. "The middle school years are especially important for parents to stay in touch with adolescent literature," says Nancy Bentley, coordinator for information and technology at Mann Middle School in Colorado Springs, Colorado. "I'm sorry to say that all adults (and that includes teachers) fall off the wagon and just don't keep reading contemporary fiction and nonfiction for older kids the way parents of elementary students do. What can parents do? Go to bookstores and libraries and ask to see award-winning books and encourage their children to 'read the best.'"

> One mistake parents make is underestimating their children's maturity and giving them books that feel "babyish" to the reader.

Middle-grade fiction can be found in bookstores and libraries in the juvenile fiction section, organized alphabetically by author (some bookstores have separate shelves for middle-grade fiction series). Nonfiction is located with all the other children's nonfiction, arranged by subject.

Young Adult

TRADITIONALLY, YOUNG ADULT fiction and nonfiction have been targeted to readers age 12 and up. In recent years, however, some books carry an age designation of 10 and up. This is because, toward the end of elementary school, kids cross back and forth between middle-grade and young adult fiction.

Young adult fiction is epitomized by a character growing from being focused on his place within his family and friends to his role in larger society. Plots deal with realistic issues (regardless of the genre: fantasy, mystery, adventure, and so on) and revolve around a character's first brush with the "real" world. Taking that first step across the threshold to adulthood, the loss of innocence and coming of age are common themes. Teens and preteens are the central focus; adults are firmly in the background.

Young adult nonfiction also has a broader worldview. Topics include sociological issues, events and people who have affected world history, and scientific principles that build on basic knowledge learned in elementary school. Information is in-depth and raises questions that inspire further study. However, the best young adult nonfiction is still written in a lively, accessible, and even hip style.

I cover engaging fiction and nonfiction for the lower end of the young adult bracket in chapter 8. Young adult fiction often has its own place in bookstores and libraries, near to but apart from the children's section. Nonfiction for young adults is generally mixed in with the rest of the children's nonfiction in bookstores, but your library might mix the young adult nonfiction in with nonfiction for adults.

And now the fun begins. You have an understanding of the qualities that appeal to reluctant readers, and you know how these books are written and where they're found in the stores. You're ready to browse, discover, and read. In the next five chapters, I give detailed critiques of some outstanding books that can help plant the reading bug in children in grades 3 through 8. These are my personal favorites, but they also serve as excellent starting points for further exploration. So cancel all your appointments and spend tomorrow at the library. And don't forget to bring your kid along.

How to Use This Book

IN CHAPTERS 4 through 8, I provide detailed critiques of the books I've recommended for reluctant readers. In the two pages or so devoted to each book, you'll find the following information:

Title

Photo of the Book Cover

Author and Illustrator

Genre (such as fantasy, historical fiction, adventure, mystery, biography, or science)

Publisher and Retail Price (The hardcover [h] or paperback [p] price is listed next to the publisher. In most cases I've given the price of the paperback edition.)

Page Length (in most cases, this is the number of pages the child actually has to read)

Type of Illustrations (color, black and white, photographs)

Suggested Reading Level (It sometimes helps to know the publisher's reading level when trying to find a book in a store. However, you'll notice that I've created my own age and reading level classifications for each book since reluctant readers often don't fall within the designated category.)

Reluctant Reader Appeal (I'll list which of the eight characteristics of Reader Appeal apply to each book. These characteristics were explained in chapter 1. They are Humor, Well-Defined Characters, Fast-Paced Plot, Concise Chapters, Suitable Text, Kid Relevance, Unique Presentation, and Visual Appeal.)

Brief Excerpt from the Text

Synopsis of the Plot (fiction) or Content (nonfiction)

(continues)

Why This Book Appeals to Reluctant Readers

Who Might Like This Book

Notes to Parents (This will appear in reviews only if the book has won a major award or covers issues or themes I feel parents might want to be aware of.)

If Your Child Liked This Book, Then Try . . . (other books by the same author, or in the same genre)

How to Narrow Down the Choices

I've DIVIDED THE next five chapters into specific reading levels. I've also listed the age of the average reader just because it might help you find the books in a store or library. You'll note that the age-groups overlap; this is because a 9-year-old with average to good reading skills may read a chapter book one day and a middle-grade novel the next. For your reluctant reader, it's best to ignore the publisher's age designation and instead choose books that closely match your child's reading ability. That's why the Genre and Reluctant Reader Appeal listings are so useful. They'll help you zero in on the literary qualities that capture your child's interest and hold his attention. If a book designed for a young reader will also appeal to an older child, I've noted that in my review.

Chapter 4, "Taking the First Step," introduces some high-interest, easy-to-read books for kids who are developing basic reading skills (and remember, I listed additional easy reader titles in chapter 3). Average age of reader: 5 to 8.

Chapter 5, "Keeping It Simple," contains longer books for kids who are starting to become comfortable reading on their own. Though they have more text than beginning easy readers, these books still feature a simple sentence structure and are heavily illustrated. Average age of reader: 6 to 9.

Chapter 6, "Making the Transition," includes books with fewer illustrations and more text than easy readers. These short novels and engaging nonfiction titles are for kids who have mastered the fundamentals of reading but aren't ready for full-length middle-grade books. Average age of reader: 7 to 10.

Chapter 7, "Stretching It Out," lists books with longer texts, more complex sentence structure, and few (or no) illustrations. These books look a lot like the books kids will be reading as adults, the main difference being that the topics are relevant to children in the middle elementary grades. Average age of reader: 8 to 12.

Chapter 8, "Ready for Anything," contains novels and non-fiction with more sophisticated themes to hold the interest of readers in upper elementary grades and middle school. Average age of the reader: 10 and up.

Within each chapter, I've listed fiction titles first, followed by nonfiction. Within those two categories, I've started with the books that are easiest to read, gradually progressing to more difficult texts.

I've also provided a list of Further Recommended Reading at the end of this book. This will give you some additional titles to try once your child has given her approval—or veto—to the choices in the previous chapters. And finally, I've given you some Resources for Parents if you want to compile other reading lists or learn more about children's literature.

Good luck. I hope you and your reluctant reader have as much fun reading these books as I did.

Chapter Four

Taking the First Step

High-interest, easy-to-read books for kids who are developing basic reading skills.

FICTION

How Big Is a Foot? by Rolf Myller · page 34

Monster Manners by Joanna Cole · page 36

Gus and Grandpa by Claudia Mills · page 38

Minnie and Moo Go to the Moon by Denys Cazet · page 40

Here Comes the Strikeout by Leonard Kessler · page 42

The Cat in the Hat by Dr. Seuss · page 44

Amelia Bedelia by Peggy Parish · page 46

The Adventures of Snail at School by John Stadler · page 48

Emma's Magic Winter by Jean Little · page 50

NONFICTION

Red-Eyed Tree Frog by Joy Cowley · page 52

Dinosaur Days by Joyce Milton · page 54

Abe Lincoln's Hat by Martha Brenner · page 56

How Big Is a Foot?

by

ROLF MYLLER

Illustrator ROLF MYLLER

Genre: Fable

Publisher: Yearling, $3.99 (p)

Page Length: 48

Type of Illustrations: Color, on every page

Reluctant Reader Appeal: Humor, Fast-Paced Plot, Suitable Text, Unique Presentation

Suggested reading level: Ages 5–8

Once upon a time
there lived a King
and his wife, the Queen.

They were a happy couple
for they had everything in the World.

However . . .
when the Queen's birthday came near
the King had a problem:

What could he give to Someone who had Everything?

Synopsis This is a clever fable about how measurements became standardized. The king comes up with the perfect birthday present for the queen—a new bed (she didn't have one because beds had not yet been invented). An apprentice is hired to build the bed but doesn't know how big it should be. The king, after much deliberation, finally determines that it must be big enough to fit the queen. He asks her to lie on the floor, and then he measures (with his own feet) a rectangle 3 feet wide and 6 feet long. The apprentice builds the bed (using *his* foot as a measurement), but when the queen tries it out, the bed is much too small. The apprentice is thrown in jail, where he has time to think and realizes that the king's feet must be bigger than his own. After a sculptor makes a marble copy of the king's foot, the apprentice gives the bed another try using his new measuring device. The bed fits the queen perfectly, and the apprentice is made a prince.

Why This Book Appeals to Reluctant Readers Though this story is short and the text takes up only a few lines on each page, it doesn't have an easy reader feel. The droll tone and the math concepts will appeal to emerging readers who don't want a "babyish" book. Instead of taking up the whole page, the illustrations consist of spot art sprinkled through the text, which also keeps the book from feeling like a picture book. The story is funny and quick but subtly makes an important statement about basic math.

Who Might Like This Book Boys and girls who are fond of fables and fairy tales or light, humorous stories.

If Your Child Liked This Book, Then Try . . . *Slower Than a Snail* by Anne Schreiber, illustrated by Larry Daste (Scholastic HELLO MATH READER! series, Level 2).

Monster Manners

by

JOANNA COLE

Illustrator JARED LEE

Genre: Humorous Fantasy

Publisher: Scholastic,
$3.99 (p)

Page Length: 48

Type of Illustrations: Color,
on every page

Reluctant Reader Appeal:
Humor, Well-Defined
Characters, Fast-Paced Plot,
Suitable Text

**Suggested
reading level:**
Ages 6–8

*Rosie had just one problem.
She was always forgetting
her monster manners.*

*Monsters are supposed
to fight with their friends
and break each other's toys.*

*Rosie played nicely with everyone.
This made her mother very unhappy.*

Synopsis Rosie Monster tries her best, but she just can't master the proper manners monsters are supposed to have. She asks her best friend, Prunella, for help, and Prunella attempts to coach Rosie on making monster faces and eating with her hands, but it's no use. Rosie's parents are unhappy, and that makes Rosie unhappy too. Then a pipe breaks in the Monsters' house, and Rosie's parents call the plumber. But when they growl into the phone, the plumber hangs up. When Rosie calls and asks very politely for the plumber to come fix the leak, he agrees. After the mess is cleaned up, Rosie's parents decide that her unusual manners do sometimes come in handy.

Why This Book Appeals to Reluctant Readers The tight story line, the ironic humor, and the zany illustrations, complete with their own jokes, are sure to entice reluctant readers who need short books with simple, spare text.

Who Might Like This Book Just about any child who appreciates a good laugh while mastering basic reading skills.

If Your Child Liked This Book, Then Try . . . *It's Not Easy Being a Bunny* by Marilyn Sadler, illustrated by Roger Bollen (Random House BEGINNER BOOKS series, Grades 1–2).

Gus and Grandpa

by

CLAUDIA MILLS

Illustrator CATHERINE STOCK

Genre: Contemporary Fiction

Publisher: Farrar, Straus & Giroux, $4.95 (p)

Page Length: 48

Type of Illustrations: Color, on almost every page

Reluctant Reader Appeal: Humor, Well-Defined Characters, Concise Chapters, Suitable Text, Kid Relevance

Suggested reading level:
Ages 6–9

*"We should only
eat one doughnut hole,"
Grandpa said.
But they both ate another.
"That's enough for us,"
Grandpa said.
But they each ate
one more.*

Synopsis Gus and Grandpa have a very special relationship. This simple, warm book contains three short stories about Gus and Grandpa's times together: "The Great Dog Trainer," in which Gus tries to train Grandpa's dog and ends up making a big mess; "The Lost Car," about when Gus and Grandpa go to the grocery store and can't find Grandpa's car; and "The Birthday Party," when Gus and Grandpa made a cake to celebrate their birthdays together. Told in short, declarative sentences, the text emphasizes the small details children appreciate, as when Gus jumps into a ditch: *Most of Gus didn't get wet. Just one foot and one ankle and one shin and one knee.* The illustrations, featuring soft greens and yellows, give the book a nostalgic glow.

Why This Book Appeals to Reluctant Readers Kids, like adults, sometimes crave books that reflect the simple pleasures in life, and one of the most endearing relationships is that between a child and grandparent. Grandpa is characterized as a witty adult who is still a kid at heart (as when they bake a birthday cake together and eat so much frosting there's not enough left to cover the sides of the cake). The three separate stories provide natural breaks for the reader and yet make the book feel heftier than it is, and the illustrations wonderfully bring the gentle nature of the text to life.

Who Might Like This Book Children who love spending time with their grandparents or kids who are drawn to slice-of-life stories rather than action-packed plots.

If Your Child Liked This Book, Then Try . . . Other books in this series include *Gus and Grandpa Ride the Train*, *Gus and Grandpa at the Hospital*, *Gus and Grandpa and the Two-Wheeled Bike*, and *Gus and Grandpa and Show-and-Tell*.

Minnie and Moo
Go to the Moon

by

DENYS CAZET

Illustrator DENYS CAZET

Genre: Humorous Fiction

Publisher: DK Ink, $3.95 (p)

Page Length: 48

Type of Illustrations: Color, on every page

Reluctant Reader Appeal: Humor, Well-Defined Characters, Concise Chapters, Fast-Paced Plot, Suitable Text

Suggested reading level: Ages 6–8

"Try the magic words," said Moo.
"The ones the farmer shouts
when the tractor won't start."
"Okay," said Minnie.

"YOU CHEESY PIECE OF JUNK!
YOU BROKEN-DOWN, NO-GOOD,
RUSTY BUCKET OF BOLTS!"
Moo turned the key.
The tractor grumbled.

Synopsis Minnie and Moo are two cows with very little brains. In fact, thinking usually gets them in trouble, like the day when Moo suggests they try to drive the farmer's tractor. Minnie explains that they have no hands or feet, but Moo insists that if they put on the farmer's boots and hat, then driving the tractor should be no problem.

When the tractor still doesn't start, Moo employs her logic again—shout the words the farmer uses and kick the tires—and miraculously (after Moo turns the key) the tractor takes off. After soaring over a hill, Minnie and Moo are convinced they've crash-landed on the moon. Their encounter with "moonsters" (read: very angry chickens) cuts their explorations short, and they quickly sail back over the hill, and land in the farmer's pond. The book ends with a very perplexed farmer gazing at his waterlogged machine and his two cows grazing innocently nearby.

Why This Book Appeals to Reluctant Readers These cows are so clueless that they take everything at face value, applying a nonsensical logic to each situation. But Minnie and Moo also completely believe in themselves, which makes them loveable. Seven very short chapters provide natural breaks for the reader and at the same time make the story feel more complex than it really is. Older kids reading below grade level will appreciate the ironic humor presented in a fast plot and short, simple sentences.

Who Might Like This Book Kids who love silly stories, wordplay, or nonsensical plots.

If Your Child Liked This Book, Then Try . . . Other Minnie and Moo books by Denys Cazet, including *Minnie and Moo Go Dancing* (DK Ink).

Here Comes the Strikeout

by

LEONARD KESSLER

Illustrator LEONARD KESSLER

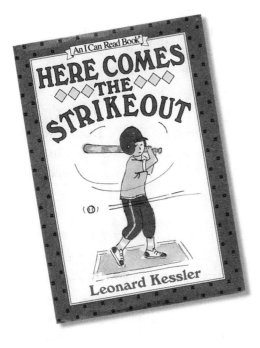

Genre: Fiction/Sports

Publisher: HarperCollins, $3.95 (p)

Page Length: 64

Type of Illustrations: Color, on every page

Reluctant Reader Appeal: Well-Defined Characters, Fast-Paced Plot, Suitable Text, Kid Relevance

Suggested reading level: Ages 6–8

It was a fast ball
right over the plate.
Bobby swung.
"STRIKE THREE!
You are OUT!"
The game was over.
Bobby's team had
lost the game.

"I did it again,"
said Bobby.
"Twenty-one times at bat.
Twenty-one strikeouts.
Take back your lucky hat, Willie.
It was not lucky for me."

Synopsis Bobby loves to play baseball. But every time he comes up to bat, the other team yells, "Here comes the strike-out!" Bobby's mother reminds him that he learned to swim and run, and he can also learn to hit if he works hard. So Bobby asks his friend Willie for help, and the two practice hitting for many days. Gradually, Bobby improves. During the final game of the summer, Bobby gets his first hit: a pop fly to the shortstop. Encouraged, Bobby vows to do better the next time at bat, and in the final inning, Bobby gets a base hit, batting in the winning run for his team.

Why This Book Appeals to Reluctant Readers Bobby's embarrassment when striking out (and the cruel shouts from other players) will be all too familiar to readers in the same situation. This book focuses on the determination and hard work necessary to accomplish something important. The story, written in spare, controlled text, ends believably with Bobby scoring just enough to satisfy himself and make a difference to his team.

Who Might Like This Book Bobby's feelings will be especially relevant to boys, but this book will also appeal to girls who like to play sports. Any beginning reader who is working hard to achieve a goal will find encouragement from this story.

If Your Child Liked This Book, Then Try . . . *Owen Foote, Soccer Star* by Stephanie Greene, illustrated by Martha Weston (Clarion).

The Cat in the Hat

by

D R .   S E U S S

Illustrator D R .   S E U S S

Genre: Humorous Fiction

Publisher: Random House, $7.99 (h)

Page Length: 72

Type of Illustrations: Color, on every page

Reluctant Reader Appeal: Humor,
  Well-Defined Characters,
  Fast-Paced Plot, Suitable Text

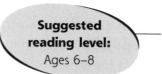

**Suggested
reading level:**
Ages 6–8

Synopsis The narrator and his sister Sally are stuck inside the house, alone and bored, on a rainy day. Suddenly in bursts a large cat wearing a bow tie and a red-and-white striped hat, claiming that he can show them how to have fun. The children are speechless, but their pet fish isn't; he scolds the cat, telling the cat he should not be here when Mother is out. The cat immediately begins his "tricks": balancing the fish's bowl on the end of his umbrella and then gradually adding more items to his balancing act as he stands on a ball. Disaster ensues when everything comes tumbling down and the fish lands in a teapot. But the cat shrugs off this setback (and the fish's renewed nagging) and brings in a large box holding his two friends: Thing One and Thing Two, who systematically destroy the house. Finally, the narrator finds his voice and tells the Things to stop just as the fish looks out the window and sees Mother coming down the sidewalk. The house is quickly cleaned up and the cat exits moments before Mother enters to find the children sitting quietly by the window, just as she left them.

Why This Book Appeals to Reluctant Readers For generations, children have sharpened their beginning reading skills with *The Cat in the Hat*. The text is made up of only 223 different words, each of which is repeated several times throughout the story, so it's easy for readers to master quickly. The rhyming format helps readers learn the rhythm of the sentences and creates a momentum that almost propels the reader forward. It's also fun to read out loud. But the real appeal of this book is the humor, the breakneck speed at which the story takes place, and its slightly subversive content. There's a climax every kid can relate to (Will we get this mess cleaned up before Mom walks in?). And finally, the last two pages make this a book that speaks directly to the reader. After Mother returns and asks the kids if they had any fun that day, Dr. Seuss ends the story by asking, "What would *you* do if your mother asked you?"

Who Might Like This Book Though *The Cat in the Hat* is often read by younger kids, children in third and fourth grades who are developing reading skills can appreciate the humor, the zany illustrations, and the "let's keep this a secret from the grown-ups" feel of the story. Despite the simple text, the story has a bona fide plot and an ending that asks the reader to think.

If Your Child Liked This Book, Then Try . . . Most Dr. Seuss books are great for beginning readers (though some books have more complicated sentences and made-up words). Two to try are *The Cat in the Hat Comes Back* and *Green Eggs and Ham* (both from Random House).

Amelia Bedelia

by

PEGGY PARISH

Illustrator FRITZ SIEBEL

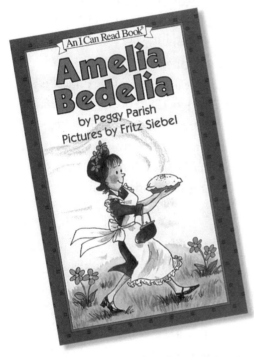

Genre: Humorous Fiction

Publisher: HarperCollins, $3.95 (p)

Page Length: 64

Type of Illustrations: Color, on every page

Reluctant Reader Appeal: Humor, Well-Defined Characters, Fast-Paced Plot, Suitable Text

Suggested reading level: Ages 6–8

Amelia Bedelia found
the green bathroom.
"Those towels are very nice.
Why change them?" she thought.
Then Amelia Bedelia remembered
what Mrs. Rogers had said.
She must do just what
the list told her.
"Well, all right,"
said Amelia Bedelia.
Amelia Bedelia got some scissors.

She snipped a little here
and a little there.
And she changed those towels.

Synopsis Amelia Bedelia is a cheerful housekeeper starting a new job with the Rogerses. There's just one problem: Amelia Bedelia takes everything literally. She follows Mrs. Rogers' list exactly: drawing the drapes when the sun comes in (with paper and pencil), putting the lights out (on the clothesline), and dressing the chicken (in a sporty pair of shorts). When the Rogerses return home, it looks like Amelia Bedelia will lose her job, until Mrs. Rogers takes a bite of Amelia Bedelia's lemon meringue pie. The Rogerses promptly decide that if Amelia Bedelia can bake such delicious pies, she must stay. And Mrs. Rogers vows that in the future she'll be much more careful about how she words her lists.

Why This Book Appeals to Reluctant Readers
Amelia Bedelia is a silly grown-up who is completely oblivious to her one fault: the inability to see shades of meaning in words. But the reader *can* understand dual meanings of common expressions and so feels smarter than the main character. *Amelia Bedelia* is told through action and dialogue, so there's no lag in the story. The illustrations give the reader clues as to the meanings of the expressions. The book feels substantial, but the amount of text on each page is easy to handle.

Who Might Like This Book Though this story is often read by first or second graders, the wordplay lets older boys and girls laugh without feeling as if they're reading a story for "little kids."

If Your Child Liked This Book, Then Try . . . Any of the other books in the AMELIA BEDELIA series, all by Peggy Parish; the GOLLY SISTERS series by Betsy Byars, illustrated by Sue Truesdell (Harper I CAN READ series, Level 3).

The Adventures of Snail at School

by

JOHN STADLER

Illustrator JOHN STADLER

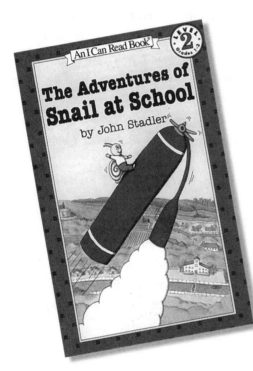

Genre: Fiction/Talking Animals

Publisher: HarperTrophy, $3.95 (p)

Page Length: 64

Type of Illustrations: Color, on every page

Reluctant Reader Appeal: Humor, Concise Chapters, Suitable Text

Suggested reading level: Ages 6–8

Snail came to the principal's office.
There was a fire extinguisher
by the door.
"This should not be here,"
he said.
"I will put it back."
Snail pushed.
Suddenly he heard
Hisssss!

He grabbed the fire extinguisher.
It started to shake, rattle, and roll.
"Yikes!" Snail cried.
"It's blasting off!"

Synopsis Snail tries his best to be a model student, but he keeps getting distracted during his errands for his teacher. In three short chapters, Snail accidentally causes a flood when he turns on the water fountain on his way to the library, takes a detour on the way to pick up a new student at the principal's office when he rides a fire extinguisher into outer space, and forms a marching band in the hallway when the music teacher doesn't arrive in time. Mrs. Harvey doesn't quite believe Snail's elaborate excuses, but the reader knows they're all true.

Why This Book Appeals to Reluctant Readers Humor, the hallmark of successful easy readers, is used in large doses; first, in the exaggerated stories (Snail really *does* surf the waves in the water fountain, he really *does* ride the fire extinguisher into outer space and land on a planet, and the instruments really *do* march down the hallway on their own) and, second, in the illustrations of tiny Snail occupying a child-size desk in class and navigating through a human-size school. Each page of text describes one clear event in the chapter, and the action is nonstop.

Who Might Like This Book Boys or girls who are still learning basic reading skills. These are nonthreatening, easy-to-grasp plots that don't talk down to the reader. The illustrations add another level of humor to the text.

If Your Child Liked This Book, Then Try . . . Any other Level 2 books from the Harper I CAN READ series, including *Soap Soup* by Karla Kuskin and *Scruffy* by Peggy Parish.

Emma's Magic Winter

by

JEAN LITTLE

Illustrator JENNIFER PLECAS

Genre: Contemporary Fiction

Publisher: HarperCollins, $3.95 (p)

Page Length: 64

Type of Illustrations: Color, on almost every page

Reluctant Reader Appeal: Well-Defined Characters, Fast-Paced Plot, Concise Chapters, Suitable Text, Kid Relevance

Suggested reading level: Ages 6–8

On Friday Mom picked Emma up from school.
She said, "We have new neighbors.
The Grays have two children.
Josh is four and Sally is your age.
You can make friends."
"I don't know how," Emma said.

Synopsis The well-meaning adults in Emma's life don't seem to understand how shy she is. When new neighbors move in next door, Emma's mother sends her over with a pie. Emma notices some boots in the neighbor's hallway that look just like hers. Then Sally appears, and Emma takes a deep breath and explains that her own boots make her invisible and help her fly. The girls quickly become friends, pretending their "magic" boots give them special powers.

The next day at school, Sally encourages Emma to ask her magic boots to make her brave so she can read in front of the class. It works. Emma and Sally play happily together all winter. When spring comes, Emma's mother gives her a new jump rope, but Emma worries Sally might not like skipping as much as she does. Could the two girls still be friends? Then Emma looks out the window and sees Sally with a jump rope just like hers. Emma declares the ropes magic, and the two skip off into a magic spring.

Why This Book Appeals to Reluctant Readers

The language is simple, but the story deals with substantial feelings many children are familiar with, such as shyness and the certainty that their friends like their possessions rather than their genuine personalities. Emma deals with these feelings in her own imaginative way, thus allowing herself—and, by association, the reader—to become empowered.

Who Might Like This Book

This is a warm, joyful story that celebrates friendship and discovering one's own strengths. Children who are drawn to texts with emotional depth will like this book. Readers—especially girls—who are shy or unsure of themselves will appreciate how Emma overcomes similar obstacles.

If Your Child Liked This Book, Then Try . . .

Meet M & M by Pat Ross, illustrated by Marilyn Hafner (Puffin Books); *Mr. Putter and Tabby Pour the Tea* by Cynthia Rylant, illustrated by Arthur Howard (Harcourt).

Red-Eyed Tree Frog

by

JOY COWLEY

Photographer NIC BISHOP

Genre: Nonfiction/Tree Frogs

Publisher: Scholastic Press, $9.95 (h)

Page Length: 32

Type of Illustrations: Color photographs, on every page

Reluctant Reader Appeal: Fast-Paced Plot, Suitable Text, Unique Presentation, Visual Appeal

Suggested reading level: Ages 4–8

Here is an iguana.
Frogs do not eat iguanas.

Do iguanas eat frogs?
The red-eyed tree frog
does not wait to find out.

It hops onto
another branch.

Synopsis As evening comes to the rain forest, the red-eyed tree frog wakes up and begins to search for food. It encounters an iguana, an ant, a katydid, a caterpillar, and a boa snake before devouring a moth. After its meal, the red-eyed tree frog settles on a leaf to go back to sleep as morning approaches. Spare text written in simple, declarative sentences is paired with extraordinary color photographs of the tree frog and other creatures of the rain forest. A "Did You Know?" informational section at the end provides more tree-frog facts.

Why This Book Appeals to Reluctant Readers The close-up, vibrant color photographs are sure to entice any reader who loves amphibians (my favorites are the two-page spread of the frog jumping and the three-photo sequence of the frog falling asleep). The text is active and draws the reader into the plot (*Will it eat the caterpillar? No!*) but remains spare (one or two sentences per page) and easy to read. The sheer detail of the photographs elevates frogs, snakes, and insects from creepy critters to things of beauty.

Who Might Like This Book Kids who find frogs and amphibians fascinating will certainly love this book, but also kids who are interested in insects, animals, or the rain forest will appreciate this work.

If Your Child Liked This Book, Then Try . . . *Dorling Kindersley Readers: Tale of a Tadpole* by Karen Wallace (DK Publishing, Level 1); *Fantastic Frogs* by Fay Robinson, illustrated by Jean Cassels (Scholastic HELLO READER! series, Level 2).

Dinosaur Days

by

JOYCE MILTON

Illustrator RICHARD ROE

Genre: Nonfiction/Dinosaurs

Publisher: Random House, $3.99 (p)

Page Length: 48

Type of Illustrations: Color, on every page

Reluctant Reader Appeal: Suitable Text, Kid Relevance, Unique Presentation, Visual Appeal

Suggested reading level: Ages 6–8

The word <u>dinosaur</u> looks hard.
But it is really easy to say.
Say: DIE-nuh-sor.
<u>Dinosaur</u> means "terrible lizard.

Millions of years ago
the world belonged
to the dinosaurs.

In the days of the dinosaurs
there were no people.
No dogs or cats.
No horses or cows.

Synopsis In simple, declarative sentences, the author introduces the reader to popular dinosaurs and plesiosaurs and discusses the different theories for how the dinosaurs died out. Each dinosaur is presented with one major characteristic that helps the reader identify it (size, number of teeth, ability to defend itself, and so on) and listed chronologically so the reader can see how dinosaurs evolved. The illustrations give a good sense of how the dinosaurs may have interacted and depict the other animals alive at that time.

Why This Book Appeals to Reluctant Readers One of the things I like about this book is that each dinosaur's name is spelled phonetically when first mentioned, so the reader can sound it out. Kids who love dinosaurs but are still learning to read will appreciate this as well as the short text. Each line on the page contains one complete thought, allowing the reader to comprehend the text in small chunks. The information isn't overwhelming, but it is substantial enough to help the child feel as if he's read a "real" book.

Who Might Like This Book Kids who are crazy about dinosaurs, of course!

If Your Child Liked This Book, Then Try . . . *Why Did the Dinosaurs Disappear? The Great Dinosaur Mystery* by Melvin and Gilda Berger, illustrated by Susan Harrison (Ideals); *Dinosaur Time* by Peggy Parish, illustrated by Arnold Lobel (Harper I CAN READ series, Level 1).

Abe Lincoln's Hat

by

MARTHA BRENNER

Illustrator DONALD COOK

Genre: Nonfiction/Biography

Publisher: Random House, $3.99 (p)

Page Length: 48

Type of Illustrations: Color, on every page

Reluctant Reader Appeal: Well-Defined Characters, Fast-Paced Plot, Suitable Text, Unique Presentation

Suggested reading level: Ages 6–8

Abe Lincoln was a smart lawyer.
People came to him
with all kinds of problems.
He helped them all.
But he had one problem himself.

He forgot to answer letters.
He forgot where
he put important papers.
A good lawyer cannot forget.

Abe wanted to be a good lawyer,
but he was not a good paper-keeper.
What could he do?

Synopsis This simple biography chronicles Abraham Lincoln's life from the time he became a lawyer until he was elected president in 1860. But rather than weigh the reader down with historical dates and events, the author conveys who Abe Lincoln was as a person through a series of incidents in his life. Framing these episodes is Abe Lincoln's hat: a tall, black silk affair that he wore to help people remember him and that he used to hold his important papers. The warm illustrations show Lincoln's poverty, his friendly personality, and his cluttered office in the days in which a tall hat could truly be a lawyer's most valuable tool.

Why This Book Appeals to Reluctant Readers Each page of text (up to about eight lines) covers one clear idea; each separate incident lasts for two to four pages. Historical details are appealing to young readers (for example, Lincoln had to speak loudly in one courthouse to be heard over the pigs who lived under the building) and to show the contrast between a lawyer's life then and now. Photographs of the principal characters at the end of the book reinforce the idea that everything the child just read really happened.

Who Might Like This Book Kids who show an interest in American history, presidents, or biographies. This is also a gentle way to introduce children with below-average reading skills to biographies in general.

If Your Child Liked This Book, Then Try . . . *The True Story of Pocahontas* by Lucille Recht Penner, illustrated by Pamela Johnson (Random House STEP INTO READING series, Step 2); *George Washington's Mother* by Jean Fritz, illustrated by DyAnne DiSalvo-Ryan (Grosset ALL ABOARD READING series, Level 3).

Chapter Five

Keeping It Simple

These are slightly longer books for kids who are starting to become comfortable reading on their own. Though they have more text than beginning easy readers, these books still feature a simple sentence structure and are heavily illustrated.

FICTION

Buggy Riddles by Katy Hall and Lisa Eisenberg · page 61

The One in the Middle Is the Green Kangaroo by Judy Blume · page 63

Purple Climbing Days by Patricia Reilly Giff · page 65

Greg's Microscope by Millicent E. Selsam · page 67

Abigail Takes the Wheel by Avi · page 69

Dragon Breath (EEK! STORIES TO MAKE YOU SHRIEK series) by Jane O'Conner · page 71

The Drinking Gourd: A Story of the Underground Railroad by F. N. Monjo · page 73

Nate the Great and Me (NATE THE GREAT series) by Marjorie Weinman Sharmat · page 75

Dinosaurs Before Dark (MAGIC TREE HOUSE series) by Mary Pope Osborne · page 77

Junie B. Jones and the Stupid Smelly Bus (JUNIE B. JONES series) by Barbara Park · page 79

Albertina the Practically Perfect by Susi Gregg Fowler · page 81

Marvin Redpost: Alone in His Teacher's House (MARVIN REDPOST series) by Louis Sachar · page 83

NONFICTION

Who Eats What? Food Chains and Food Webs (LET'S-READ-AND-FIND-OUT SCIENCE series) by Patricia Lauber · page 85

I Wonder Why I Blink and Other Questions About My Body by Brigid Avison · page 87

I Am Rosa Parks by Rosa Parks with Jim Haskins · page 89

The Titanic: Lost . . . and Found by Judy Donnelly · page 91

Moonwalk: The First Trip to the Moon by Judy Donnelly · page 93

Dig and Sow! How Do Plants Grow? (AT HOME WITH SCIENCE series) by Janice Lobb · page 95

Baseball's Greatest Hitters by S. A. Kramer · page 97

Buggy Riddles

by

KATY HALL AND LISA EISENBERG

Illustrator SIMMS TABACK

Genre: Riddles

Publisher: Puffin Books, $3.99 (p)

Page Length: 48

Type of Illustrations: Color, on every page

Reluctant Reader Appeal: Humor, Suitable Text, Kid Relevance, Visual Appeal

Suggested reading level: Ages 7–9

> *How do you keep a mosquito from biting you on Monday?*
> *Swat it on Sunday.*

> *What do spiders like with their hamburgers?*
> *French flies!*

Synopsis Puns and wordplay abound in this collection of 42 simple riddles involving insects.

Why This Book Appeals to Reluctant Readers The nonsense of puns and double meanings delights kids in the early and middle elementary grades. These riddles are simple in that each is only two sentences long, but much of the humor comes from basic knowledge of bug behavior, which appeals to the older reluctant reader (for example, in order to get one joke, the child must know that termites eat wood). However, the illustrations provide additional information about the punch lines if the reader needs it. These are the kinds of riddles kids love to memorize and then torture their parents with over and over.

Who Might Like This Book Obviously, children who love jokes, riddles, and puns, but also kids who are fond of bugs or those who haven't been able to finish a whole book up to now. This text can be breezed through very quickly, and the laughs on each page ensure that the child will have a good time while reading.

Notes to Parents Except for some of the names of bugs, a younger child with emerging reading skills should be able to handle most of the text.

If Your Child Liked This Book, Then Try . . . Other books in this series by the same authors: *Fishy Riddles, Snakey Riddles,* and *Grizzly Riddles.* Also try *Spooky Riddles* by Marc Brown (Random House BEGINNER BOOKS series, Grades 1–2).

The One in the Middle Is the Green Kangaroo

by

JUDY BLUME

Illustrator IRENE TRIVAS

Genre: Contemporary Fiction

Publisher: Atheneum, $16.00 (h); Dell, $5.99 (p)

Page Length: 42

Type of Illustrations: Color (hardcover) or black and white (paperback), on every page

Reluctant Reader Appeal: Humor, Well-Defined Characters, Fast-Paced Plot, Concise Chapters, Kid Relevance

Suggested reading level: Ages 6–9

Then one day Freddy heard about the school play. Mike had never been in a play. Ellen had never been in a play. This was his chance to do something special. Freddy decided he would try it.

He waited two whole days before he went to his teacher. "Ms. Gumber," he said. "I want to be in the school play."

Ms. Gumber smiled and shook her head. "I'm sorry, Freddy,"
she said. "The play is being done by the fifth and sixth graders.
The big boys and girls, like Mike."

Freddy looked at the floor and mumbled. "That figures!" He
started to walk away.

Synopsis Freddy is a middle child, and he's tired of feeling like "the peanut butter part of a sandwich." His older brother Mike gets new clothes while Freddy has to wear Mike's hand-me-downs; his little sister Ellen gets her own room. So one day Freddy decides to do something Mike and Ellen have never done: try out for the school play. He's cast as the green kangaroo and to his delight discovers he's the only kangaroo in the play! For the first time, Freddy's the center of attention.

Why This Book Appeals to Reluctant Readers Judy Blume is known for writing children's books with humor and honesty, and this book is no exception. Middle children will recognize how Freddy feels, and they'll appreciate how he takes matters into his own hands and solves his problem. Freddy's in second grade, but his story will ring true for kids through fourth grade who prefer reading short chapter books. The story's satisfying, feel-good ending gives a positive spin on the whole reading experience.

Who Might Like This Book Boys and girls who are middle children or kids who have felt the need to stand out from the crowd. It's also a nice story for any kid who just wants to feel special.

Notes to Parents The new hardcover edition has been redesigned to look like a picture book. If your child prefers a book with an "older" feel, try the paperback edition (shelved with the easy readers or in juvenile fiction).

If Your Child Liked This Book, Then Try . . . *Freckle Juice* by Judy Blume, illustrated by Sonia O. Lisker (Dell).

Purple Climbing Days

(THE KIDS OF THE POLK STREET SCHOOL series)

by

PATRICIA REILLY GIFF

Illustrator BLANCHE SIMS

Genre: Contemporary Fiction

Publisher: Dell, $3.99 (p)

Page Length: 70

Type of Illustrations: Black
and white, one per chapter

Reluctant Reader Appeal:
Humor, Well-Defined
Characters, Fast-Paced
Plot, Suitable Text,
Kid Relevance

**Suggested
reading level:**
Ages 6–9

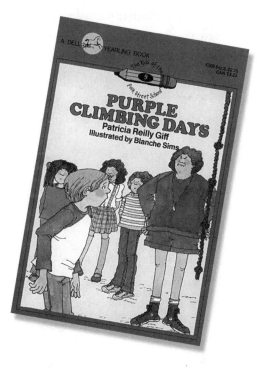

Climbing day.
He had forgotten all about it.
He was supposed to climb the rope in the gym.
Climb it to the top.
He didn't even like to climb the monkey bars.
  "Today I'm going to climb that rope . . ." Matthew began.
"Today I'm going right up there."
Richard put his books in his desk.
  Today was the day he was going to fall off the gym
ceiling. He was going to break his neck.

Synopsis Richard Best is having a "purple Monday." He forgot his lunch money, he thought it was the day his class was getting a pet skink (that's Wednesday), and it's climbing day in gym. To top it off, Mrs. Miller is teaching gym today, and she's the meanest substitute teacher in school. But Richard's saved when Mrs. Miller announces they're going to play "a tisket, a tasket" instead. When the skink finally arrives later that week, Richard is sure it knows that he's afraid to climb the rope. And though he keeps making excuses, his classmates are starting to catch on as well. But with some unexpected help from Mrs. Miller (and some inspiration from the skink), Richard soon learns to climb the rope halfway to the top. But more important, he's learned that there's no shame to admitting his fears because everyone is afraid of something.

Why This Book Appeals to Reluctant Readers Though Richard's in second grade, the author deftly uses him to represent every elementary school kid who suffers from the anxiety of being embarrassed in front of his or her classmates. The dialogue between Richard and his peers is succinct and authentic; the author conveys Richard's feelings and his perceptions of the adults in his life without ever slowing the pace of the plot. Declarative sentences and paragraphs that average one or two sentences long help the reader breeze through this story.

Who Might Like This Book Children who are just starting to feel the effects of peer pressure or the desire to fit in. The male protagonist will be especially relevant to boys who aren't as athletic as their classmates. THE KIDS OF THE POLK STREET SCHOOL series is very popular with boys and girls who have outgrown easy readers but aren't quite ready for full-length chapter books.

If Your Child Liked This Book, Then Try . . . Other books in THE KIDS OF THE POLK STREET SCHOOL series by Patricia Reilly Giff, including *The Beast in Ms. Rooney's Room, Fish Face, The Candy Corn Contest, In the Dinosaur's Paw,* and *Say "Cheese."*

Greg's Microscope

by

MILLICENT E. SELSAM

Illustrator ARNOLD LOBEL

Genre: Contemporary Fiction

Publisher: HarperCollins, $3.95 (p)

Page Length: 64

Type of Illustrations: Color, on almost every page

Reluctant Reader Appeal: Fast-Paced Plot, Suitable Text, Kid Relevance, Visual Appeal

Suggested reading level: Ages 7–9

Greg's mother came in.
"Let me see that salt," she said.
She looked through the microscope.
"My goodness," she said.
"The salt looks like rocks.
Come into the kitchen, Greg.
Let's look for more tiny things."
Greg did not go right away.
He just kept looking at the salt.

Synopsis Greg wants a microscope, just like his friend Billy. After some discussion, Greg's father brings home a microscope but tells Greg he'll have to make his own slides of "tiny things" to look at. Greg and his mother find items from around the house—salt, sugar, hair, thread—and discover that these things look very different when magnified 100 times. The next week, Greg takes his microscope to school and learns that everything is made out of cells. He then looks at a plant and water from his fish tank and discovers that he can see tiny, one-celled animals swimming on the slide. Illustrations show realistic images of what Greg sees when looking through the microscope's lens and introduce children to a fascinating molecular world right under their noses.

Why This Book Appeals to Reluctant Readers Greg's excitement over his microscope is contagious, and it's nice to see his parents share his enthusiasm. The uncomplicated text imparts simple scientific principles in a fictional format (mainly through characters' dialogue); Greg learns that salt crystals look like blocks, but when they're dissolved in water and then dried, they resemble prisms. The illustrations show precisely what the reader would see through a microscope, inspiring the reader to beg for one of her own.

Who Might Like This Book Some kids love looking at the "tiny things" around them; these children, who are curious about the world, will identify with Greg's fascination with his new microscope. This book, paired with a microscope, would make a great gift for a beginning reader.

If Your Child Liked This Book, Then Try . . . *Yuck! The Big Book of Little Horrors* by Robert Snedden (Simon & Schuster).

Abigail Takes the Wheel

by

A V I

Illustrator D O N   B O L O G N E S E

Genre: Historical Fiction

Publisher: HarperCollins,
$3.95 (p)

Page Length: 64

Type of Illustrations: Color,
on every page

Reluctant Reader Appeal:
Fast-Paced Plot, Concise
Chapters, Suitable Text

**Suggested
reading level:**
Ages 8–9

*Suddenly [Mr. Oliver] said, "Abigail, you'd better take over. I'm
really sick." With a groan he staggered out of the pilot house.*

Abigail grabbed the wheel again.

"What do we do now?" Tom asked.

"How many times have we gone to New York?" Abigail asked.

"A million, maybe," Tom said.

*"Then we must know the way," Abigail said. She gripped the
wheel tightly. "I need to keep both hands on the wheel. Swing the
speaking tube toward you, Tom. Tell the engineer we need more
power."*

Synopsis It's 1880, and Abigail and her brother Tom live aboard the freight boat *Neptune,* where their father is captain. Every morning, the *Neptune* delivers vegetables from New Jersey to New York City. It also takes Abigail and Tom to school.

One morning as the *Neptune* is entering the narrow channel leading toward New York, two other ships collide. One ship, the *Bonnie Brea,* lost its sails in the crash and can't go on under its own power. The crew of the *Bonnie Brea* ask the *Neptune* to tow them into the city. Abigail's father agrees and climbs aboard the damaged ship to steer it while in tow.

But soon after the ships are under way, the **Neptune's** first mate gets sick and asks Abigail to take the wheel. In a tension-filled climax, Abigail steers the *Neptune* through a busy harbor and docks it, as well as the *Bonnie Brea,* at Pier Forty-two in New York City. An author's note at the end of the book gives more information about water traffic in the port of New York during this time and says that this book is based on a story originally published in 1881 in the children's magazine *St. Nicholas.*

Why This Book Appeals to Reluctant Readers
Though this story is brief, it contains many compelling details about ships and the atmosphere of the New York harbor in the 1880s. The six short chapters each end on a high point in the action. The book looks hefty but the large typeface and substantial room given to the dramatic illustrations means the pages will turn quickly. This story offers an interesting slice of history, action, and excitement.

Who Might Like This Book
Abigail will appeal to girls as a heroine, but the story itself—along with the information about ships and harbor life—will intrigue boys and girls alike.

If Your Child Liked This Book, Then Try . . .
Finding the Titanic by Robert D. Ballard with Nan Froman, illustrated by Ken Marschall (Cartwheel).

Dragon Breath

(EEK! STORIES TO MAKE YOU SHRIEK series)

by

JANE O'CONNOR

Illustrator JEFF SPACKMAN

Genre: Spooky Fiction

Publisher: Grosset & Dunlap,
$3.99 (p)

Page Length: 48

Type of Illustrations: Color,
on most pages

Reluctant Reader Appeal:
Fast-Paced Plot, Well-
Defined Characters,
Suitable Text

**Suggested
reading level:**
Ages 6–8

Owen was the keeper of the castle.

*"It's called Wyllylldrygyn, same as our town," Owen told me.
"It means <u>in the shadow of the dragon</u>."*

"Cool!" I said. Then I asked if there really was a dragon.

*"Oh, I believe in the dragon. I do indeed, lad," Owen said.
"But you are only here for a week. You will not have a chance to
find out for yourself. And this is lucky too."*

Synopsis When the narrator arrives with his parents for vacation in the Welsh town of Wyllylldrygyn, he notices the place

smells like smoke. The boy also notices that the few children he sees are all girls, and everyone in town seems to be staring at him strangely. To pass the time, he visits Owen, the keeper of the town's castle, and sees a huge stone statue of a dragon whose eyes seem to follow him around the room. When the boy points out a book in the castle—*History of the Dragon*—Owen tells him, "There are things in that book you do not need to know."

The next morning, the boy and his parents are told they must leave Wyllylldrygen at once. The boy sneaks off to say good-bye to Owen, but the castle's empty. Only the dragon statue remains, and the boy realizes the smoke he's been smelling is filling the room. Just as he's about to leave, he sees the book again and can't help but read it.

He learns that the dragon is asleep inside the stone stuatue, but wakes once every 50 years to spread fire over the land. The only way to stop the dragon is if a young boy forces it to see its own face. Then it will die.

The boy suddenly realizes that this chain of events is playing itself out before his eyes. In a quick, tension-filled climax, the boy saves himself but doesn't stop the dragon from spreading fire and returning to the rock for another 50 years.

Why This Book Appeals to Reluctant Readers A third or fourth grader won't get nightmares from this spooky series, but the fast-paced plot with the promise of something creepy just around the corner will keep the pages turning.

Who Might Like This Book We tend to think of boys as the market for scary stories, but girls like them too. These are perfect for sleep-overs with friends, read with a flashlight.

If Your Child Liked This Book, Then Try . . . Other books in this series, such as *The Spooky Sleepover* by Joan Holub, illustrated by Cynthia Fisher, and *Creep Show* by Jennifer Dussling, illustrated by Jeff Spackman.

The Drinking Gourd:
A Story of the
Underground Railroad

by

F. N. MONJO

Illustrator FRED BRENNER

Genre: Historical Fiction

Publisher: HarperCollins.
$3.95 (p)

Page Length: 64

Type of Illustrations: Color,
on almost every page

Reluctant Reader Appeal:
Well-Defined Characters,
Fast-Paced Plot, Concise
Chapters, Suitable Text

**Suggested
reading level:**
Ages 7–9

Dan'l Webster stamped his hoof.
Tommy climbed back into the loft
to see what had made the noise.
"Who's there?" Tommy hollered.

"Stop right there!" said a deep voice.
"You won't take us alive!"
A black man stood up, covered with hay.
He had an axe in his hand.

Synopsis When Tommy's father sends him home one Sunday for misbehaving in church, Tommy discovers a runaway slave family in his barn. The slaves explain that Tommy's barn is a stop on the Underground Railroad, which leads all the way to Canada. Later that night, Tommy and his father hide the slaves under hay bales in their wagon and set off for the river. Tommy's father is searching through the trees along the riverbank when a U.S. marshal shows up. Tommy confronts the marshal alone and says that he's running away because his father got mad at him in church. The marshal laughs and tells Tommy to go on home. Once the coast is clear, Tommy's father takes the slaves across the river in a rowboat, to the next stop on the Underground Railroad.

Back home, Tommy and his father discuss slavery and when the law might be wrong. An author's note at the end explains how the Underground Railroad worked and the laws that kept slaves captive and finally were changed to make them free.

Why This Book Appeals to Reluctant Readers Using a boy as the viewpoint character helps present moral questions from a child's perspective: Is it okay to lie to save someone's life? Can you justify breaking a law if you feel the law is wrong? The plot is broken into six short chapters, each with a climactic moment of its own. One illustration, depicting a reward poster, provides very real tension and shows the danger Tommy and his father face.

Who Might Like This Book Kids interested in American history, African American history, or those studying this period of time in school.

If Your Child Liked This Book, Then Try . . . The Hatmaker's Sign: A Story by Benjamin Franklin, retold by Candice Fleming, illustrated by Robert Andrew Parker (Orchard).

Nate the Great and Me

(NATE THE GREAT series)

by

MARJORIE WEINMAN SHARMAT

Illustrator MARC SIMONT

Genre: Mystery

Publisher: Delacorte,
$4.50 (p)

Page Length: 64

Type of Illustrations: Color,
on almost every page

Reluctant Reader Appeal:
Humor, Well-Defined
Characters, Fast-Paced
Plot, Concise Chapters,
Suitable Text

**Suggested
reading level:**
Ages 6–8

*I, Nate the Great, said to Annie,
"First you have to remember.
Remember if there was
anything different
about Fang today.
Any reason why he might run away.
Then remember where you last saw him.
Remember what he was doing.
Remember who was there."*

Synopsis Nate the Great, boy detective and lover of pancakes, has been engaging young readers for years with his deadpan delivery and clever observations. In this story, Nate's friend's dog is missing, and even though it's Nate's day off, he can't help but solve the case. This book is different from others in the series in that the text contains asides to the reader asking about clues (*Did you notice that Fang wasn't there?*), sharing private jokes, or giving assignments. By the time the dog is found, the reader has gotten a crash course in detective work and become an active part of the story. The book includes detective tips, a secret code, and activities and recipes that tie in with the story.

Why This Book Appeals to Reluctant Readers Young readers love mysteries, and this book elevates the reader from observer to participant. Though Nate the Great takes the reader step-by-step through the mystery, the reader does have the opportunity to collect clues and solve the case before Nate gives the answer. Short sentences, humorous dialogue, a quick plot, and a large typeface with lots of white space on each page make this book easy to read and allow the reader to concentrate on the content of the story.

Who Might Like This Book Kids who like mysteries or who imagine themselves as detectives. Boys and girls who appreciate funny dialogue and interesting, smart characters should get a kick out of this book.

If Your Child Liked This Book, Then Try . . . Other Nate the Great detective stories including *Nate the Great, Nate the Great and the Phony Clue, Nate the Great and the Missing Key, Nate the Great Stalks Stupidweed, Nate the Great Goes Down in the Dumps,* and *Nate the Great Saves the King of Sweden.*

Dinosaurs Before Dark

(MAGIC TREE HOUSE series)

by

MARY POPE OSBORNE

Illustrator SAL MURDOCCA

Genre: Fiction/Time Travel

Publisher: Random House,
$3.99 (p)

Page Length: 68

Type of Illustrations: Black
and white, every few pages

Reluctant Reader Appeal:
Humor, Well-Defined
Characters, Fast-Paced
Plot, Concise Chapters,
Suitable Text

**Suggested
reading level:**
Ages 6–9

Jack looked back at the Tyrannosaurus.

> *Good. The monster still didn't seem to know he was there.*

> *Don't panic. Think.* Think. *Maybe there's information in
the book.*

> *Jack opened the dinosaur book. He found Tyrannosaurus rex.
He read:*

> Tyrannosaurus rex was the largest meat-eating land
> animal of all time.

> If it were alive today, it would eat a human in one bite.

> *Great. The book was no help at all.*

Synopsis Jack and his younger sister Annie are walking home one evening when Annie disappears into the woods. Jack finds Annie at the base of a rope ladder that disappears into a large oak tree. The children climb the ladder and find a mysterious tree house filled with books. Jack opens a dinosaur book and points to a picture of a pteranodon. "I wish I could see a Pteranodon for real," Jack whispers.

Suddenly, the tree house starts to shake and spin. When things settle down again, the children look out the window to see a real pteranodon flying by. They're back in the time of the dinosaurs!

The children are off on an extraordinary adventure, meeting friendly (and not-so-friendly) dinosaurs before they return home. But one mystery still remains: Jack found a gold medallion engraved with the letter "M" laying in the grass near a triceratops. Someone else had used the tree house before them. But who?

Why This Book Appeals to Reluctant Readers This story has all the elements of an enticing read: time travel, dinosaurs, and a hint of mystery wrapped up in a quick, exciting plot. The children are juxtaposed from the expected characterizations: Jack, the older brother, is studious and cautious, while Annie is impulsive, curious, and brave. The chapters are short, and the text is broken up with full-page illustrations to facilitate quick reading. This is a good choice for kids reading slightly below grade level or those who don't want to work too hard for their stories.

Who Might Like This Book Kids who like fantasy, adventure, mysteries, or (for this book in the series) dinosaurs. The MAGIC TREE HOUSE series is very popular with boys and girls alike.

If Your Child Liked This Book, Then Try . . . Other books in the series, all by Mary Pope Osborne, including *The Knight at Dawn, Pirates Past Noon, Night of the Ninjas, Afternoon on the Amazon, Sunset of the Sabertooth,* and *Midnight on the Moon.*

Junie B. Jones and the Stupid Smelly Bus

(JUNIE B. JONES series)

by

BARBARA PARK

Illustrator DENISE BRUNKUS

Genre: Contemporary Fiction

Publisher: Random House, $3.99 (p)

Page Length: 72

Type of Illustrations: Black and white, about two per chapter

Reluctant Reader Appeal: Humor, Well-Defined Characters, Fast-Paced Plot, Concise Chapters, Kid Relevance

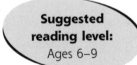

Suggested reading level:
Ages 6–9

The bus made a big roar. Then a big puff of black smelly smoke came out the back end of it. It's called bus breath, I think.

Mr. Woo drove for a while. Then the brakes made that loud, screechy noise again. I covered my ears so it wouldn't get inside my head. 'Cause if loud, screechy noises get inside your head, you have to take an aspirin. I saw that on a TV commercial.

Synopsis Junie B. Jones is a precocious kindergartner whose first day of school starts out badly: She dreads riding the "stupid smelly bus," but her mother insists. Things go downhill from there: Junie can't sit where she wants on the bus and makes an enemy out of a classmate before she even gets to school, the red chair she had claimed for her own is taken in the classroom, and she writes her name too big on her name tag and can't fit the "B." But worst of all, her hall buddy tells Junie that when she rides the bus home, kids will pour chocolate milk on her head. Junie is determined not to let that happen, so she hides in the classroom as the other kids file out to the bus at the end of the day. She entertains herself in the empty school as only a kindergartner can, but then she has to go to the bathrom and the doors are locked. Since this is surely an emergency, Junie dials 911 on the nurse's phone. Help arrives, and in true Junie B. Jones fashion, everything turns out okay in the end.

Why This Book Appeals to Reluctant Readers Though Junie is a kindergartner, her funny, literal, and to-the-point observations about the world have been entertaining second, third, and fourth grade readers for years. Readers quickly find themselves getting caught up in her whirlwind activity and marveling at how Junie pulls off each escapade through sheer strength of will.

Who Might Like This Book Girls, especially those with younger siblings or a connection with 5- and 6-year-old kids, which helps the reader identify with Junie and see the perfect authenticity of her personality.

If Your Child Liked This Book, Then Try . . . Other books in the series, including *Junie B. Jones and a Little Monkey Business, Junie B. Jones and the Yucky Blucky Fruitcake,* and *Junie B. Jones and Some Sneaky Peeky Spying* (all from Random House). Also try *Ivy Green, Cootie Queen* by Joan Holub (Troll).

Albertina the Practically Perfect

by

SUSI GREGG FOWLER

Illustrator JIM FOWLER

Genre: Contemporary Fiction

Publisher: Greenwillow Books,
$15.00 (h)

Page Length: 80

Type of Illustrations: Color
spot illustrations, every few
pages

Reluctant Reader Appeal:
Well-Defined Characters,
Fast-Paced Plot, Concise
Chapters, Suitable Text,
Kid Relevance

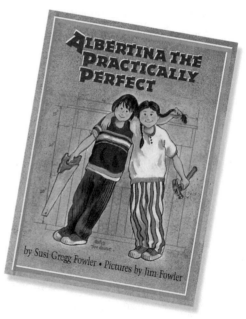

**Suggested
reading level:**
Ages 6–9

*Albertina looked at Grandpa. "We had the same wonderful idea at
exactly the same time. My daddy says when that happens, it's a sign."*

"Oh?" said Grandpa. "A sign of what, may I ask?"

*"A sign that we should do it if it is at all possible," Albertina
said. We grabbed each other's hands and squeezed tightly.*

*"Would anyone like to tell me what we are talking about
here?" Grandpa asked.*

*"Building a tree house!" Albertina and I said at the very same
time.*

Synopsis The first day Molly explores her new neighborhood, she meets some local girls led by Violet, who greets Molly with an attempted karate kick. The other girls laugh, all except Albertina. She's friendly, doesn't bow to peer pressure, and has an infectious laugh; in other words, Albertina is perfect. She and Molly become instant best friends and spend the rest of the summer together building a tree house.

But Molly's bothered that Albertina's still friends with Violet. One day at school, Molly overhears Albertina telling Violet about Molly's nightlight, thus divulging Molly's deepest secret: She's afraid of the dark. Molly's sure Albertina has betrayed her and stops speaking to her friend. But in the end the two girls patch things up, and Molly learns that even tough Violet has fears of her own.

Why This Book Appeals to Reluctant Readers The plot doesn't break any new ground, but this gentle story of making friends, worrying about what others think, and relying on first impressions will seem new to readers who are experiencing these things for the first time. Molly's and Albertina's delight in their blooming friendship is presented from an authentic childlike viewpoint (they have the same ideas simultaneously); Molly fears their bond will be broken as quickly as it was formed. The uncomplicated sentence structure makes the text accessible.

Who Might Like This Book Because of Molly's first-person narration, this book will be most appealing to girls, especially those who are moving to a new neighborhood or who have a best friend with whom they share everything.

If Your Child Liked This Book, Then Try . . . *Best Enemies Again* by Kathleen Leverich, illustrated by Walter Lorraine (Beech Tree Books).

Marvin Redpost: Alone in His Teacher's House

(MARVIN REDPOST series)

by

LOUIS SACHAR

Illustrator BARBARA SULLIVAN

Genre: Contemporary Fiction

Publisher: Random House, $3.99 (p)

Page Length: 84

Type of Illustrations: Black and white, one per chapter

Reluctant Reader Appeal: Humor, Well-Defined Characters, Fast-Paced Plot, Concise Chapters, Suitable Text, Kid Relevance

---

Suggested reading level:
Ages 6–9

"You were alone in her house?" Stuart exclaimed.
Marvin nodded.
"Oh, man, what'd you do?" asked Nick.
Marvin shrugged.
They were out on the playground. School hadn't started yet.
"Let me see the key," said Stuart.
"Did you look in her closet?" asked Nick.
"No," said Marvin. Why would he look in her closet?

Synopsis When Marvin Redpost's third-grade teacher, Mrs. North, goes away for a week, she asks Marvin to feed her dog. Marvin is shocked, not only at the prospect of earning $25 but also because he'll get a key to his teacher's house. When he goes home with Mrs. North to meet Waldo, he's surprised to find out she lives in an ordinary home (there's not even a flagpole out front!) and is affectionate toward her dog, almost like a normal person. Marvin takes his job very seriously but on the sixth day, something terrible happens: Waldo dies.

Marvin calls the vet, who comes right over and assures him that Waldo was very old and it wasn't Marvin's fault, but Marvin can't help but feel he did something wrong. He spends the next 24 hours terrified of what Mrs. North will do when she gets home (Will she think he killed her dog? Will she flunk him from third grade?) The story ends on a reassuring note. After all, Mrs. North is an understanding person, and Marvin had tried his best.

Why This Book Appeals to Reluctant Readers The author has humorously captured the interactions between third graders and their belief that teachers can't possibly have normal lives outside the classroom. Marvin is a very endearing character; he's not a saint, but he often acts as the level-headed straight man to his friend's zanier antics. There's also substantial emotion and tension to this story, making it appealing to readers even older than the designated age-group.

Who Might Like This Book This series is a good choice for boys who are reluctant readers and refuse to read stories featuring girls.

Notes to Parents If you feel the topic of this story is too heavy for your child, try other books in this series, listed below.

If Your Child Liked This Book, Then Try . . . Other books in the MARVIN REDPOST series by Louis Sachar.

Who Eats What? Food Chains and Food Webs

(LET'S-READ-AND-FIND-OUT SCIENCE series)

by

PATRICIA LAUBER

Illustrator HOLLY KELLER

Genre: Nonfiction/Ecology

Publisher: HarperCollins, $4.95 (p)

Page Length: 32

Type of Illustrations: Color, on every page

Reluctant Reader Appeal: Suitable Text, Unique Presentation, Visual Appeal

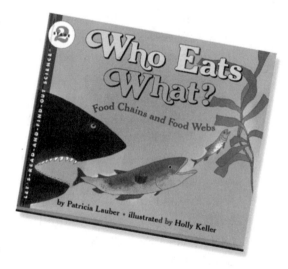

Suggested reading level:
Ages 5–9

The hawk is the top of the food chain, because no other animal attacks and eats hawks. The animal at the top of a food chain is always the last eater—the one nobody else eats.

Suppose you eat an apple off the tree. That makes you part of a short food chain—the apple and you. You are the top of the food chain.

Or suppose you drink a glass of milk. Now you are the top of a slightly longer food chain. The milk came from a cow, and the cow ate grass. So this chain is grass, cow, you.

Synopsis What do humans and tuna have in common? They're both at the top of a food chain that begins with a tiny green plant. *Who Eats What?* explains different food chains from the animal kingdom, all of which begin with plants, the only living things that do not have to eat something else for their survival. Colorful illustrations clearly depict the sequence of events, sometimes showing one creature inside another, inside another, inside another, and so on. The author encourages readers to draw their own food chains for familiar animals and people; examples of these drawings are done in marker and crayon, as if created by a child. The reader comes away with a solid understanding of how food chains merge into food webs and an appreciation for how all species are dependent on one another for their very existence.

Why This Book Appeals to Reluctant Readers The LET'S-READ-AND-FIND-OUT SCIENCE series teaches important scientific concepts to elementary school children through easy-to-read text. Short paragraphs with controlled sentence structure contain solid information that will interest even older readers who feel overwhelmed by more difficult books. The illustrations are clearly labeled and offer precise drawings without looking too much like a textbook. Readers are gently encouraged to participate in the book with fun nonreading activities.

Who Might Like This Book Kids who love to observe and learn about animals, children who are concerned about the environment, and readers who have their own gardens or bug collections will be curious to see how their hobbies and interests are linked to life all over the planet.

If Your Child Liked This Book, Then Try . . . Other titles in this series, including *Why Do Leaves Change Color?*, *Where Does the Garbage Go?*, *How Do Birds Find Their Way?*, *What Happens to a Hamburger?*, and *How Mountains Are Made.*

I Wonder Why I Blink and Other Questions About My Body

by

BRIGID AVISON

Illustrator VARIOUS ILLUSTRATORS

Genre: Nonfiction/Anatomy

Publisher: Kingfisher,
$7.95 (p)

Page Length: 32

Type of Illustrations: Color,
on every page

Reluctant Reader Appeal:
Suitable Text, Kid
Relevance, Unique
Presentation, Visual Appeal

**Suggested
reading level:**
Ages 5–9

Why do I feel dizzy when I spin around?

Inside each ear, you have three loop-shaped tubes with watery liquid in them. This swishes around when you spin. Special nerves pick up this movement and tell the brain you are spinning. If you stop suddenly, the liquid goes swishing around for a little longer. Your brain gets the wrong message and you feel dizzy!

Synopsis This book answers common questions children have about how their bodies work. The table of contents lists each question for easy reference; the text provides one paragraph of general information, with additional details conveyed through well-annotated illustrations. Questions are worded to reflect a child's sensibilities (*What are goose bumps? Why can't I see in the dark? Why do I need shots?*). The answers, formatted in a large, easy-to-read typeface, convey substantial information in simple language that never condescends to the reader.

Why This Book Appeals to Reluctant Readers Kids always have questions about their bodies. This book poses the questions kids would ask themselves and gives just enough of an answer to satisfy a child's curiosity without overwhelming the reader. The illustrations (some funny, some realistic) add a great deal to the understanding of the text. Generous white space on each page makes for a pleasing layout and helps strike a balance between the text and illustrations.

Who Might Like This Book Boys and girls who are curious about how their bodies work or who are starting to study human anatomy and physiology in school.

Notes to Parents This book could easily be read to a younger child (ages 5–7) or read by an older child who prefers a simple text.

If Your Child Liked This Book, Then Try . . . *You Can't Smell a Flower with Your Ear! All About Your Five Senses* by Joanna Cole, illustrated by Mavis Smith (Grosset ALL ABOARD READING series, Level 2). Also try other books in the I WONDER WHY . . . series from Kingfisher, including *I Wonder Why Camels Have Humps and Other Questions About Animals, I Wonder Why Castles Had Moats and Other Questions About Long Ago,* and *I Wonder Why Stars Twinkle and Other Questions About Space.*

I Am Rosa Parks

by

ROSA PARKS WITH JIM HASKINS

Illustrator WIL CLAY

Genre: Nonfiction/Biography

Publisher: Puffin, $3.99 (p)

Page Length: 48

Type of Illustrations: Color, on almost every page

Reluctant Reader Appeal: Suitable Text, Concise Chapters, Kid Relevance

Suggested reading level: Ages 6–9

When we rode a bus,
we could only sit in the back seats.
The front seats
were just for white people.

If all the front seats were filled
with white people,
we black people
had to give up our seats
to the next white people
who got on the bus.

Synopsis One day in 1955, Rosa Parks refused to give up her seat on a bus to a white man. She was arrested, and her act spurred the start of the civil rights movement. In this book, Rosa Parks tells in her own words how she worked with others in her community to help black people win their rights. Broken into four short chapters, it chronicles how Parks got arrested; how she grew up; how Parks's arrest led to a yearlong boycott of buses by blacks in Montgomery, Alabama, and eventually to the Supreme Court decision to end segregation; and how her life has been different since the boycott. And though the book ends on a hopeful note, she points out that there is still much work to be done because though the laws have changed, "there are still many people who have not changed their hearts."

Why This Book Appeals to Reluctant Readers Parks paints herself not as a celebrity but as an ordinary person standing up for her rights. She simply lays out the facts and states that she wouldn't give up her seat that day because she was just tired of giving in. Young children have an innate sense of fairness, and reluctant readers will appreciate that Parks allows them to draw their own conclusions about what life might be like for themselves and their friends if she hadn't stood her ground all those years ago.

Who Might Like This Book This book ties in beautifully with school assignments kids may have on the civil rights movement. Kids who have questions about racial prejudice can gain some perspective from this biography. Girls who are looking for strong women role models may also enjoy this book.

Notes to Parents *I Am Rosa Parks* plants the seeds for some interesting discussions on human rights and prejudice. It also provides a window into what society was like during your own childhood or that of your parents, when civil rights were not taken for granted.

If Your Child Liked This Book, Then Try . . . *Great Black Heroes: Five Notable Inventors* by Wade Hudson, illustrated by Ron Garnett (Scholastic HELLO READER! series, Level 4).

The Titanic: Lost . . . and Found

by

JUDY DONNELLY

Illustrator KEITH KOHLER

Genre: Nonfiction/Shipwrecks

Publisher: Random House, $3.99 (p)

Page Length: 48

Type of Illustrations: Color, on almost every page

Reluctant Reader Appeal: Fast-Paced Plot, Concise Chapters, Suitable Text, Visual Appeal

Suggested reading level:
Ages 7–8

It is almost midnight. The ship is quiet. The sea is smooth as glass. The air is biting cold.

The passengers have had a good dinner. Some of them are still up playing cards. Most are asleep in their rooms.

It is a good night to be inside. But the lookout must watch for danger. He is high above the ship in the crow's-nest. He stares into the darkness.

Suddenly the lookout sees a dark shape. It is a mountain of ice! And the Titanic is heading right into it! The lookout rings an alarm. He calls, "Iceberg straight ahead!"

Synopsis This book chronicles the journey of the great "unsinkable" ship *Titanic:* the excitement surrounding its maiden voyage from England on April 10, 1912, its demise off the Canadian coast four days later, and its eventual discovery on the ocean floor by Robert Ballard in 1985. In direct, vivid language, the author describes the ship's opulent decor, its sinkproof design, and the people—rich and poor—who lined up to travel to America. When the *Titanic* hits an iceberg and begins to sink, the text takes on a breathless, tense quality and focuses on the human details that made the event so tragic (for example, another ship, the *Californian,* was only 10 miles away but had turned off its radio and so did not receive the *Titanic's* distress calls). The illustrations have an intimate quality, conveying both the vastness of the ocean and the terrified faces of the passengers as the ship sinks into the icy waters.

Why This Book Appeals to Reluctant Readers This book brings the *Titanic's* fate to life on an emotional as well as a factual level and clearly explains how the ship sunk and why so few passengers survived. The tension of the events will capture any kid who is fascinated with sunken ships and buried treasure.

Who Might Like This Book The *Titanic's* story is interesting to just about everyone, but especially to kids who love ships, adventure stories, or treasure hunts.

If Your Child Liked This Book, Then Try . . . *Pompeii . . . Buried Alive!* by Edith Kunhardt, illustrated by Michael Eagel (Random House STEP INTO READING series, Step 3); *Finding the Titanic* by Robert D. Ballard with Nan Froman, illustrated by Ken Marshall (Scholastic HELLO READER! series, Level 4).

Moonwalk: The First Trip to the Moon

by

JUDY DONNELLY

Illustrator DENNIS DAVIDSON

Genre: Nonfiction/
  Space Travel

Publisher: Random House,
  $3.99 (p)

Page Length: 48

Type of Illustrations: Color
  illustrations and photographs, on almost every
  page

Reluctant Reader Appeal:
  Fast-Paced Plot, Suitable
  Text, Visual Appeal

**Suggested
reading level:**
Ages 7–9

*Nothing moves. There is no wind or weather. No sign of life
anywhere.*

*Bright sunshine lights up the surface of the moon. But the
sky is black. And way off in the distance hangs a tiny, shining
blue-white Earth.*

*It is time to explore. Together the two astronauts walk into
the gray-white world. The ground is covered with a powdery
dust. With almost every step they leave footprints—footprints on
the moon! If no one comes to disturb them, they will stay just as
they are for millions of years.*

Synopsis Mankind's first trip to the moon is outlined in five tight chapters: "Moon Launch," about the blastoff of *Apollo 11* on July 16, 1969; "How Do You Get to the Moon?" explains different attempts people have made at space travel over thousands of years; "Wanted: Astronauts" describes the training astronauts undertake; "Destination Moon" comes back to *Apollo* and chronicles how the landing craft *Eagle* separated from the command module and landed on the moon; and "Moonwalk," about man's first steps on the moon and the astronauts' return to earth. Illustrations are seamlessly combined with photographs of the astronauts.

Why This Book Appeals to Reluctant Readers The author skillfully conveys the excitement and awe that surrounded the first moon trip, which may be news to young readers who have seen several rocket launches on television. Interesting, kid-appealing details are sprinkled throughout (the *Apollo* crew was in quarantine for three weeks after returning to earth in case they brought back "moon germs"). The typeface is large enough to be easily read, but there's a substantial amount of text on each page, which helps the reader feel he's mastered a hefty book.

Who Might Like This Book The early space program was male-dominated, so girls won't find any female role models in this book, but any child interested in space travel, astronomy, or the moon will still find this account fascinating and exciting.

Notes to Parents If you want to sneak a little personal history into the mix, read this book with your child and then discuss your own memories of watching the first astronauts on television.

If Your Child Liked This Book, Then Try . . . *To the Top! Climbing the World's Highest Mountain* by S. A. Kramer, illustrated by Thomas LaPadula (Random House STEP INTO READING series, Step 4).

Dig and Sow!
How Do Plants Grow?

(AT HOME WITH SCIENCE series)

by

JANICE LOBB

Illustrators PETER UTTON AND
ANN SAVAGE

Genre: Nonfiction/Plants

Publisher: Kingfisher,
$10.95 (h)

Page Length: 32

Type of Illustrations: Color,
on every page

Reluctant Reader Appeal:
Humor, Concise Chapters,
Suitable Text, Kid
Relevance, Unique
Presentation, Visual Appeal

**Suggested
reading level:**
Ages 5 and up

Why don't trees fall down?

*Like most plants, trees need to grow upward to get as much light
as possible. To keep them from falling down, plants have roots
that spread out under the ground and support them as they grow.
As well as supporting the plant, roots also suck up water from
the soil. Trees need thick, woody roots to support their heavy
trunks, but smaller plants have thinner roots.*

Synopsis Using questions to begin each two-page chapter, this book explains simple scientific concepts about the plant, insect, and animal life found in an ordinary backyard. Each question is posed from a child's viewpoint (*Why is grass green? How do seeds grow? What do worms do all day?*); the answer is given in one general paragraph of text and then expanded on with annotated illustrations. Twelve "See for yourself!" experiments offer step-by-step instructions to easy activities that reinforce the information. Animal cartoon characters, named after famous scientists, cavort through the pages and start off each new topic with a joke (*Why wasn't the butterfly invited to the dance? Because it was a moth ball!*). Interesting insect trivia is scattered throughout, and a glossary rounds out this fun, informative book.

Why This Book Appeals to Reluctant Readers The information is presented in a straightforward manner that's accessible to young children, and the uncomplicated sentence structure won't overwhelm older readers who prefer easier texts. The humor and fascinating facts keep the interest level high, and the experiments allow readers to see the scientific principles at work. The fact that this book is about things the reader can find close to home makes the topic especially relevant to kids.

Who Might Like This Book Kids who love to garden, those who are interested in bugs and plants, and children who like to do experiments with materials found around the house and yard.

If Your Child Liked This Book, Then Try . . . Other AT HOME WITH SCIENCE books by Janice Lobb, including *Splish! Splosh! Why Do We Wash?* and *Listen and See! What's on TV?* Also try the HANDS-ON SCIENCE series from Kingfisher, including *Sound and Light* by Jack Challoner and *Forces in Motion* by John Graham.

Baseball's Greatest Hitters

by

S.A. KRAMER

Illustrator JIM CAMPBELL

Genre: Nonfiction/Baseball

Publisher: Random House, $3.99 (p)

Page Length: 48

Type of Illustrations: Color illustrations combined with color and black-and-white photographs

Reluctant Reader Appeal: Concise Chapters, Suitable Text, Kid Relevance, Visual Appeal

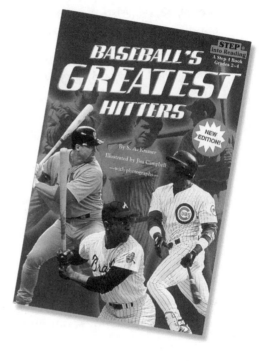

Suggested reading level: Ages 7–9

Babe is baseball's first power hitter. By clouting homer after homer, he has changed the game more than anyone else. But he's 37 now. Is he too old to hit anymore? Babe, however, still believes in himself.

Cub fans boo as Babe steps into the batter's box. Players on the Cub bench heckle him. When the first pitch is a strike, some shout "Baboon! Potbelly!" Babe, who is overweight, grins and raises one finger.

Synopsis This book profiles the most spectacular hitters in the history of baseball: Ty Cobb, Babe Ruth, Ted Williams, Hank Aaron, Mark McGwire, and Sammy Sosa. Each chapter starts with a pivotal moment that helped define the player's career, then backtracks to the player's childhood and how he got started in professional baseball. A page at the end of the chapter provides the player's statistics and highlights his greatest feats. Photographs and illustrations depict the players at their best.

Why This Book Appeals to Reluctant Readers Sports fans love to collect statistics and trivia on their favorite players, and this book provides such facts at a glance. The text brings alive the tension and excitement of the game from the batter's perspective, helping readers feel as if they're standing in the batter's box facing down the pitcher. The chapters are short and concentrate mostly on the game, which easily holds the attention of reluctant readers, but the biographical information also illustrates the sheer determination of each player and why he's earned his hero status.

Who Might Like This Book Baseball fans, of course, especially those who enjoy spouting the stats of their favorite players.

Notes to Parents Even older kids who are below-average readers but love baseball can enjoy this book. By the way, comparing baseball statistics between players or figuring out how stats are calculated is an easy way to connect reading and math.

If Your Child Liked This Book, Then Try . . . *Baseball's Greatest Pitchers* by S. A. Kramer, illustrated by Jim Campbell; *Baseball's Best: Five True Stories* by Andrew Gutelle, illustrated by Cliff Spohn (both Random House STEP INTO READING series, Step 4).

Chapter Six

Making the Transition

With fewer illustrations and more text than easy readers, these short novels and engaging nonfiction titles are for kids who have mastered the fundamentals of reading but aren't ready for full-length middle-grade books.

FICTION

Horrible Harry in Room 2B by Suzy Kline · page 101

The Chalk Box Kid by Clyde Robert Bulla · page 103

Flat Stanley by Jeff Brown · page 106

Cam Jansen and the Mystery of the Stolen Corn Popper (CAM JANSEN series) by David A. Adler · page 108

Amber Brown Is Not a Crayon by Paula Danziger · page 111

The Adventures of Captain Underpants (CAPTAIN UNDERPANTS series) by Dav Pilkey · page 114

Parachuting Hamsters and Andy Russell (ANDY RUSSELL series) by David A. Adler · page 117

What's the Matter with Herbie Jones? (HERBIE JONES series) by Suzy Kline · page 120

Sarah, Plain and Tall by Patricia MacLachlan · page 123

Fat Men from Space by Daniel Manus Pinkwater · page 126

Not My Dog by Colby Rodowsky · page 128

Your Mother Was a Neanderthal (THE TIME WARP TRIO series) by Jon Scieszka · page 130

Little Fox's Secret: The Mystery of Bent's Fort by Mary Peace Finley · page 133

Oh, No, It's Robert by Barbara Seuling · page 135

Little Wolf's Book of Badness by Ian Whybrow · page 137

NONFICTION

Amazing Snakes (EYEWITNESS JUNIORS series) by Alexandra Parsons · page 140

The Magic School Bus Inside the Earth by Joanna Cole · page 142

Steam, Smoke, and Steel: Back in Time with Trains by Patrick O'Brien · page 145

The Top of the World: Climbing Mount Everest by Steve Jenkins · page 147

Pond Life: A Close-Up Look at the Natural World (LOOK CLOSER series) by Barbara Taylor · page 149

Pirates! (EYEWITNESS READERS series) by Christopher Maynard · page 151

Barry: The Bravest Saint Bernard by Lynn Hall · page 153

Fire! by Joy Masoff · page 155

Questions and Answers About Weather by M. Jean Craig · page 157

How to Talk to Your Dog by Jean Craighead George · page 159

Tornadoes! (THE WEATHER CHANNEL PRESENTS series) by Sally Rose · page 161

Horrible Harry in Room 2B

by

SUZY KLINE

Illustrator FRANK REMKIEWICZ

Genre: Humorous Fiction

Publisher: Puffin Books,
$3.99 (p)

Page Length: 56

Type of Illustrations: Black
and white, about every
other page

Reluctant Reader Appeal:
Humor, Well-Defined
Characters, Fast-Paced
Plot, Concise Chapters,
Kid Relevance

**Suggested
reading level:**
Ages 7–10

*When I first met Harry out on the playground, he had a shoe-
box. I asked him, "What's in there?"*

"Something. What's your name?"

"Doug," I said.

"Want to see a girl scream, Doug?"

*Before I could say anything, Harry took off after Song Lee.
When he trapped her by a tree, he opened up his box and dan-
gled a garter snake in her face.*

Song Lee screamed!

That's the first time I saw Harry do something horrible.

Synopsis Second grade is pretty exciting for Doug, the narrator of this book and Harry's best friend. Doug is constantly in awe of Harry's horrible ways, such as when he shakes hands with Sidney, telling him the goop on his hand is a squashed bug (it's really banana), or hides "stub" people in the teacher's desk. Sometimes Harry's plans backfire (the teacher thinks the stub people are cute), and sometimes he makes Doug mad. But all in all, Harry's a pretty good friend.

Why This Book Appeals to Reluctant Readers Though Harry's in second grade, his antics are daring and entertaining enough to amuse older kids. Each chapter reads like a stand-alone short story, so the book can easily be read in small chunks. The characters are distinctive and funny, and Harry's jokes, often involving bugs, snakes, or some sort of slime, directly appeal to elementary school kids' sense of humor. Finally, everyone knows (or is) a Harry, making this book immediately relevant to readers' lives.

Who Might Like This Book Any kids who love humor and practical jokes, but especially boys. The short paragraphs and larger type size make this a good transition book for kids who want to move up to chapter books but are still not ready for more complex sentence structure.

Notes to Parents Don't worry—Harry's not a model for bad behavior. He doesn't do anything your kid hasn't already thought of on his own. Not every joke comes off as Harry had planned, but he does prove to be a loyal friend.

If Your Child Liked This Book, Then Try . . . Other books in this series, including *Horrible Harry and the Ant Invasion* and *Horrible Harry's Secret* (all from Puffin Books).

The Chalk Box Kid

by

CLYDE ROBERT BULLA

Illustrator THOMAS B. ALLEN

Genre: Contemporary Fiction

Publisher: Random House,
$3.99 (p)

Page Length: 60

Type of Illustrations: Black
and white, about every
other page

Reluctant Reader Appeal:
Well-Defined Characters,
Concise Chapters, Suitable
Text, Kid Relevance

**Suggested
reading level:**
Ages 7–10

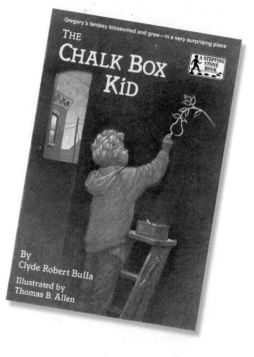

At noon a boy named Vance came up to him on the playground.
Vance was the biggest boy in Room 3.

"Did you say you went to North Lake School?" he asked.

"Yes," said Gregory.

"What made you say it's a big school?" asked Vance.

Some other boys and girls had come by. They were listening.

"It is a big school," said Gregory.

"No, it isn't," said Vance. "I've been there, and it's not as big
as this."

"It looks bigger," said Gregory.

"Well, it isn't," said Vance. "You like to brag, don't you?"

"I wasn't bragging," said Gregory. "I just said it was bigger. I didn't say it was better."

He stopped. No one was listening. Vance and the others had gone away.

Synopsis On Gregory's ninth birthday, his family moves to a small house across the city because Gregory's father has to start a new job. It doesn't have a yard, but Gregory is thrilled to have his own room. His privacy, however, is short-lived: Uncle Max comes to stay with them because he's out of work, and Gregory and Max must bunk together. Gregory comforts himself by drawing pictures and hanging them on his walls, until Uncle Max covers them with car posters.

Then Gregory starts his new school and somehow gets off on the wrong foot. The only person Gregory even talks to is Ivy, a shy girl who is the best artist in class. One day, Gregory investigates the building behind his house, which turns out to be an abandoned chalk factory that had burned down. Gregory finds a few boxes of chalk and begins to draw on the blackened walls.

When his class learns about plants, Gregory decides he'll create a garden for himself at the chalk factory. He spends days drawing flowers, vegetables, trees, and a pool. He tells his classmates that he has a wonderful garden, but some children think he's bragging. They follow him home and see that his garden is really made of chalk drawings, which gives them more reason to think he's strange. But Ivy tagged along as well, and once she starts telling adults about Gregory's garden, things finally begin to fall into place in Gregory's life.

Why This Book Appeals to Reluctant Readers In simple, eloquent text, the author has captured the feelings of a child trying to cope with change. Caught at the age when he's too old to cry to his parents but too young to really express how he feels, Gregory deals with his loneliness in a very believable, poignant way. The book conveys deep emotion without being overly sentimental yet sticks close to a child's perspective. And every child appreciates the importance of having your own special, secret place. The short chapters give just enough information to tell the story but still allow the reader to fill in the underlying meanings (for example, the author just shows that Gregory's parents are too busy to see his garden but doesn't dwell on how Gregory feels about their brush-offs). This makes it easy for readers to project themselves onto Gregory, especially if they've ever felt that the world is spinning beyond their control.

Who Might Like This Book Readers who like thoughtful books with emotional resonance or those who have felt shy, new, or out of place and need to see their feelings reflected in a character who finds a way to solve his problem on his own. Even though the protagonist is a boy, this book should appeal to boys and girls alike.

If Your Child Liked This Book, Then Try . . . Shoe-shine Girl by Clyde Robert Bulla (HarperTrophy).

Flat Stanley

by

JEFF BROWN

Illustrator STEVE BJORKMAN

Genre: Humorous Fiction

Publisher: HarperTrophy, $4.25 (p)

Page Length: 58

Type of Illustrations: Black and white, on almost every page

Reluctant Reader Appeal: Humor, Fast-Paced Plot, Concise Chapters, Suitable Text

Suggested reading level: Ages 7–10

When Stanley got used to being flat, he enjoyed it. He could go in and out of rooms, even when the door was closed, just by lying down and sliding through the crack at the bottom.

Mr. and Mrs. Lambchop said it was silly, but they were quite proud of him.

Arthur got jealous and tried to slide under a door, but he just banged his head.

Synopsis One day Stanley Lambchop's bulletin board falls on him while he's sleeping, and suddenly he's flat—one-half inch thick, to be exact. Stanley finds his new shape quite enjoyable. He can slide into rooms under closed doors, be rolled up and carried like a rug, or flown like a kite. He can even be airmailed to visit a friend in California. Best of all, Stanley volunteers to pose as a painting in the museum to catch some art thieves, and he becomes a hero.

But Stanley soon discovers there are two problems with being flat. First, his younger brother Arthur is jealous of all the attention Stanley gets. And second, once the novelty wears off, Stanley is teased by the other kids and called names. When Stanley finally confides his problems to Arthur, his younger brother comes up with the perfect way to make Stanley boy-shaped once again.

Why This Book Appeals to Reluctant Readers
Though the story (first published in 1964) might seem a bit tame by today's standards, it provides gentle, easygoing entertainment. The funniest aspect of the book is the fact that no one (especially Stanley's parents) seems particularly worried about Stanley's condition. It's considered more interesting than alarming. The author knows exactly what kids will find intriguing about Stanley: It's not his flatness but what he does with it that makes him special.

Who Might Like This Book Boys and girls in third and fourth grade who like to breeze through a story that's light, entertaining, and not weighed down by a lesson or moral (and don't mind when the author pushes the boundaries of reality) should enjoy this book.

If Your Child Liked This Book, Then Try . . . Other books by Jeff Brown, published by HarperTrophy: *Stanley and the Magic Lamp* and *Invisible Stanley*. Also try *The Boy with the Helium Head* by Phyllis Reynolds Naylor, illustrated by Kay Chorao (Dell Yearling FIRST CHOICE CHAPTER BOOK series).

Cam Jansen and the Mystery of the Stolen Corn Popper

(CAM JANSEN series)

by

DAVID A. ADLER

Illustrator SUSANNA NATTI

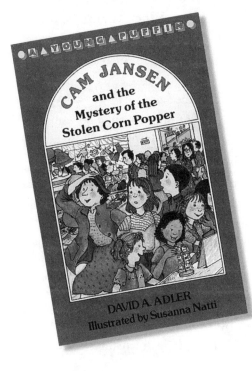

Genre: Mystery/Fiction

Publisher: Viking, $11.10 (h);
Puffin Books, $3.99 (p)

Page Length: 58

Type of Illustrations: Black
and white, about two per
chapter

Reluctant Reader Appeal:
Well-Defined Characters,
Fast-Paced Plot, Concise
Chapters, Suitable Text

**Suggested
reading level:**
Ages 7–10

*Eric was reaching for a pack of pencils when Cam tapped him on
his shoulder. She pointed to a woman in the candy department
and whispered, "She's been looking over here for a long time."*
    "So?"

"I remember her. She was here when the man's shopping bag was stolen."

Eric took a pack of pencils from the display. Then he found the pens and erasers.

"Put those things down," Cam told him. "That woman is holding a shopping bag, and I'll bet she has a corn popper in there."

Synopsis Jennifer "Cam" Jansen is a fifth-grade girl with a photographic memory. She looks at something, closes her eyes and says "Click," and the image is stored in her brain like a snapshot to be studied later. In this book, Cam and her friend Eric are in Binky's Department Store buying school supplies when a man standing next to them announces that someone has stolen his shopping bag. It contained a popcorn popper wrapped in gold paper with a green bow. As the security guards are instructed to stop anyone leaving the store with such a package, Cam takes a "picture" of the scene. Then she sees a suspicious-looking woman whom she and Eric follow through the store. The woman puts down her shopping bag in the toy department and moves away. Cam is just peering into the woman's bag when a girl yells from another aisle that her bag was stolen as well.

Cam eventually determines who the thief is, but it takes her and Eric several attempts to convince the security guards to take them seriously and to figure out how the woman is stealing from the store. Once the thief is caught, Cam and Eric are rewarded for their efforts.

Why This Book Appeals to Reluctant Readers Middle graders have always loved mysteries; these books add another compelling element to the plot and help the reader become involved in the story. The Cam Jansen mysteries are perfect for reluctant readers because they're quick, they take place over a short period of time, and Cam's photographic memory is an interesting hook.

However, Cam's memory simply assists in gathering clues; the final leap to solving the crime is done with old-fashioned observation and deduction, which the reader can accomplish as well as Cam. This keeps the reader thinking, hoping to solve the mystery before the characters do. These bite-size mysteries introduce readers to the genre with ordinary, everyday crimes whose solutions are within the reach of an average kid.

Who Might Like This Book As a character, Cam Jansen appeals to boys and girls. Readers who are easily bored with contemporary fiction might find that the simple mystery element of these books holds their attention.

If Your Child Liked This Book, Then Try . . . Other books in the series, such as *Cam Jansen and the Mystery of the U.F.O, Cam Jansen and the Mystery of the Dinosaur Bones, Cam Jansen and the Ghostly Mystery,* and *Cam Jansen and the Mystery of Flight 54* (all from Viking/Puffin Books).

Amber Brown
Is Not a Crayon

by

PAULA DANZIGER

Illustrator TONY ROSS

Genre: Contemporary Fiction

Publisher: Putnam, $14.99
(h); Little Apple, $3.99 (p)

Page Length: 80

Type of Illustrations: One
or two black-and-white
illustrations per chapter

Reluctant Reader Appeal:
Humor, Well-Defined
Characters, Fast-Paced Plot,
Concise Chapters, Kid
Relevance, Suitable Text

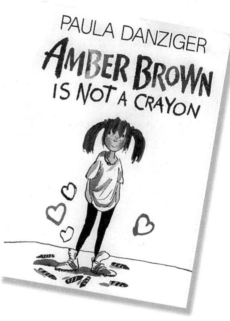

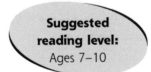

**Suggested
reading level:**
Ages 7–10

*I don't look so bad, and anyway, I forgot that the pictures were
being taken that day, even though Mr. Cohen told us a million
times, and even though he had written two million reminders
on the blackboard.*

So I'm a little forgetful.

And Hannah Burton isn't always totally right. I don't comb my hair with a rake. Maybe my fingers sometimes but never a rake.

"I like your picture." Justin grins at me. "It looks exactly like you, not just the way you look but the way you act."

"You mean messy." Hannah laughs.

I want to pull off the stupid little bow that she's wearing on her head.

"Don't you dare." Justin pulls on my arm.

I like the way that Justin usually knows what I'm thinking and I usually know what he's thinking.

Synopsis Amber Brown and Justin Daniels have been best friends since preschool. Justin helps Amber with fractions, and Amber cleans up his messy writing. They always sit next to each other in class, play together every day, and have been building a giant chewing gum ball for years. Justin was there when Amber's parents got divorced, and Amber is there now when Justin misses his dad because his father had to take a new job far away. The only problem is that Justin's family will be joining his dad as soon as they sell their house. Amber hopes that the house will never sell and Justin won't have to move, but then one day it happens. The two best friends only have a few weeks left, and suddenly they can't get along anymore. They fight, they sit with other people at school, and Amber worries they'll never make up in time. Will her friendship with Justin survive his move?

Why This Book Appeals to Reluctant Readers Amber Brown is a very real, funny, smart, no-nonsense third grader. She and Justin delight in each other's company and typical third-grade activities. Their banter rings true, and any readers of this age will see themselves in the two characters. Amber's dilemma is also relevant to kids of this age, when long-standing friendships often start to break down as kids go off in different directions. Her problems, and their solutions, are presented in a genuine, child-like manner. The chapters move quickly with lots of action and dialogue. The author is able to show the concerns of children in middle elementary grades without imposing an adult perspective.

Who Might Like This Book Boy or girls who appreciate humor, real-life situations, and seeing kids just like themselves in their books.

Notes to Parents Paula Danziger is a very popular author with middle-grade readers, mainly because her characters and dialogue are so true to life. She has many longer novels as well as the Amber Brown series.

If Your Child Liked This Book, Then Try . . . There are many other books featuring Amber Brown, including *Amber Brown Goes Fourth* and *You Can't Eat Your Chicken Pox, Amber Brown* (all from Putnam).

The Adventures of Captain Underpants

(CAPTAIN UNDERPANTS series)

by

DAV PILKEY

Illustrator DAV PILKEY

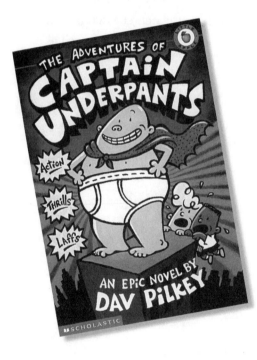

Genre: Humorous Fiction

Publisher: Blue Sky Press/ Scholastic, $3.99 (p)

Page Length: 124

Type of Illustrations: Black and white, on every page

Reluctant Reader Appeal: Humor, Well-Defined Characters, Fast-Paced Plot, Concise Chapters, Suitable Text, Visual Appeal

Suggested reading level: Ages 7–10

Over the years, [George and Harold] had created hundreds of their own comics, starring dozens of their own superheroes. First there was "Dog Man," then came "Timmy the Talking Toilet," and who could forget "The Amazing Cow Lady"?

But the all-time greatest superhero they ever made up had to be "The Amazing Captain Underpants."

George came up with the idea.

"Most superheroes look *like they're flying around in their underwear,"* he said. *"Well, this guy actually* is *flying around in his underwear!"*

Synopsis George and Harold, fourth graders at Jerome Horwitz elementary school, are best friends with an uncontrollable "silly streak" that manifests itself through practical jokes and assorted pranks. They spend time each afternoon creating comic books featuring Captain Underpants and sell the comics at school for 50 cents apiece.

Their school principal, Mr. Krupp, is sick of George and Harold's mischief and determined to catch them in the act. One day he gets his chance: After installing surveillance cameras all over school, Mr. Krupp videotapes the boys as they elaborately sabotage the school football game. In order to prevent Mr. Krupp from turning over the tape to the football team, George and Harold agree to the principal's list of demands. The boys are sure they're doomed to years of hard labor until George sees a magazine ad for a 3-D Hypno-Ring. They send for the ring and, when it arrives, use it to hypnotize Mr. Krupp.

While under hypnosis, Mr. Krupp hands over the videotape. Then George and Harold decide to have some fun. They entertain themselves by giving the principal several hypnotic suggestions, ending with telling him he's Captain Underpants. Mr. Krupp, having read every one of the boys' comics, immediately tears off all his clothes (except his underpants, of course), dons a red curtain as a cape, and takes off across the playground. After several adventures involving a bank robbery, robots, a giant laser and fake doggie doo, Goerge and Harold dehypnotize Mr. Krupp but don't use the proper technique because they fail to read the ring's instructions. As a result, Mr. Krupp unexpectedly turns back into Captain Underpants every time he hears someone snap their fingers.

This book's hilarious illustrations add yet another level to the story. "The Extremely Graphic Violence Chapter," for example, begins with a humorous disclaimer about the following "graphic" scenes, followed by "Flip-O-Rama" pictures of George and Harold that the reader can flip quickly back and forth to create the appearance of animation. And this doesn't even begin to cover all the hidden jokes and puns contained in the cartoon-style, exaggerated drawings

Why This Book Appeals to Reluctant Readers The title alone is appealing; what third- or fourth-grade boy would turn down the chance to read about a character named Captain Underpants? This story flies along and has a decidedly subversive undertone, mostly at the expense of the school principal. Dav Pilkey's winks to the reader make the child feel as if he's in on the joke, as when George and Harold watch Dr. Evil's robots rob the Rare Crystal Shop:

"Did I just see two ROBOTS *get into a van?"* asked Harold.

"You know," said George, *"up until* now *this story was almost* believable!"

Who Might Like This Book This book is a natural for boys, especially those with a rollicking sense of humor. Girls will like it too (though the older ones might not be as apt to admit it).

Notes to Parents Though George and Harold's humor may seem a bit crude at times, it never goes overboard. Some of the text in the boys' Captain Underpants comic book is misspelled, but it's clear from the illustrations that this is the writing of George and Harold and not to be taken literally.

If Your Child Liked This Book, Then Try . . . Other books in the CAPTAIN UNDERPANTS series, published by Scholastic: *Captain Underpants and the Attack of the Talking Toilets, Captain Underpants and the Invasion of the Incredibly Naughty Cafeteria Ladies from Outer Space, Captain Underpants and the Perilous Plot of Professor Poopypants,* and *Captain Underpants and the Wrath of the Wicked Wedgie Woman.*

Parachuting Hamsters and Andy Russell

(ANDY RUSSELL series)

by

DAVID A. ADLER

Illustrator WILL HILLENBRAND

Genre: Mystery

Publisher: Gulliver Books/
Harcourt, $14.00 (h)

Page Length: 112

Type of Illustrations: Black
and white, two per chapter

Reluctant Reader Appeal:
Humor, Well-Defined
Characters, Fast-Paced
Plot, Concise Chapters,
Suitable Text

**Suggested
reading level:**
Ages 7–10

*Uncle Terence smiled and told Andy and Tamika, "Now comes
the best part of the meal, the dessert, and I know just what we'll
have." He signaled to Jacques and told him, "We'll all have*
mousse au chocolat meringuée."

"Mouse!" Andy exclaimed. "I don't eat mouse."

"No," Tamika told him, "it's mousse, not mouse."

*"And I don't eat moose, either. I don't eat animals. Why can't
I have a real dessert, like cake, ice cream, or pudding?"*

"Mousse au chocolat meringuée is *pudding,*" Uncle Terence explained. "*It's rich chocolate pudding layered with baked egg whites that have been sweetened and whipped. It's delicious.*"

"Oh," Andy said. "*It's just that I like to know what I'm eating before I eat it.*"

Synopsis Fourth-grader Andy Russell is spending the weekend in New York City with his friend Tamika and her Aunt Mandy and Uncle Terence. Aunt Mandy has no kids or pets, frequents museums, and is a stickler for good manners.

Andy's convinced the weekend will be a bore, but while he and Tamika are waiting for Aunt Mandy in the lobby of her posh apartment building, something strange happens: Hamsters, tied to colorful silk handkerchiefs, parachute down to the driveway from the top floor. Andy decides he's going to find out the identity of the person who would do such a thing to helpless animals.

The evening progresses to dinner at a fancy French restaurant (Andy tries to use his best manners but nevertheless ends up making a big mess) and then back to Aunt Mandy's building, where they discover someone has buttered all the buttons in the elevator. The next day, Andy and Tamika accompany Aunt Mandy to an art museum and the ballet, along with Jason, a boy who lives upstairs. Jason, who is rude and aloof, insists on carrying his backpack wherever he goes. It's soon clear to Andy that Jason is probably the hamster-tossing, button-buttering culprit, but how can he prove it? Things get tense for a while as Jason makes it look like Andy's the one causing trouble, but Andy manages to come up with evidence that links Jason to the crimes. The weekend ends with a cozy, candlelit dinner at Aunt Mandy's, where Uncle Terence, dressed as a snooty waiter, serves them pancakes.

Why This Book Appeals to Reluctant Readers Unlike David Adler's Cam Jansen mystery series for this same age-group (see page 108), the mystery is just a small part of this story.

As a result, this book will please both mystery lovers (though it's clear halfway through that Jason is the perpetrator, seeing how Andy will prove it keeps the suspense going) and those kids who want a funny read. Though Andy tries to stay out of trouble, it just seems to find him. The scene at the French restaurant is hilarious, and Andy's attempts to understand modern art perfectly capture the unpretentious interpretations of a fourth grader. The uncluttered text, quick pacing, and short chapters make this book a breeze to read.

Who Might Like This Book Boys will be drawn to Andy, especially his comical efforts at affecting fancy manners. Kids who are just starting to read mysteries or books over 100 pages will find this easy to handle. Readers who like realistic, funny characters or any child who has ever spent the weekend getting "cultured" by relatives will appreciate this book.

If Your Child Liked This Book, Then Try . . . Other books in the ANDY RUSSELL series by David A. Adler: *The Many Troubles of Andy Russell, Andy and Tamika,* and *School Trouble for Andy Russell* (Harcourt).

What's the Matter with Herbie Jones?

(HERBIE JONES series)

by

SUZY KLINE

Illustrator RICHARD WILLIAMS

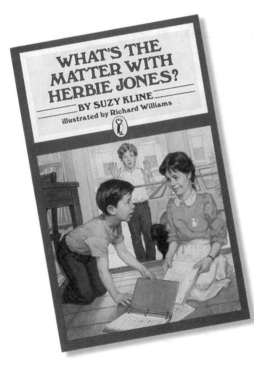

Genre: Contemporary Fiction

Publisher: Puffin Books, $4.99 (p)

Page Length: 111

Type of Illustrations: Black and white, about one every other chapter

Reluctant Reader Appeal: Humor, Fast-Paced Plot, Concise Chapters, Suitable Text, Kid Relevance

---

Suggested reading level: Ages 8–12

"How many pennies did you bring?"

"Uh . . . two . . ." Herbie stammered.

"Two?"

". . . two hundred or so."

"Oh, Herbie! What a wonderful surprise!" And then Annabelle closed her eyes and waited. "I'll start wishing just as soon as you put them in."

Them? Herbie thought. He dropped four pennies into the water.

Annabelle opened up one eye. "All of them."

"All of them?" Herbie squeaked.

Synopsis Herbie Jones and Annabelle Hodgekiss aren't exactly on speaking terms, until he writes her a poem in a get-well card and then unwittingly becomes her partner in the class dance contest. Suddenly, Annabelle is paying attention to Herbie, and he likes it. Herbie's best friend, Ray, is worried about whatever has come over Herbie, but he needn't be—after only a couple of days, Annabelle gets bossy and possessive, and Herbie's had enough. The trouble is, now he can't get rid of her.

Herbie's efforts at giving Annabelle the brush-off are unsuccessful, but then the boys come up with a plan: If they can beat the girls in the class spelling bee, Annabelle won't ever speak to any of the boys again (she *hates* losing). And best of all, they can get the list of words before the contest! But though Herbie goes along with the plan at first, he doesn't feel right about cheating and eventually convinces the boys to come clean with the teacher. The class competes and Herbie wins the spelling bee fair and square, ensuring that Annabelle is out of his life for good.

Why This Book Appeals to Reluctant Readers
Though this book isn't profoundly literary, it's a light, funny story about how boys and girls in third or fourth grade relate to each other, as seen from a boy's point of view. Herbie is an average, happy-go-lucky kid who is discovering his talents (he's not great at spelling but likes to write poems) and for a while enjoys basking in the glow of female attention. But, true to his age, this doesn't last long. The short chapters move quickly and are full of believable dialogue; the gentle moral message is woven seamlessly into the story.

Who Might Like This Book The Herbie Jones books are great for kids who want easier text but a longer story. Boys read them because of the male protagonist, but the author's take on how boys and girls interact should appeal to both genders. If your child doesn't want to read a story about boy/girl relationships, there are several more titles in the Herbie Jones series, some of which are listed below.

Notes to Parents The publisher lists these books for ages 8 to 12, but I feel the content appeals to a slightly younger audience, and the text is not overwhelming. This series is good if you want your child to read books with subtle moral messages wrapped in an entertaining format. Since many of the books were written in the early to mid-1980s, some details are dated (Herbie types a note to Annabelle on a typewriter and they dance to music on a record player). However, these are minor points and don't detract from the story.

If Your Child Liked This Book, Then Try . . . Other books in the HERBIE JONES series by Suzy Kline, including *Herbie Jones and Hamburger Head, Herbie Jones and the Class Gift, Herbie Jones and the Dark Attic,* and *Herbie Jones and the Monster Ball.*

Sarah, Plain and Tall

by

PATRICIA MacLACHLAN

Genre: Historical Fiction

Publisher: HarperTrophy,
$4.95 (p)

Page Length: 58

Type of Illustrations: None

Reluctant Reader Appeal:
Well-Defined Characters,
Concise Chapters, Suitable
Text, Kid Relevance

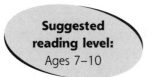

Suggested reading level:
Ages 7–10

"Dear Mr. Jacob Witting,

"I am Sarah Wheaton from Maine as you will see from my letter. I am answering your advertisement. I have never been married, though I have been asked. . . .

No one spoke when Papa finished the letter. He kept looking at it in his hands, reading it over to himself. Finally I turned my head a bit to sneak a look at Caleb. He was smiling. I smiled, too.

"One thing," I said in the quiet of the room.

"What's that?" asked Papa, looking up.

I put my arm around Caleb.

"Ask her if she sings," I said.

Synopsis Anna's mother died the day after her brother Caleb was born. Their house on the prairie is quiet now since her Papa doesn't sing anymore. Then one day Papa places an advertisement for a wife in the newspaper and gets a letter from Sarah Wheaton, who lives in Maine. Papa and the children exchange letters with Sarah, and Sarah agrees to come visit for a month to see how things work out. She'll come by train, her letter states, and wear a yellow bonnet. "I am plain and tall."

When Sarah arrives, she's everything the children expected. She slides down haystacks, dries flowers for the winter, and learns to plow. And she sings. But Anna and Caleb can tell that Sarah misses the sea, and they're worried she won't want to stay. Then, after Sarah insists that Papa teach her to drive the wagon, Sarah heads into town alone. The children wait anxiously all day for her return. Will she come back? Finally, at dusk, they see the dust from Sarah's wagon. She's brought colored pencils from town so she can draw the sea. And she's decided to stay for good.

Why This Book Appeals to Reluctant Readers It's hard to believe that so much story is packed into so few pages. The reading is effortless, but the impact of this book is profound. The reader learns a lot about the characters from their letters to each other: Sarah is forthright and unpretentious; Anna misses having her mother around the house; and Caleb wants to know about Sarah's cat, if she can keep a fire going at night, and if she snores. Anna's struggle to hold on to the past and yet embrace the future are themes that crop up again and again, providing a strong emotional pull to the story. Short chapters move the reader quickly through the month of Sarah's visit and weave details of the simple yet sometimes harsh prairie life in the late 1800s into the bigger story of how people work together to create a family.

Who Might Like This Book Girls in particular will be drawn to this book, though boys who like stories about families might appreciate it as well. Readers who love historical fiction or books with strong emotional undertones will find this to be a great read.

Notes to Parents *Sarah, Plain and Tall* has won many awards, including the 1986 Newbery Medal. This is a wonderful book to read out loud if you have children of different ages (kids as young as 5 who will sit through a story of this length can follow it easily). It can spark some lively discussions about blended families and how the time period and setting dictated that Anna's family needed a woman around and perhaps also affected how Anna and Caleb welcomed their potential stepmother.

If Your Child Liked This Book, Then Try . . . *Skylark* by Patricia MacLachan (HarperTrophy, sequel to *Sarah, Plain and Tall*). Also try the AMERICAN GIRL series of historical fiction, published by Pleasant Company (various authors—the whole series is shelved together in the bookstore).

Fat Men from Space

by

DANIEL MANUS PINKWATER

Illustrator DANIEL MANUS PINKWATER

Genre: Humorous Science Fiction

Publisher: Dell Yearling, $3.99 (p)

Page Length: 57

Type of Illustrations: Black and white, every few pages

Reluctant Reader Appeal: Humor, Well-Defined Characters, Fast-Paced Plot, Suitable Text

Suggested reading level: Ages 8–12

The spacemen weren't at all what William had expected. They looked like ordinary earth-people, except that they were fatter than most. William guessed that they weighed at least 350 pounds apiece. . . . All the spacemen were wearing plaid sports jackets, and dacron slacks. They had knitted neckties, and black-and-white shoes with thick rubber soles. They all had crew cuts and they all wore eyeglasses made of heavy black plastic. The only thing about their clothing that was sort of nifty and space-manlike was their belts. . . .

Synopsis Much to his delight, William discovers that the new filling in his tooth picks up radio broadcasts from all over the country. One evening, William tries running a wire from his tooth to a chain-link fence to improve his reception and hears radio signals from alien spacecrafts. But the aliens are on to him and soon abduct him in their saucer-shaped ship. The creatures, who look like fat men in polyester suits, explain their mission: to invade Earth, eat all the junk food available, and then enslave humans and force them to create junk food forever. William monitors reports of the invasion on his tooth-radio, listening for hours as stories of fat men raiding refrigerators and streets snarled with junk-food containers beam up to him through the atmosphere. Then, suddenly, the mission is aborted and William is returned home. Things eventually return to normal, though humans are confined to a diet of lean meat, fish, fruits, and vegetables for many months until the planet's supply of junk food can be reestablished.

Why This Book Appeals to Reluctant Readers This story reads like a humorous *Twilight Zone* episode: It doesn't really make sense, but that doesn't matter. The droll, over-the-top tone and the absurd plot twists will keep readers glued to the pages. Some of the disjointed radio broadcasts coming from William's mouth are laugh-out-loud funny. This slim novel feels more like a long short story—a quick, entertaining read with no message or moral attached.

Who Might Like This Book Kids who appreciate offbeat, slightly weird comedy; readers who like humorous science fiction; and children who are in the mood for witty dialogue and a light story that doesn't require wading through heavy subtext.

If Your Child Liked This Book, Then Try . . . *Lizard Music* by Daniel Manus Pinkwater (Bantam).

Not My Dog

by

COLBY RODOWSKY

Illustrator THOMAS F. YEZERSKI

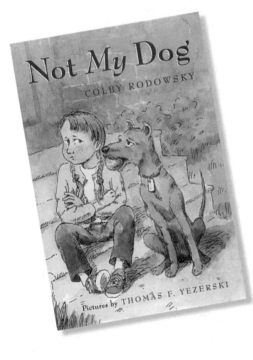

Genre: Contemporary Fiction

Publisher: Farrar, Straus & Giroux, $4.95 (p)

Page Length: 69

Type of Illustrations: Black and white, one or two per chapter

Reluctant Reader Appeal: Humor, Well-Defined Characters, Concise Chapters, Kid Relevance, Suitable Text

Suggested reading level: Ages 7–10

When Ellie went to bed that night, she closed her eyes and tried to think about the perfect puppy, maybe one with curly hair and soft floppy ears and a stubby tail. But no matter how hard she tried, all she could think of was the way Great-aunt Margaret had looked when she said goodbye to Preston. And she wondered if right this very minute Great-aunt Margaret and the sort of square, boring brown dog with sticking-up ears and a skinny tail who was downstairs in the family room were thinking about each other.

Synopsis For years, Ellie Martin has wanted a puppy more than anything. But Ellie's parents don't think she's ready—she'll have to wait until she's 9.

Then one day a few months before Ellie's ninth birthday, her parents make an announcement: They will be adopting Great-aunt Margaret's dog because Margaret is moving into an apartment building that doesn't allow pets. Ellie is crushed. She wants a puppy with soft, floppy ears, not some old mutt with pointy ears and a skinny tail.

Ellie refuses to think of Preston as her dog, but she can't help feeling sorry for him because he obviously misses Great-aunt Margaret. Slowly, Ellie admits that Preston has his uses (he's good company while watching scary movies and loves to play fetch), though she's still not ready to let him take the place of her puppy. Then one day, Ellie decides to take the long way home from a friend's and gets lost. She panics until Preston starts barking and pulling on the leash. Ellie follows Preston and soon finds herself safely back home. The next day at school, Ellie writes a story about Preston, her dog.

Why This Book Appeals to Reluctant Readers This is an engaging, modest story with emotional depth. Ellie's disappointment is genuine and believable. The simple text easily conveys the complexity of Ellie's feelings: She's torn between giving up her lifelong dream of having a puppy and her compassion for the dog she's been given.

Who Might Like This Book Readers who are drawn to books in which the action is more emotionally based than physical, dog lovers, or those kids who have been asked to compromise on their dreams will all relate to this story.

If Your Child Liked This Book, Then Try . . .
Shiloh by Phyllis Reynolds Naylor (Atheneum, ages 8–12).

Your Mother Was a Neanderthal

(THE TIME WARP TRIO series)

by

JON SCIESZKA

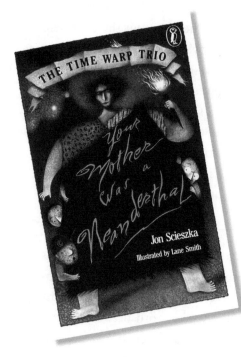

Genre: Humorous Fiction/ Time Travel

Publisher: Viking, $13.50 (h); Puffin Books, $4.99 (p)

Page Length: 78

Type of Illustrations: Black and white, about two per chapter

Reluctant Reader Appeal: Humor, Well-Defined Characters, Fast-Paced Plot, Concise Chapters, Suitable Text

Suggested reading level: Ages 7–10

It was like nothing on earth we had ever seen before. Fred, Sam, and I stood in front of a forest of strange trees and giant ferns. A rocky cliff rose behind us. A volcano smoked ahead of us.

But we really didn't notice any of that at first. The first thing we noticed was that the three of us were standing around completely, unbelievably, and absolutely naked.

"We lost everything," yelled Fred. He dove behind the nearest fern.

"I don't understand it," said Sam. "This never happens in those other time travel books."

Synopsis Joe (the narrator), Sam, and Fred are three pals who have a unique way of getting out of doing their math homework: They travel to different points in the past or future using The Book, a mysterious present given to Joe by his uncle.

In this installment of THE TIME WARP TRIO series, the boys decide if they travel back to the time of the cavemen and bring some modern trinkets with them, they'll be considered magicians and kings. But their plans go awry when they land in the Stone Age with nothing but Fred's baseball cap, Sam's glasses, and a straw Joe is holding. The Book is nowhere to be seen.

The boys are soon discovered by a clan of Cro-Magnon cave-women whose leader ("Ma") bears a striking resemblance to Joe's mother. The boys are locked into a sort of cave jail, where they wonder why they haven't seen any men in the clan and if the women are cannibals. The boys escape during a sunset clan ritual, but while stumbling through the dark forest they fall into a hole in the ground that turns out to be the home of a clan of Neanderthal men. The men are much cruder than the women; they speak in grunts, wear smelly animal skins, and relish eating maggot-infested meat.

In a hilarious, action-packed adventure, the boys outwit some prehistoric beasts, bring the clans together, find a way home, and even get to put their math skills to use.

Why This Book Appeals to Reluctant Readers The Time Warp Trio mixes adventure, clever humor, magic, and slapstick to create a fast-paced series that sneaks in a math concept in each book. The three main characters are sharply drawn: Joe is the leader of the group, the most level-headed except when he gets engrossed in his magic tricks; Sam's the brain, with a head full of random facts and trivia that often come in handy; and Fred's the energetic goofball who acts first and thinks later. Their dialogue and interactions perfectly capture the mind-set of typical fifth-grade boys. The "history" in these books is meant to be taken with a grain of salt; their primary purpose is to entertain and show how math really can be useful in everyday life.

Who Might Like This Book Any child who appreciates a goofy story full of sharp humor and action. The Time Warp Trio especially appeals to boys who want to read fiction but haven't found many books they like.

Notes to Parents Each book contains several multiple-choice math problems at the end, only a few of which are meant to be taken seriously.

If Your Child Liked This Book, Then Try . . . The Time Warp Trio travels to many points in the past and future, including *Knights of the Kitchen Table* (the first in the series), *2095, The Good, the Bad, and the Goofy,* and *The Not-So-Jolly Roger* (all published by Viking/Puffin Books).

Little Fox's Secret:
The Mystery of Bent's Fort

by

MARY PEACE FINLEY

Illustrator MARTHA JANE SPURLOCK

Genre: Historical Fiction

Publisher: Filter Press,
  $5.95 (p)

Page Length: 58

Type of Illustrations: Black
  and white, every few pages

Reluctant Reader Appeal:
  Well-Defined Characters,
  Fast-Paced Plot, Concise
  Chapters, Suitable Text

**Suggested
reading level:**
Ages 8–10

*Even from this distance, Little Fox could hear the ring of the
blacksmith's anvil and the shouts of men and the screech of giant
birds with fanning blue feathers that Robert called "peacocks."
There was not a cloud in the sky, but a cold shadow shivered
across Little Fox's shoulders.* What will happen down there?
What will I have to do? *He raised up higher on Frijol's back,
trying to see Robert.*

*"Look well," Gray Owl said, twisting on his saddle blanket
to face the five braves. "You will not see this Fort again."*

Synopsis In the summer of 1849 Little Fox, an 11-year-old Cheyenne brave, is excited about his village's yearly trading expedition to Bent's Fort. He's been training for months to beat his friend Robert Bent at their annual footrace. But the night before they leave, Gray Owl calls his people together for a meeting. He's had a vision—white men have been slaughtering the buffalo, fouling the water, and bringing disease to the Plains. Bent's Fort will be destroyed, and the Cheyenne will never trade there again.

William Bent, who built and runs the trading post, is married to a Cheyenne woman and so is considered family. Gray Owl takes five braves to travel to the Fort to warn Bent of his vision. And he brings Little Fox along as well. Soon Little Fox learns why he was chosen to go along: Gray Owl has seen that Little Fox will be the one to bring down the Fort!

Why This Book Appeals to Reluctant Readers Little Fox and Robert and William Bent are all well-written characters who clearly portray the relationship Bent had with the Cheyenne in the 1840s. The real cause of the destruction of Bent's Fort in 1849 is a mystery, but this book offers one plausible explanation. The rich language, fast-paced plot, and tight chapters keep the action moving, with the tension mounting as Little Fox discovers that he will have a hand in the Fort's ruin. Historical facts at the end of the book summarize what's actually known about Bent's Fort.

Who Might Like This Book Any child interested in the history of the American West will enjoy this book, but it's an especially good historical novel for boys. Kids who like shorter adventure stories will also find this book compelling.

If Your Child Liked This Book, Then Try . . . *Thunder at Gettysburg* by Patricia Lee Gauch, illustrated by Stephen Gammell (Putnam); *Kate Shelley and the Midnight Express* by Margaret K. Wetterer, illustrated by Karen Ritz (Carolrhoda).

Oh No, It's Robert

by

BARBARA SEULING

Illustrator PAUL BREWER

Genre: Contemporary Fiction

Publisher: Front Street/ Cricket Books, $14.95 (h)

Page Length: 118

Type of Illustrations: Black and white, about two per chapter

Reluctant Reader Appeal: Humor, Well-Defined Characters, Fast-Paced Plot, Concise Chapters, Suitable Text, Kid Relevance

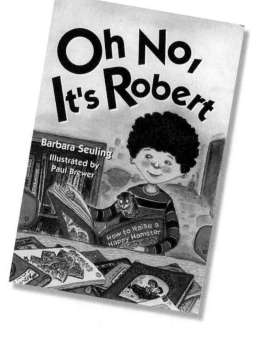

Suggested reading level:
Ages 7–10

Robert went up to the front of the room and picked up a piece of chalk. He drew a circle on the blackboard. Then he drew another circle inside that one.

"It's a doughnut!" called Matt Blakey. "That's a great invention!"

"Be quiet, class," said Mrs. Bernthal.

Robert added another circle above the first one. He drew in a bottom.

He wrote the water closet *in big letters next to it.*

"Oh, no," whispered Susanne Lee loudly. "He's talking about the toilet!" The rest of the class burst out laughing.

Synopsis Robert Dorfman is in the slow reading group, hates math, and his homework always comes back with the dreaded pig stamp that says "could be neater." So when his teacher announces a classroom achievement contest, Robert wants to win the prize more than ever. Robert and his friend Paul come up with a plan to become super helpers to teachers. Robert passes out flyers advertising his services, and business takes off.

One of Robert's jobs is as the classroom library monitor, and he desperately wants to solve the mystery of who is scribbling in all the books. At first he thinks it's Lester, the class bully. Then Robert has the opportunity to get to know Lester a little better and realizes that though Lester has problems, being the Scribbler isn't one of them. All the evidence now points to his friend Paul, and Robert has a dilemma: Is being a super helper and winning the prize more important than tattling on his best friend? Robert solves his problem in a thoughtful way and is rewarded for his hard work.

Why This Book Appeals to Reluctant Readers Robert represents every ordinary, good kid who tries hard but never seems to stand out from the crowd. His blunders are humorous but always believable. Each of the well-paced chapters ends on a dramatic or suspenseful note, drawing the reader further into the story. The substantial typeface not only is easy to read but also helps give the book the length and heft of a novel for older readers. The quirky, appealing illustrations add to the comic nature of the story.

Who Might Like This Book Boys and girls who are drawn to humorous, realistic books about the trials of just being a kid. Kids who are struggling to carve out a niche for themselves or trying to find what they're good at will identify with Robert.

If Your Child Liked This Book, Then Try . . . *All About Stacy* by Patricia Reilly Giff, illustrated by Blanche Sims (Dell Yearling).

Little Wolf's Book of Badness

by

IAN WHYBROW

Illustrator TONY ROSS

Genre: Humorous/Talking Animals

Publisher: Carolrhoda Books, $6.95 (p)

Page Length: 130

Type of Illustrations: Black-and-white spot art throughout

Reluctant Reader Appeal: Humor, Well-Defined Characters, Fast-Paced Plot, Kid Relevance, Suitable Text (see Notes to Parents below)

Suggested reading level:
Ages 7–10

Dear Mom and Dad,
. . . You just think I am a goody-goody, I bet. Is that why I have to go away for badness lessons? But I told you I only brushed my teeth last week for a joke. And combing my fur and going to bed early were just tricks to trick you! You ask my cousin Yeller. It was his idea. He said, "Let's pretend being good." I just

said OK. So I pretended. . . . But no, you would not listen. You did not understand. You said I must go to Cunning College, and I must live in Frettnin Forest until I get my BAD badge and learn Uncle Bigbad's 9 Rules of Badness.

Synopsis Little Wolf has a problem: He's too good. So he's sent by his father to the Cunning College for Brute Beasts, run by Uncle Bigbad Wolf. There, he'll learn the 9 Rules of Badness and earn his BAD badge. After a harrowing, solitary journey, Little Wolf arrives at the college located in the Frettnin Forest. The story, told through a series of letters from Little Wolf to his parents, recounts his education at the paws of his miserly, fearsome uncle (whose bark is often worse than his bite). Little Wolf uses his cunning to extract the 9 Rules of Badness from Uncle Bigbad, who would rather just be left alone. Along the way, Little Wolf meets a pack of Cub Scouts, and his friendly, good nature wins out. He decides to join the Scouts and earn merit badges for things like Navigating and Exploring. In the end, instead of returning home, Little Wolf uses gold he's inherited from his uncle (who met an untimely death) to open a new college in Frettnin Forest: Adventure Academy.

Why This Book Appeals to Reluctant Readers The layout of this book—short letters surrounded by illustrations and lots of white space—allows readers to zip right through the story. Though the basic plot is simple, Little Wolf has many sideline adventures along the way. Uncle Bigbad thinks he's threatening and mean, but he's such a doofus that he's actually funny. Little Wolf is earnest and sincere; he unwittingly plays the straight man to his uncle's bumbling wrath. Little Wolf's letters home perfectly capture the voice of a child sent off to camp against his will; he lays the guilt on his parents for sending him away while telling them how much he misses them.

Readers will also appreciate references to classic fairy tales, especially Little Red Riding Hood. Though some elements of the story verge on that slightly subversive grossness in which third and fourth graders revel, they are not dwelled on. The story remains on a very humorous, tongue-in-cheek level.

Who Might Like This Book Any child—but especially boys—who enjoys irreverent, physical comedy; ironic humor; and seeing both good and nasty characters getting just what they deserve.

Notes to Parents The text is written in fairly simple sentences, but some of the words are intentionally misspelled (these are, after all, Little Wolf's actual letters). However, the misspelled words are easy to figure out. Uncle Bigbad does die at the end of the book (he explodes from eating too many baked beans), but Little Wolf deals with this event as matter-of-factly as he deals with everything else that comes his way. None of these characters are meant to be taken seriously.

If Your Child Liked This Book, Then Try . . . *Little Wolf's Diary of Daring Deeds* and *Little Wolf's Haunted Hall for Small Horrors* by Ian Whybrow (Carolrhoda).

Amazing Snakes

(EYEWITNESS JUNIORS series)

by

ALEXANDRA PARSONS

Photography JERRY YOUNG

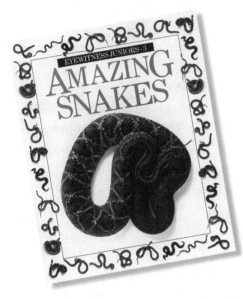

Genre: Nonfiction/Snakes

Publisher: Knopf, $9.99 (p)

Page Length: 32

Type of Illustrations: Color photographs and drawings, on every page

Reluctant Reader Appeal: Concise Chapters, Suitable Text, Kid Relevance, Unique Presentation, Visual Appeal

Suggested reading level: Ages 7–9

The Vine Snake

The vine snake lies very still in its tree, waiting for something tasty to pass by. Wrapped around a branch, it looks like a harmless piece of jungle vine.

Watching and waiting

The vine snake has very good eyesight. Both of its eyes face forward, like human eyes, so the snake can judge distances as it goes in for the kill. Its head is long and pointed, like the nose of a fighter plane.

Synopsis This book provides an intimate look at some of the world's most amazing snakes. Each "chapter" (one two-page spread) focuses on either a specific aspect of snakes or a particular variety of the species. Fascinating facts—each presented with a bold subheading and a short paragraph of information—are wound around striking photographs or illustrations. Interesting snake trivia is sprinkled throughout, and the stunning photographs on the end pages practically slither out of the book.

Why This Book Appeals to Reluctant Readers There's just enough information to entice reptile lovers without burying them under facts. The text is simple but lively; statistics, such as the size or speed of snakes, are presented within a context meaningful to children. The incredible photographs show every detail of the snakes and beg to be studied over and over. The content is substantial yet interesting; the reader finishes this book feeling like he's really learned something.

Who Might Like This Book Snake and reptile lovers, of course, or anyone interested in animal facts and behavior. This series is also an excellent supplement to science textbooks in the early to middle elementary grades.

Notes to Parents There are over 25 titles in the EYEWITNESS JUNIORS series, so if your child gets squeamish about snakes, try looking up another book under a different topic. If your child wants to learn more, move up to the regular Eyewitness books (also shelved by topic in the bookstore or library), which follow the same format but are longer and more in-depth.

If Your Child Liked This Book, Then Try . . . Other books in this series, including *Birds, Mammals, Spiders, Cats, Frogs & Toads, Fish, Monkeys, Animal Disguises,* and *Animal Babies.* There are also some nonanimal subjects covered, such as *Flying Machines, Boats,* and *Bikes.*

The Magic School Bus Inside the Earth

(THE MAGIC SCHOOL BUS series)

by

JOANNA COLE

Illustrator BRUCE DEGEN

Genre: Nonfiction/Geology

Publisher: Scholastic,
$4.99 (p)

Page Length: 40

Type of Illustrations: Color,
on every page

Reluctant Reader Appeal:
Humor, Well-Defined
Characters, Fast-Paced Plot,
Suitable Text, Unique
Presentation, Visual Appeal

> **Suggested
> reading level:**
> Ages 6–9

*You never know
what will happen
on a trip with Ms. Frizzle.
Her new dress
was a trip in itself.
At first the old school bus
wouldn't start.
But finally we were on our way.*

When we came to the field,
all the kids wanted
to get out of the bus.
But suddenly,
the bus began to spin like a top.
That sort of thing doesn't happen
on most class trips.

Synopsis Ms. Frizzle is an enthusiastic science teacher who loves field trips. Her less-than-enthusiastic class unwittingly goes along for the ride when they board the Magic School Bus, which can transport them to any place or time imaginable. In this book, the children travel inside the earth, landing first in an underground limestone cave, then moving through the earth's layers to its metal core. Finally, they emerge back on top of the earth through a volcano. The children are happily collecting rocks on the earth's surface when the volcano erupts, sending the bus and its occupants out to sea on a river of lava. A bit nervous (though not terrified—these children have experienced Ms. Frizzle's class trips before), the children sit back as the bus rises on a huge cloud of steam and magically lands back in the school parking lot. The book ends with an illustration of the class's rock collection, a pronunciation guide of the terms introduced in the story, and a fictional dialogue between the author and a reader in which the author defends and explains her portrayal of the bus's journey inside the earth.

But there's more to this short, information-packed book. The children's dialogue is presented in speech bubbles, as in a comic book. Each child writes a school report explaining one facet of the book's subject, and these are displayed on the outer margin of each page. The result is a science lesson embedded within a humorous story.

Why This Book Appeals to Reluctant Readers Children can read this book on several levels: the story of the class's journey depicted in the text, the dialogue and jokes in the speech bubbles, or the scientific information in the school reports. There's so much happening on each page that new facts or humorous details will still be discovered after several readings. The class remains consistent with each book in the series, so kids can meet their favorite characters over and over. And the juxtaposition of Ms. Frizzle's zeal for exploration with the children's reluctant participation provides a sophisticated humor that's perfect for third and fourth graders.

Who Might Like This Book Boys and girls alike love The Magic School Bus. Kids interested in all aspects of science will find a book in this series that speaks to them. Those who aren't science lovers will still learn while they laugh.

Notes to Parents Because of the action-packed illustrations, THE MAGIC SCHOOL BUS books can also be read aloud to younger children or read with a child who can't handle the text alone. If your child is a fan of the series but is ready for longer text and fewer illustrations, try THE MAGIC SCHOOL BUS SCIENCE CHAPTER BOOK series, based on the same characters (reading level ages 6–9, about 80 pages long). One title: *The Search for the Missing Bones* by Eva Moore, illustrated by Ted Enik (Scholastic).

If Your Child Liked This Book, Then Try . . . Any of the numerous other books in THE MAGIC SCHOOL BUS series, covering topics ranging from the human body to dinosaurs to the solar system. These books are often displayed together in the children's nonfiction section of bookstores or shelved by topic in the nonfiction section of the library. Make sure you choose the original MAGIC SCHOOL BUS books written by Joanna Cole and illustrated by Bruce Degen and not those based on the animated television series (which are smaller in size and called *Scholastic's The Magic School Bus* and aren't nearly as good as the real thing).

Steam, Smoke, and Steel: Back in Time with Trains

by

PATRICK O'BRIEN

Illustrator PATRICK O'BRIEN

Genre: Nonfiction/Trains

Publisher: Charlesbridge, $6.95 (p)

Page Length: 32

Type of Illustrations: Color, on every page

Reluctant Reader Appeal: Fast-Paced Plot, Suitable Text, Unique Presentation, Visual Appeal

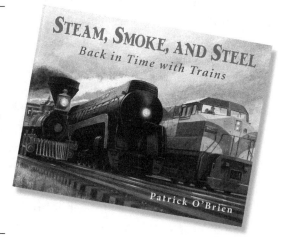

Suggested reading level: Ages 4–9

I think my dad's got the best job in the world. He's an engineer. Up in the cab of his giant locomotive he controls ten thousand tons of rolling steel. Coal, oil, lumber, cars—whatever needs to be carried by rail, he hauls it with his 4,400-horsepower diesel engine. One day I counted more than a hundred freight cars lined up behind his engine. That train was more than a mile long!

Synopsis The narrator of this book takes the reader back through seven generations of his family, all train engineers. The six men and one woman are briefly profiled along with the trains they drove. Details about the types of engines, how the trains were powered, what they were used for, and how they affected commerce and transportation help the reader compare the different trains within their own time period. The reader feels pulled along an unbroken track to the birth of trains in this country and the beginning of a family tradition of engineers.

Why This Book Appeals to Reluctant Readers I like the pacing of this book and the way the story links each previous generation to an earlier model of train. The illustrations and a narrative device nudge the reader back in time (*When my dad was a kid in the 1960's, he sometimes got to ride on* his *dad's train.*), and anecdotes from the engineer's experiences to present a colorful picture of the time period. The illustrations depict each train against the same landscape, showing how the wilderness grew to a town and finally a city behind the train tracks.

Who Might Like This Book Kids with a budding interest in trains who appreciate the history of the locomotive but don't want (or need) too much technical detail.

Notes to Parents The publisher's listed age range includes nonreaders who would listen to the book being read out loud. For independent readers, the writing is slightly beyond the easy-reader stage. However, many bookstores and libraries will shelve this with picture books. If you can't find it in nonfiction under "Trains," look in the fiction section under the author's name.

If Your Child Liked This Book, Then Try . . . *Train* by John Coiley (Dorling Kindersley EYEWITNESS BOOKS); *Cars, Bikes, Trains, and Other Land Machines* by Ian S. Graham (HOW THINGS WORK series by Kingfisher Books).

The Top of the World: Climbing Mount Everest

by

STEVE JENKINS

Illustrator STEVE JENKINS

Genre: Nonfiction/
Mountaineering

Publisher: Houghton Mifflin,
$16.00 (h)

Page Length: 32

Type of Illustrations: Color,
on every page

Reluctant Reader Appeal:
Suitable Text, Unique
Presentation, Visual Appeal

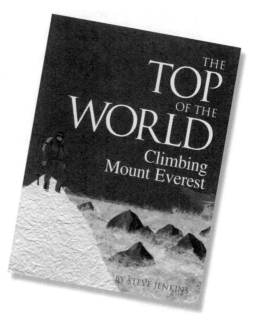

**Suggested
reading level:**
Ages 8–11

Mount Everest

Its summit is the highest point on earth, 5 1/2 miles above sea level. For thousands of years, the mountain has been a sacred place for those who live in its shadow. The rest of the world, however, wasn't really aware of the mountain until about 180 years ago. Ever since that time, climbers, scientists, and adventurers have been fascinated by this peak. Many have tried to climb it. Some have succeeded, but many more have failed. Some have died trying.

Synopsis With spare text, this book describes the conditions and terrain of Mount Everest and the attempts that have been made to scale its peak, and gives some general information about the equipment needed, the techniques used, and the dangers involved in mountain climbing. While the text will be of interest to current or would-be mountain climbers, the real appeal of this book is its illustrations. The author/illustrator uses dramatic cut-paper collages to depict the mountain, the climbers, and their equipment. The result is visually stunning images that have a texture and depth not ordinarily found in picture book illustrations.

Why This Book Appeals to Reluctant Readers The artwork alone makes this a book that begs to be read over and over. Though the book is not text heavy, the author puts Mount Everest in context with the geography of the rest of the world and the cultures of Nepal and Tibet. This will be enough to whet the appetite of those kids who want to learn more about mountaineering or Himalayan cultures without boring those readers who have only a passing interest.

Who Might Like This Book Boys or girls who dream of climbing the world's highest peaks and those who enjoy high-altitude winter sports. It will also be appealing to budding artists who want to see examples of beautiful illustration techniques.

Notes to Parents If your child likes Steve Jenkins's artwork, try his some of his other nonfiction picture books from Houghton Mifflin: *Hottest, Coldest, Highest, Deepest* and *What Do You Do When Something Wants to Eat You?*

If Your Child Liked This Book, Then Try . . . *Black Whiteness: Admiral Byrd Alone in the Arctic* by Robert Burleigh, illustrated by Walter Lyon Krudop (Simon & Schuster).

Pond Life: A Close-Up Look at the Natural World

(LOOK CLOSER series)

by

BARBARA TAYLOR

Photography FRANK GREENAWAY

Genre: Nonfiction/Pond Flora and Fauna

Publisher: Dorling Kindersley, $4.95 (p)

Page Length: 48

Type of Illustrations: Color photographs, on every page

Reluctant Reader Appeal: Concise Chapters, Suitable Text, Unique Presentation, Visual Appeal

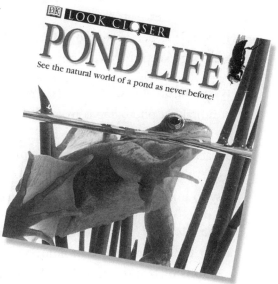

Suggested reading level:
Ages 6–10

Flying Dragon

The large, powerful wings of the dragonfly help it zoom backward and forward over the pond with lightning speed, like a tiny helicopter. About 300 million years ago, there were dragonflies with wings as big as gulls' wings, but the dragonflies that live today are only the size of large butterflies. The dragonfly's wings beat up and down about 20 times per second, pushing it along at up to 20 miles per hour. . . .

Synopsis Dorling Kindersley's trademark photographs against a white background give readers an up-close and intimate view of life in a pond. Cleverly shot to show the perspective from under the water as well as above, the photos place the reader eye-to-eye with diving beetles, newts, frogs, and sticklebacks. Each two-page spread covers a different topic; a paragraph of general information is followed by several shorter paragraphs containing more details scattered around the photos. Catchy subtitles (Tadpole Terrors, Flipper Feet, Floating Food) and interesting trivia on each page keep the tone light and engaging.

Why This Book Appeals to Reluctant Readers The breathtaking photographs make the reader feel like he's actually in the pond swimming with the frogs. The photos are the centerpiece of each page, with the text acting almost as elaborate captions. As a result, the clear, short paragraphs of information are broken into easy-to-understand chunks and presented in a visually dynamic way.

Who Might Like This Book Readers who are curious about the natural world or enjoy seeing dramatic, close-up photographs of plants, animals, fish, and insects. Kids who love to learn interesting, unusual facts about nature will find the LOOK CLOSER series enthralling.

Notes to Parents This series is suitable for reading aloud to younger children and also is good for children in the upper elementary grades or middle school who read below grade level.

If Your Child Liked This Book, Then Try . . . Other titles in the LOOK CLOSER series, which features a variety of habitats, including *Rain Forest, Meadow, Desert Life, Forest Life, Tree Life, River Life,* and *Tide Pool.* They can be found shelved under the appropriate subject headings in the library or bookstore.

Pirates!

(EYEWITNESS READERS series)

by

CHRISTOPHER MAYNARD

Illustrator PETER DENNIS

Genre: Nonfiction/Pirates

Publisher: Dorling Kindersley, $3.95 (p)

Page Length: 48

Type of Illustrations: Color illustrations and photo-graphs, on every page

Reluctant Reader Appeal: Well-Defined Characters, Concise Chapters, Suitable Text, Unique Presentation, Visual Appeal

Suggested reading level:
Ages 7–9

Let me tell you the story of my brilliant career as a buccaneer. My name is John Dunn. I started out, like so many in the Caribbean, living off the land and hunting wild cattle on the island of Hispaniola. We buccaneers were a rough bunch, but we lived by our wits and were free men. That is, until the Spanish killed off the cattle and drove us away. That's when we became pirates.

We attacked Spanish ships until they sailed in fleets we couldn't beat. Then we turned to raiding Spanish towns. And that's when Henry Morgan first crossed my path.

Synopsis The stories of five famous pirates, told in fictionalized first-person accounts by people who knew the men, constitute this book. Each story is given its own chapter, which includes illustrations of the pirates, their ships, and their treasures. The margins of each page present short paragraphs of information about the pirates and the time periods in which they lived. One chapter is devoted to Oak Island off the Canadian coast, rumored to be where Captain Kidd buried his treasure. A glossary clearly defines many of the terms used in the book.

Why This Book Appeals to Reluctant Readers Children are exposed to pirates early on through stories and movies and have always been fascinated with the adventurous, dangerous lives of these men. The chapters stand alone as individual short stories; the generous text size and abundant illustrations allow for easy reading of each page. Because the pirates profiled span from the Roman Empire to the early 1700s, readers also get an overview of the food, money, weapons, and laws from different time periods.

Who Might Like This Book Boys and girls who are interested in pirates or sailors or who simply like true-life adventure stories.

Notes to Parents Though the stories in this book are fictionalized accounts of real people, it's considered nonfiction and shelved in that section of the library. It will be found with other easy readers shelved by series in most bookstores.

If Your Child Liked This Book, Then Try . . . *True-Life Treasure Hunts* by Judy Donnelly, illustrated by Thomas LaPadula (Random House STEP INTO READING series, Step 4); other books in the EYEWITNESS READERS series, such as *Going for Gold!*, and *Secrets of the Mummies.*

Barry:
The Bravest Saint Bernard

by

LYNN HALL

Illustrator ANTONIO CASTRO

Genre: Nonfiction/
Rescue Dogs

Publisher: Random House,
$3.99 (p)

Page Length: 48

Type of Illustrations: Color,
about every other page

Reluctant Reader Appeal:
Fast-Paced Plot, Suitable
Text, Unique Presentation

**Suggested
reading level:**
Ages 7–9

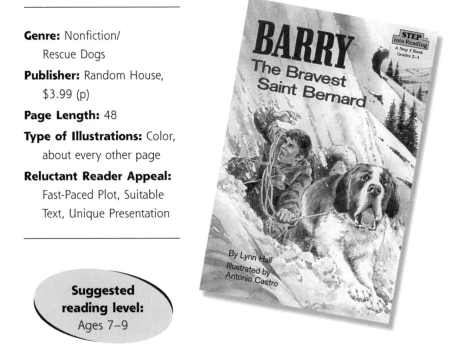

*By the end of that winter, it was clear that Barry was the best
rescue dog the monks had ever had. When an avalanche struck,
Barry was the first to find people buried under the snow. He was
the fastest to dig them out. Barry worked hardest to warm them
up. Sometimes the other dogs gave up. But Barry would go on
licking a frozen face until there was some movement. Then the
great dog would go wild with joy.*

Synopsis The monks of the Saint Bernard Monastery, high in the mountains of Switzerland, are known for breeding a special kind of dog to rescue people trapped in avalanches. This book tells the story of Barry, the Saint Bernard whose name, to this day, honors the best dog at the monastery.

Though the author doesn't specify exactly when Barry lived, she does say it was at a time when the only way over the Swiss mountains was through the Saint Bernard Pass, either on horseback or by foot. The monks helped guide travelers over the pass and sent out search parties for missing people. The book pairs Barry's life with the story of Werner, a boy who grew up in the monastery and later became a monk and trainer of rescue dogs. He and Barry were best friends.

Barry's life is chronicled through a series of incidents that depict his years as a rescue dog, saving over 40 avalanche victims. After his death, the monks of Saint Bernard waited 100 years before they had another dog great enough to be named Barry. Today, there is a dog at the monastery who bears the honored name.

Why This Book Appeals to Reluctant Readers Animal stories are perennially appealing to kids, and what better hero than Barry, a gentle, loyal, lovable beast of a dog whose greatest joy is to save someone's life? Though this book isn't divided into chapters, the pages break at high points in the action, which gives the text a fast pace and encourages readers to keep going.

Who Might Like This Book Fans of animal stories, true adventures, or those into winter mountain sports who understand the dangers of avalanches will find this book interesting.

If Your Child Liked This Book, Then Try . . . *Buddy: The First Seeing Eye Dog* by Eva Moore, illustrated by Don Bolognese (Scholastic HELLO READER! series, Level 4).

Fire!

by

JOY MASOFF

Photograpy JACK REZNICKI AND

BARRY D. SMITH

Genre: Nonfiction/Fire Fighting

Publisher: Scholastic, $16.95 (h)

Page Length: 48

Type of Illustrations: Color photos, on every page

Reluctant Reader Appeal: Concise Chapters,
Suitable Text, Kid Relevance,
Unique Presentation, Visual Appeal

Suggested reading level:
Ages 7–11

When you arrive for your shift, you pull out your gear and set it up near your rig. If you're going to be working at night, you make your bed and help clean up the station house. There are usually training sessions to attend. You might even shop for groceries and cook dinner. There's always lots to do.

*The calls will come in to **DISPATCH** via the 911 network, and you never know what they will be. A child locked in a bathroom, a car that hit a stop sign, a burst pipe, a funny smell, a cat stuck inside a wall . . . people call the fire department for help with everything.*

Synopsis There are many books that describe fire-fighting vehicles and equipment; this book shows the reader what it feels like to be a firefighter. Broken into five short chapters that cover everything from tools of the trade to the different classifications of firefighters, *Fire!* takes the reader through training sessions, life at the station house, and along on the adrenaline-pumping, sometimes terrifying job of fighting fires. Each two-page spread focuses on a specific element of the job (Incredible Rescues, Smoke Jumpers & Hotshots, Fire Detectives), with red subheadings that break up the information into smaller pieces. The pages are heavily illustrated with dramatic photographs of firefighters, equipment, and fire fighting throughout history. The last four pages explain 12 things readers can do to avoid fires at home and lists resources to learn more about fighting fires.

Why This Book Appeals to Reluctant Readers The author clearly has great respect and admiration for the men and women who fight fires and perform heroic rescues, and this feeling comes across in the text. She includes small details that children will find fascinating (firefighters use golf tees to plug leaks in oil drums) and also places the reader in the position of firefighter on several occasions (*What does it feel like to hold an attack line? Ask your best friend to push against you as hard as possible. Now you push back with the same force*). No detail is missed, but the information is presented in such an appealing way that kids won't even know how much they're reading.

Who Might Like This Book Kids who have always been fascinated with fire engines, even gear junkies who love learning about equipment and special tools used for different jobs.

Notes to Parents This book can easily be shared with a younger child who is interested in the subject. It's also a good pick for older kids who don't want to read longer nonfiction.

If Your Child Liked This Book, Then Try . . . Other titles by Joy Masoff: *American Revolution, 1700–1800* (Scholastic CHRONICLE OF AMERICA series); *Oh, Yuck: The Encyclopedia of Everything Nasty* (Workman Publishing).

Questions and Answers About Weather

by

M. JEAN CRAIG

Illustrator LEN EBERT

Genre: Nonfiction/Weather

Publisher: Scholastic, $5.99 (p)

Page Length: 48

Type of Illustrations: Color, on every page

Reluctant Reader Appeal: Concise Chapters, Suitable Text, Kid Relevance, Unique Presentation

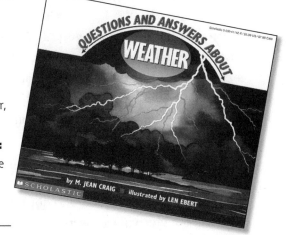

Suggested reading level: Ages 7–10

Q. Why does the sky look blue when the sun is shining?

We call ordinary sunlight white light, because we cannot see any color in it. But sunlight is really a mixture of many different colors of light.

The sunlight that reaches us passes through air and dust high above the earth. Some of the blue rays of the sunlight make the air and the dust look blue. When we look at a clear blue sky, what we really see are very tiny bits of air and very tiny specks of dust glowing with a blue light.

Synopsis The title of this book says it all. Divided into eight broad sections, such as "Hot, Cold, and In Between" and "Fair Today, but Rain Tomorrow," the text comprises answers to the kinds of questions kids ask about the weather (*Why do we have seasons? Why is it so cold inside a deep cave? Do clouds freeze in cold weather?*). The contents lists every question in the book so kids can go straight to the information they want. The answers are clear, concise, and to the point. While the illustrations don't add new information, they do provide a colorful backdrop to the words.

Why This Book Appeals to Reluctant Readers
Elementary school children are innately curious about the world around them, and the weather is something that directly affects their lives every day. The questions have a very childlike perspective: It's as if the reader is standing outside, looking around, and asking about what she sees. Kids will appreciate that the answers provide enough information to explain the concept but don't go into unnecessary detail. Though the text is clearly written, it's not simplistic—even older kids who don't want to read longer nonfiction will get satisfying answers to their weather-related questions.

Who Might Like This Book Kids who ask questions about the world around them, those who like to keep track of weather forecasts, and even those who are interested in the outdoors and the environment.

Notes to Parents *Questions and Answers About the Weather* can be used as a simple reference book. Take it along when you're hiking or picnicking with your child and looking at clouds or keep it next to the television while watching the weather forecast.

***If Your Child Liked This Book, Then Try* . . .** *The Magic School Bus Inside a Hurricane* by Joanna Cole, illustrated by Bruce Degen (Scholastic).

How to Talk to Your Dog

by

JEAN CRAIGHEAD GEORGE

Illustrator SUE TRUESDELL

Genre: Nonfiction/Animal
Behavior

Publisher: HarperCollins,
$9.95 (h)

Page Length: 32

Type of Illustrations: Color,
on every page

Reluctant Reader Appeal:
Humor, Suitable Text,
Kid Relevance, Unique
Presentation

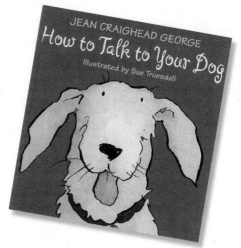

**Suggested
reading level:**
Ages 7–11

*To say hello to your dog, sniff toward his nose. That's dog talk.
He will answer by pulling his ears back and close to his head.
What he is saying is "Hello, leader."*

*There is also the joyous hello. When you return home, your
dog greets you bounding, tail wagging, body swishing, and with
his head lowered in deference to you. He might lick you to seal
the welcome. You don't have to lick back. That would please
him, but he will love you even if you don't. A hug or head pat is
your "joyous hello" to your dog.*

Synopsis Jean Craighead George understands the special relationship children can have with their dogs, and she uses this bond to teach basic, easy-to-apply aspects of animal/human communication. Through uncluttered text that acknowledges the delight children take in their pets, she explains how to convey "hello," "good-bye," "good night," "I am the boss," "no," "I am the leader," and "let's play" using body language and noises dogs understand. She also describes how to recognize dogs' different emotions by their facial expressions, barks, and body postures. The illustrations combine photographs of the author with drawings of dogs, adding a playful note to the book. All in all, this book is a terrific introduction to the nature of dogs and lays a good groundwork for future obedience training.

Why This Book Appeals to Reluctant Readers This hands-on guide allows children to read a short section, try out the techniques on their dogs, and then read some more. The author truly respects dogs and doesn't write down to the reader, giving the child a sense of learning something important and worthwhile. And this book reinforces what many kids already believe—that dogs really do make the best listeners.

Who Might Like This Book Any child who views her or his dog as a full-fledged member of the family.

Notes to Parents The clearly described techniques in *How to Talk to Your Dog* can be understood by younger children, making this a great read-aloud book. And children in the upper elementary grades will still find the information fascinating without feeling like they're reading a book below their level.

If Your Child Liked This Book, Then Try . . . If your child is a cat lover, Jean Craighead George has also written *How to Talk to Your Cat*, illustrated by Paul Meisel (HarperCollins).

Tornadoes!

(THE WEATHER CHANNEL PRESENTS series)

by

SALLY ROSE

Genre: Nonfiction/Weather

Publisher: Simon Spotlight, $3.99 (p)

Page Length: 64

Type of Illustrations: Insert of color photographs

Reluctant Reader Appeal: Concise Chapters, Suitable Text, Kid Relevance, Unique Presentation, Visual Appeal

---

Suggested reading level: Ages 7–10

A tornado, also called a "twister," produces some of the most powerful winds in nature. But it wields its power in a very localized, or small, area. Most tornadoes are less than fifty yards wide and travel less than a mile. In rare instances, a tornado may reach one mile across and travel many miles. In contrast, hurricanes can be hundreds of miles across and travel for thousands of miles.

Did You Know?

A tornado's effect is usually limited to a local area. A tornado can destroy one side of a street and leave the other alone. There *have been reports of leaves and bark being stripped from one side of a tree and left untouched on the other. People have reported being stripped naked by a tornado—but left unhurt.*

Synopsis This book presents tornadoes through fascinating facts (including how tornadoes are formed, how they're predicted by weather forecasters, and accounts of some of the worst tornadoes in history) and eyewitness accounts from kids and professional storm chasers. Blue boxes containing "Did You Know?" tornado trivia pop up on almost every page; a dramatic color photo insert of tornadoes and their aftermath appears in the center of the book. A chapter on tornado safety, Web site addresses for further information, and a glossary round out this informative and entertaining book.

Why This Book Appeals to Reluctant Readers The chapters are short, with blue subtitles that break up the information into smaller sections. The writing is tight, lively, and fast-paced; anecdotes of actual tornado events give a personal slant to the topic. The scientific information is presented in a straightforward, easy-to-understand manner, and the author's awe of these exciting and dangerous weather systems inspires the reader to do further research on his or her own.

Who Might Like This Book Boys and girls who are interested in the weather, nature, or natural disasters. Kids who live in areas that get tornadoes or who have experienced one firsthand might also be intrigued by this book.

If Your Child Liked This Book, Then Try . . . Other books in THE WEATHER CHANNEL PRESENTS series from Simon Spotlight: *Lightning! and Thunderstorms, Hurricanes!,* and *Floods.*

Chapter Seven

Stretching It Out

With longer texts, more complex sentence structure, and few (or no) illustrations, these books look a lot like the books kids will be reading as adults. The main difference is that the topics are relevant to children in the middle elementary grades.

FICTION

The Whipping Boy by Sid Fleischman · page 166

All Day Nightmare (GIVE YOURSELF GOOSEBUMPS series) by R. L. Stine · page 168

Sideways Stories from Wayside School by Louis Sachar · page 170

Math Rashes by Douglas Evans · page 172

Bunnicula: A Rabbit-Tale of Mystery by Deborah and James Howe · page 174

Arthur, for the Very First Time by Patricia MacLachlan · page 176

My Teacher Is an Alien by Bruce Coville · page 178

Cockroach Cooties by Laurence Yep · page 180

Smart Dog by Vivian Vande Velde · page 182

Charlie and the Chocolate Factory by Roald Dahl · page 184

On My Honor by Marion Dane Bauer · page 186

The Kid Who Only Hit Homers by Matt Christopher · page 189

Little House on the Prairie (LITTLE HOUSE series) by Laura Ingalls Wilder · page 192

Dear Mrs. Ryan, You're Ruining My Life by Jennifer B. Jones · page 195

Peppermints in the Parlor by Barbara Brooks Wallace · page 197

The Trolls by Polly Horvath · page 199

Tuck Everlasting by Natalie Babbitt · page 201

The Boys Start the War by Phyllis Reynolds Naylor · page 203

Charlotte's Web by E. B. White · page 206

The Doll People by Ann M. Martin and Laura Godwin · page 209

From the Mixed-Up Files of Mrs. Basil E. Frankweiler by E. L. Konigsburg · page 212

The Journal of Wong Ming-Chung: A Chinese Miner, California, 1852 (MY NAME IS AMERICA series) by Laurence Yep · page 215

A Long Way from Chicago: A Novel in Stories by Richard Peck · page 218

Lily's Crossing by Patricia Reilly Giff · page 221

For YOUR Eyes Only! by Joanne Rocklin · page 224

Revenge of the Snob Squad (THE SNOB SQUAD series) by Julie Anne Peters · page 227

The Lion, the Witch and the Wardrobe (THE CHRONICLES OF NARNIA) by C. S. Lewis · page 230

Maniac Magee by Jerry Spinelli · page 233

The Invasion (ANIMORPHS series) by K. A. Applegate · page 235

Ella Enchanted by Gail Carson Levine · page 238

Harry Potter and the Sorcerer's Stone (HARRY POTTER series) by J. K. Rowling · page 241

NONFICTION

It's Disgusting and We Ate It! True Food Facts from Around the World by James Solheim · page 244

My Pony Book by Louise Pritchard · page 246

Find the Constellations by H. A. Rey · page 248

. . . If You Lived at the Time of the American Revolution by Kay Moore · page 250

Brain Surgery for Beginners and Other Major Operations for Minors: A Scalpel-Free Guide to Your Insides by Steve Parker · page 253

Lives of the Presidents: Fame, Shame (and What the Neighbors Thought) by Kathleen Krull · page 255

In the Huddle with . . . John Elway by Matt Christopher · page 258

Dr. Fred's Weather Watch: Create and Run Your Own Weather Station by Fred Bortz, Ph.D., with J. Marshall Shepherd, Ph.D. · page 260

The Whipping Boy

by

SID FLEISCHMAN

Illustrator PETER SIS

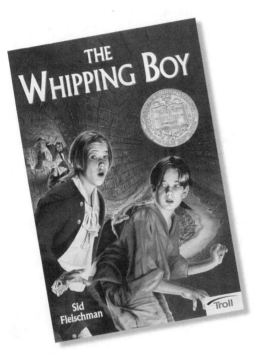

Genre: Humorous Fiction/
Adventure

Publisher: Greenwillow,
$16.95 (h); Troll, $4.95 (p)

Page Length: 90

Type of Illustrations: Black
and white, every few pages

Reluctant Reader Appeal:
Humor, Well-Defined
Characters, Fast-Paced
Plot, Concise Chapters,
Suitable Text

**Suggested
reading level:**
Ages 8–12

*Prince Brat knew he had nothing to fear. He had never been
spanked in his life. He was a prince! And it was forbidden to
spank, thrash, cuff, smack, or whip a prince.*

*A common boy was kept in the castle to be punished in his
place.*

"Fetch the whipping boy!"

*The king's command traveled like an echo from guard to
guard up the stone stairway to a small chamber in the drafty
north tower.*

Synopsis Prince Brat delights in being as naughty as possible. But he's not worried because princes can't be punished. Instead, a whipping boy is smacked with a cane in his place. Jemmy, however, won't give the prince the satisfaction of crying out when he's whipped and secretly plots to escape back to the sewers the first chance he gets. Then one night, the prince tells Jemmy he's running away and demands Jemmy come with him. Soon lost in the fog, the boys are kidnapped by the famous robber Hold-Your-Nose Billy and his sidekick, Cutwater, who think they'll get a hefty ransom for the prince. The boys eventually escape and make their way back to the city, but are followed by Billy and Cutwater. After a suspenseful chase through dark, rat-infested sewers, the boys finally rid themselves of the outlaws and return safely to the castle and a happy ending.

Why This Book Appeals to Reluctant Readers The broadly comic, tongue-in-cheek style of the narrative is immediately entertaining and belies the underlying theme of compassion that gives substance to this story. Small details, like a ballad seller with songs sold by the yard, give the setting a medieval atmosphere. The chapters are very short, with funny titles that add to the tall tale nature of the story.

Who Might Like This Book There's much about this book that will appeal to boys, especially those who like funny, almost slapstick adventure stories. The fairy tale quality of the plot will be a draw for girls as well.

Notes to Parents *The Whipping Boy* won the Newbery Medal in 1987.

If Your Child Liked This Book, Then Try . . . Other novels by Sid Fleischman, including *By the Great Horn Spoon!* (Little, Brown); *Bandit's Moon* and *The 13th Floor: A Ghost Story* (both from Greenwillow).

All Day Nightmare

(GIVE YOURSELF GOOSEBUMPS series)

by

R. L. STINE

Genre: Mystery/Horror

Publisher: Scholastic, $3.99 (p)

Page Length: 137

Type of Illustrations: None

Reluctant Reader Appeal: Fast-Paced Plot,
Concise Chapters, Suitable Text,
Unique Presentation

> **Suggested
> reading level:**
> Ages 8–12

Synopsis You wake up with a jolt. What a terrible nightmare! You were trapped in a strange house, being chased by short, creepy men, and there was some sort of spinning wheel of fire. You're sure glad that's over.

But, as you look around the room, you realize you have no idea where you are. Not only that, but you can't remember your name. To make matters worse, there's someone else in the house.

What happens next is up to the reader in this heart-pounding, goose-bump-raising tale. At the bottom of key pages, the reader can choose which direction the story will take (*To answer the door, turn to page 34. To stay hidden, turn to page 98.*). The result is over 20 very different stories in one book.

Why This Book Appeals to Reluctant Readers
There's a very high level of reader involvement in this book, from the second-person text (using "you," which makes the reader the main character) to allowing the reader to pick the plot twists

along the way. Each page contains one tight, tension-filled event, and then the reader is forced to turn the page to see what happens next. This book is all action; it's like riding a roller coaster with a big drop around every turn.

Who Might Like This Book Kids who love scary stories. This book *is* scary, as are all the GOOSEBUMPS books, but they've obviously hit a nerve with kids because GOOSEBUMPS is the biggest-selling series of all time. Depending on which choices the reader makes along the way, some of the endings in this book are funny, some happy, and others spine-tingling. But if your child likes to tell ghost stories around the campfire or rents *Friday the Thirteenth* at the video store, he'll love this book.

If Your Child Liked This Book, Then Try . . . R. L. Stine is such a popular author that he practically has his own section at the bookstore. The GIVE YOURSELF GOOSEBUMPS series has one shelf (there are nearly 50 titles), and the regular GOOSEBUMPS series (more traditionally written horror stories) has another. If your child's ready for slightly older, longer horror books, R. L. Stine's also written the FEAR STREET series for young adults.

Sideways Stories
from Wayside School

by

LOUIS SACHAR

Illustrator JULIE BRINCKLOE

Genre: Humorous
  Contemporary Fiction

Publisher: Avon Camelot,
  $4.95 (p)

Page Length: 124

Type of Illustrations: Black
  and white, one per chapter

Reluctant Reader Appeal:
  Humor, Well-Defined
  Characters, Fast-Paced
  Plot, Concise Chapters,
  Suitable Text

**Suggested
reading level:**
Ages 8–12

*"It's a difficult job," said Mrs. Jewls. "But you can do it. You
must turn the lights on every morning and turn them off at the
end of the day."*

"What?" asked Myron.

*"As a class president you must learn to listen," said Mrs.
Jewls. "I'll repeat myself one more time. You must turn the lights
on every morning—"*

*"I heard you the first time," said Myron. "It just doesn't
sound like much of a job."*

"It certainly is!" said Mrs. Jewls. "Without light I can't teach, and the children can't learn. Only you can give us that light. I think it is a very important job."

"I guess so," said Myron. He wasn't convinced.

Synopsis Wayside School was built wrong. Instead of being a one-story building with 30 rooms, it's 30 stories of one room each! Such a sideways school might host some strange goings-on, and that's exactly what happens in the classroom on the 30th floor. This book features 30 short chapters, one devoted to each student and teacher who spends the day on the top floor of Wayside School: kids like Joe, who never counts correctly but always gets the right answer; Jason, who gets stuck to his chair by a wad of bubble gum; and Nancy, who hates his name so much that he trades names with a girl named Mac. Some stories are silly, some clever, and others have a subtle lesson attached. They're all a little weird, but very funny.

Why This Book Appeals to Reluctant Readers Teachers have told me that the Wayside School books are big hits when they're read aloud in third- and fourth-grade classrooms, and it's probably because the broad humor and plotlines that don't always evolve logically appeal perfectly to middle-grade sensibilities. Each short chapter stands alone as a separate story, so kids can read just one chapter per sitting or page through the book and choose a chapter at random. The short, declarative sentences and liberal use of dialogue make this a good introduction to middle-grade novels.

Who Might Like This Book All kinds of kids love the Wayside School books, but they seem to have special appeal to boys who aren't enthusiastic readers.

If Your Child Liked This Book, Then Try . . . Other Wayside School books by Louis Sachar, including *Wayside School Gets a Little Stranger* and *Wayside School Is Falling Down* (Avon).

Math Rashes

by

DOUGLAS EVANS

Illustrator LARRY DI FIORI

Genre: Humorous Contemporary Fiction

Publisher: Front Street, $15.95 (h)

Page Length: 112

Type of Illustrations: Black-and-white spot illustrations, on almost every page

Reluctant Reader Appeal: Humor, Well-Defined Characters, Fast-Paced Plot, Concise Chapters

Suggested reading level: Ages 8–11

The recess minutes ticked away. Perhaps Andrew would have doodled the entire time if a loud whistle hadn't startled him. He paused to listen. Yes, someone very close was whistling "Yankee Doodle."

Andrew squinted at his math sheet. Was he seeing things? Every doodle on the paper was now moving. The pirate flag fluttered. The doodle springs coiled and uncoiled. The doodle race car's tires spun, and the doodle jets dropped doodle bombs that made doodle explosions at the bottom of the page.

Synopsis Every year a New-School-Year Moon shines over W. T. Melon Elementary the night before school starts. But this year, the moon was different. It sent a beam of light across the floor to the third-grade classroom at the end of the hall.

The third graders hear this story from the school custodian on the first day of school, and they wonder what's in store for the year ahead. They soon find out. Theirs is no ordinary classroom; magical events bring inanimate objects to life. Lunchboxes, doodles, and pencil sharpeners come alive and teach lessons specially designed for the students who need them the most. The kids in this classroom end up learning about life in ways that aren't found in books.

Why This Book Appeals to Reluctant Readers This episodic novel is written in chapters that stand alone as individual, action-packed short stories. The conflicts are typical of third grade and very familiar to the readers—a playground bully, a girl who can't stop losing her pencils, a boy who spends his class time doodling and so misses recess—but the solutions are straight out of a child's imagination. Each character is taught how to solve his or her problem by the objects in the school itself, using abundant humor and magic.

Who Might Like This Book Kids who like school stories, especially those that border on the silly or absurd. This book is very plot-oriented and so is great for readers with short attention spans.

Notes to Parents This is a terrific book to read out loud to kids in third, fourth, or fifth grade who might be reading well below grade level or to several kids of different ages (children as young as first grade will laugh at the characters' predicaments).

If Your Child Liked This Book, Then Try . . . The Classroom at the End of the Hall by Douglas Evans (Apple Paperbacks; featuring the same characters as *Math Rashes*).

Bunnicula:
A Rabbit-Tale of Mystery

by

DEBORAH AND JAMES HOWE

Illustrator ALAN DANIEL

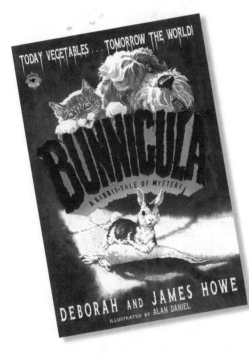

Genre: Mystery/Animal Characters

Publisher: Atheneum, $16.00 (h); Avon, $3.99 (p)

Page Length: 48

Type of Illustrations: Black and white, about two per chapter

Reluctant Reader Appeal: Humor, Well-Defined Characters, Fast-Paced Plot, Concise Chapters, Suitable Text

Suggested reading level:
Ages 8–12

"A white tomato. Very significant," Chester murmured.

"So it's a white tomato," I said, edging my way back to the kitchen door. "What does that have to do with Bunnicula?"

"I can tell you one thing," Chester said. "I got a good look at the tomato. There were very suspicious marks on the skin."

Synopsis Harold the dog and Chester the cat have a very ordinary, comfortable life with the Monroe family until one night when the Monroes return from the movies with a new pet. Someone left a rabbit on Toby Monroe's seat with a note tied to his neck that said, "Take good care of my baby." The Monroes name the rabbit Bunnicula in honor of the Dracula movie they were viewing. Bunnicula seems harmless, but Chester thinks otherwise.

Chester's suspicions grow when strange things begin to happen around the Monroe household. Vegetables turn white, sucked dry of their colorful juices. Bunnicula sleeps all day and wakes at sunset. The bunny's markings look like a cape, and Chester spies fangs in the rabbit's mouth. Could Bunnicula be a vampire rabbit? Chester's convinced, and now he must find a way to warn the Monroes before it's too late. Chester's warnings, which are misinterpreted by the humans, add another hilarious element to this madcap mystery.

Why This Book Appeals to Reluctant Readers
Harold is the perfect character to narrate this story. His droll, self-deprecating voice provides a humorous contrast to Chester's educated yet excitable personality. The plot whizzes along as the tension mounts, mostly because of Chester's active imagination. Bunnicula never says a word, but he still emerges as a full character who is more than an ordinary bunny.

Who Might Like This Book
Readers who love animal characters, mysteries, and humorous banter between characters.

Notes to Parents
The mystery and vampire themes are presented in a light and funny manner, which makes this book a good choice to read out loud to younger children.

If Your Child Liked This Book, Then Try . . .
Other books by James Howe featuring Harold and Chester, including *Bunnicula Strikes Again, The Celery Stalks at Midnight,* and *Howliday Inn* (all published by Atheneum/Avon).

Arthur, for the Very First Time

by

PATRICIA MacLACHLAN

Illustrator LLOYD BLOOM

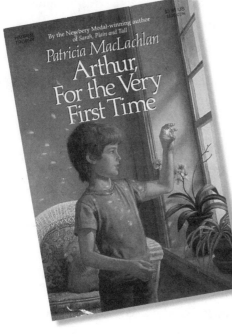

Genre: Contemporary Fiction

Publisher: HarperTrophy, $4.95 (p)

Page Length: 117

Type of Illustrations: Black and white, every few chapters

Reluctant Reader Appeal: Humor, Well-Defined Characters, Concise Chapters, Suitable Text, Kid Relevance

Suggested reading level: Ages 8–11

Aunt Elda sat Arthur at a round oak table in her kitchen. Its legs were chicken feet that grasped round balls.

"Here's your list, Arthur. Check off the food you don't like, and we'll see what we can do about it."

"You mean I don't have to eat what I don't like?" Arthur asked. He thought about tuna-noodle casserole and spinach that grew cold on his plate.

"I said we'll see what we can do about it," said Aunt Elda.

Synopsis Ten-year-old Arthur Rasby spends most of his time recording observations in his notebook. He's especially interested in things that are *real*. One of the things he's noticed lately is that his parents don't listen to him—they're too busy arguing—and his mother is going to have a baby (even though no one's told him yet). When he goes to spend the summer with his Great-Aunt Elda and Great-Uncle Wrisby on their farm, Arthur's forced to see the world in a new way.

First of all, his aunt and uncle are unlike any adults Arthur has ever known. They each have a unique way of looking at life, and they *listen* to Arthur. Moira, a girl who lives with her grandfather because her parents deserted her, urges Arthur to stop taking notes and start *doing* things. And that's exactly what Arthur does, in a summer that changes his life.

Why This Book Appeals to Reluctant Readers

Arthur is a sensitive, thoughtful boy who's not adverse to hard work. It's nice to see a male character in a middle-grade novel who has heart without being characterized as a geek. Arthur's astute observations about his world capture the sensibilities of a child who feels his family stability shifting beneath him. The characters who populate this novel are wonderfully warm and unique, and they perfectly match the small-town country setting. Above all, Arthur's growth comes from the inside, leaving the reader with a full, satisfied feeling at the end of the book.

Who Might Like This Book

This is a book that celebrates the human spirit and so is best for kids who like quiet, thoughtful books rather than action-packed, suspenseful plots.

If Your Child Liked This Book, Then Try . . .

Other books by Patricia MacLachlan, including *Cassie Binegar* and *Unclaimed Treasures* (published by Harper).

My Teacher Is an Alien

by

BRUCE COVILLE

Illustrator MIKE WIMMER

Genre: Contemporary Fiction/
Science Fiction

Publisher: Simon & Schuster,
$4.99 (p)

Page Length: 123

Type of Illustrations: Black
and white, about every
other chapter

Reluctant Reader Appeal:
Humor, Well-Defined
Characters, Fast-Paced
Plot, Concise Chapters,
Suitable Text

**Suggested
reading level:**
Ages 8–12

*When I finally got the nerve to sneak a look around the bottom
edge of the door, I saw Mr. Smith sitting at a little makeup
table, looking in a mirror. Stacey was right. The man really
was handsome. He had a long, lean face with a square jaw, a
straight nose, and cheekbones to die for.*

*Only it was a fake. As I watched, Mr. Smith pressed his fin-
gers against the bottom of his eyes. Suddenly he ran his fingertips
to the sides of his head, grabbed his ears, and started peeling off
his face!*

Synopsis When their teacher Ms. Schwartz doesn't return from spring break, Susan's class is stuck with a substitute. Mr. Smith is a polite but humorless, by-the-book kind of teacher who can't stand music. When Mr. Smith confiscates a note Susan wrote about him in class, she follows him home, hoping to swipe the note from his briefcase before he reads it. Intrigued by the strange noises coming from his house, Susan creeps inside and witnesses Mr. Smith peeling off his face to expose an alien face underneath.

Susan confides in the one classmate who will believe that their teacher is an alien—the brainy Peter. Susan and Peter break into Mr. Smith's house again and discover Ms. Schwartz trapped in a force field in the attic. They also learn that Mr. Smith has plans to kidnap five students and take them back to his planet.

In a humorous, pulse-pounding climax, Susan and Peter must find a way to rescue Ms. Schwartz and save their classmates before Mr. Smith's departure at the end of the school year.

Why This Book Appeals to Reluctant Readers This is not highly technical science fiction—the alien and his device for communicating with his ship are right out of a comic book. The plot contains enough tension to keep the pages turning but won't cause any nightmares. Susan and Peter, rather than the adults, are the heroes here—they save earth from alien invasion by using their wits and tools that are at any kid's disposal.

Who Might Like This Book Boys and girls who like funny school stories, fans of science fiction who aren't ready to wade through a book packed with highly technical contraptions, or kids who think their teacher must come from another planet.

If Your Child Liked This Book, Then Try . . . *My Teacher Fried My Brains, My Teacher Glows in the Dark,* and *My Teacher Flunked the Planet* (Minstrel Books). All four titles also have been published together in a 10th-anniversary edition by Simon & Schuster.

Cockroach Cooties

by

LAURENCE YEP

Genre: Contemporary Fiction

Publisher: Hyperion Books
for Children, $5.99 (p)

Page Length: 135

Type of Illustrations: None

Reluctant Reader Appeal:
Humor, Well-Defined
Characters, Concise
Chapters, Suitable Text,
Kid Relevance

**Suggested
reading level:**
Ages 8–12

Suddenly I heard Arnie's roar. Arnie had a big voice—as in monster big. Not just Frankenstein big. Godzilla big. You could hear his voice across the school yard.

"You're weird, Bobby," Arnie said.

"It takes one to know one," Bobby said.

Everyone thinks Bobby is the sweet one of us. That's why everyone likes him. When my grandmother talks about him, she always beams.

Me, I'm the normal one. I talk back and get into fights. When my grandmother mentions me, she just shakes her head and sighs.

However, right now Bobby was sounding like . . . well, me.

Synopsis Nine-year-old Teddy tolerates his younger brother Bobby, whom he sees as sweet but weird and annoying. But when Bobby antagonizes his large classmate Arnie, Teddy feels obligated to step in and defend his brother. Teddy and Bobby then both become Arnie's targets and spend the rest of the day dodging him in San Francisco's Chinatown. But the next day Bobby makes a discovery: Arnie's afraid of cockroaches, and his pet cockroach Hercules will protect them from Arnie. However, during a family birthday celebration at a local Chinese restaurant (complete with fish eyes and prawns that look like crickets), Hercules escapes from Bobby's pocket and is squished by Bobby's father. Without their protector, Teddy's sure he's doomed to becoming mush in Arnie's hands for the rest of the school year. But then Bobby devises another way to get Arnie off their backs for good. Bobby's plan works, and the boys not only discover why Arnie beats kids up but also begin to forge a cautious friendship.

Why This Book Appeals to Reluctant Readers Like real brothers, Teddy and Bobby are often at odds with each other, and yet are acutely aware of their family ties. This exploration of brotherly love, along with the message that to understand someone you must try to see the world through his eyes, is a nice twist on the traditional bully story. Set against the background of Chinese American life in modern San Francisco, this book has enough bug trivia to entice fans of six- and eight-legged creatures. The short chapters and tight, active sentence structure make it easy reading for those just moving from chapter books to middle-grade novels.

Who Might Like This Book Boys who want a middle-grade novel that's a fairly quick read, especially if they have an older or younger brother with whom they don't always get along. Kids who love bugs or those who appreciate reading about ways to use their brains instead of their fists in tense situations.

If Your Child Liked This Book, Then Try . . . Yep's first book about Teddy and Bobby: *Later, Gator* (Hyperion).

Smart Dog

by

VIVIAN VANDE VELDE

Genre: Humorous
Contemporary Fiction
Publisher: Harcourt Brace,
$4.50 (p)
Page Length: 146
Type of Illustrations: None
Reluctant Reader Appeal:
Humor, Well-Defined
Characters, Concise
Chapters, Fast-Paced
Plot, Suitable Text, Kid
Relevance

**Suggested
reading level:**
Ages 8–12

Amy said, "And you belong to someone at the college?"

Again F-32 shook his head, pulling the tag out from Amy's hand. He scratched himself—but discreetly, for a dog. "I belong to the college itself," he corrected.

To the Research Department, *Amy thought. And then suddenly everything was clear to her. "You're a science experiment," she guessed, which was the only explanation for why the dog was smart enough to talk. "And you're—"*

F-32 nodded. "Running away," he finished. "Yes. Will you help me?"

Synopsis Amy Prochenko doesn't exactly love fifth grade. She's lonely and unpopular, and she's also the target of torments from the bratty and beautiful Kaitlyn Walker. One day, while walking to school, Amy meets a dog who is able to speak. Amy discovers that Sherlock is the product of a science experiment at the local college, and he ran away after overhearing the head researcher say he was going to dissect Sherlock's brain. Amy agrees to hide Sherlock and, with the help of a nerdy classmate, convinces her parents to allow her to keep Sherlock as a pet. Sherlock tries his best to act like an ordinary "outside" dog, speaking only to Amy and her friend Sean, and engaging in typical doggie games. In fact, Sherlock is so lovable that Amy finds herself becoming popular for the first time in her life.

Then one day a college research assistant spies Sherlock in Amy's yard. The tension and lies escalate as Amy and Sherlock repeatedly elude the college staff, until Amy's lies hilariously unravel. But eventually Amy does get to keep her pet in a feel-good ending that's sure to satisfy dog lovers.

Why This Book Appeals to Reluctant Readers
The author nicely balances humor with the pain that comes from not being part of the "in" crowd, a concern that starts to take shape around fifth grade. Amy also learns that Kaitlyn gets her power by putting others down, a realization that will be relevant (and empowering) to many kids. But this book is really more a celebration of the reciprocal love children share with their pets. The plot zooms along, and the tension mounts quickly, ensuring that readers will stick with the story to see what happens next.

Who Might Like This Book
Dog lovers and kids who have, at some point in their lives, been relegated to the outer fringes of the popular crowd.

If Your Child Liked This Book, Then Try . . .
The Puppy Sister by S. E. Hinton, illustrated by Jacqueline Rogers (Bantam); *The Rumpelstiltskin Problem* by Vivian Vande Velde (Houghton Mifflin; humorous alterations of fairy tales).

Charlie and the Chocolate Factory

by

ROALD DAHL

Illustrator QUENTIN BLAKE

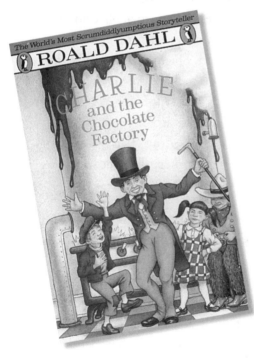

Genre: Humorous Fantasy

Publisher: Puffin Books, $5.99 (p)

Page Length: 162

Type of Illustrations: Black and white, every few pages

Reluctant Reader Appeal: Humor, Well-Defined Characters, Fast-Paced Plot, Concise Chapters, Kid Relevance

Suggested reading level:
Ages 8–12

"An important room, this!" cried Mr. Wonka, taking a bunch of keys from his pocket and slipping one into the keyhole of the door. "This is the nerve center of the whole factory, the heart of the whole business! And so beautiful! I insist upon my rooms being beautiful! I can't abide ugliness in factories! In we go then! But do be careful, my dear children! Don't lose your heads! Don't get overexcited! Keep very calm!"

Synopsis Willy Wonka, a candy-making genius, announces that he'll open up his magical factory to five children who find golden tickets hidden in the wrappers of his chocolate bars. One by one, the first four tickets are claimed. Then Charlie Bucket, a poor, starving waif, finds a dollar on the street, buys a candy bar, and discovers the final ticket. When the big day arrives, Charlie and his Grandpa Joe line up with the other winners outside the factory gates. Their once-in-a-lifetime adventure is about to begin!

Inside the factory, the children encounter magic delicacies like they've never imagined: a chocolate river, Everlasting Gobstoppers and square candies that look round. But Charlie's fellow winners—greedy Augustus Gloop, spoiled Veruca Salt, gum-chewing Violet Beauregarde, and couch-potato Mike Teavee—can't behave themselves and gradually disappear. Soon Charlie's the only one left, and he gets the best prize of all!

Why This Book Appeals to Reluctant Readers Willy Wonka's chocolate factory is straight out of a child's imagination (it's hard to believe a grown-up conceived it!); the quirky characters, though a shade one-dimensional, represent a variety of basic human traits. Children, with their innate sense of fairness, will appreciate that the greedy, the lazy, and the selfish get punished (in a very humorous way) while sweet, pure Charlie is rewarded. The plot careens along with the text flowing into illustrations and back out the other side, one chapter barely ending before the next begins.

Who Might Like This Book Kids who like books with lots of action, dialogue, and humor, or those who appreciate offbeat, even bizarre characters and colorful settings.

If Your Child Liked This Book, Then Try . . . Other books by Roald Dahl, including *Charlie and the Great Glass Elevator* (Knopf), *Matilda* (Viking), and *James and the Giant Peach* (Knopf).

On My Honor

by

MARION DANE BAUER

Genre: Contemporary Fiction

Publisher: Clarion, $15.00 (h); Yearling, $4.99 (p)

Page Length: 90

Type of Illustrations: None

Reluctant Reader Appeal: Fast-Paced Plot, Concise Chapters, Kid Relevance, Suitable Text

Suggested reading level: Ages 9–12

Joel stared. "In the river?" he demanded. "You want to go swimming in the river?"

Tony shrugged elaborately. "Where else?"

"You might as well go swimming in your toilet."

"Who says?"

"My dad says! That's who."

"My dad says," Tony mimicked, his voice coming out high and girlish.

Joel decided to ignore the taunt. He decided, also, not to remind Tony of the promise he had been required to make to his father before they left. "You know we're not allowed to swim in *the Vermillion. Nobody is. It's dangerous . . . sink holes and currents. Whirlpools, sometimes! Besides being dirty."*

Synopsis Twelve-year-old Joel promises his father that he's going for a bike ride with his best friend Tony to the state park and back and nowhere else. On the way, Tony stops on a bridge and proposes they instead swim in the treacherous river. At first, Joel tries to dissuade his reckless friend, but then, in an effort to teach Tony a lesson, he challenges Tony to a race to the sandbar in the center of the river. However, Tony disappears into the murky water. After attempting to find his friend, Joel finally rides home and decides to keep the truth of Tony's whereabouts a secret. As Joel comes to terms with the realization that his best friend is probably dead, he concocts a story of becoming too tired to ride all the way to the park and turning back while Tony went on alone. All that day, Joel wrestles with tough questions: Should he have known Tony couldn't swim? Did he try hard enough to talk Tony out of it? Is it his fault since he challenged Tony to race? Is it his dad's fault for letting them ride 12 miles to the state park in the first place? Once the police find Tony's bike and clothes on the bridge, Joel finally tells Tony's frantic parents the truth.

Why This Book Appeals to Reluctant Readers This is a very tight story, told from start to finish in less than 24 hours. As a result, the tenion is high, pulling the reader through the book quickly. Its heavy moral issues are presented in a very thoughtful and compelling manner. Joel is in a position many readers can sympathize with: being torn between looking good in front of his friend and obeying his father. The author raises basic questions of right and wrong and yet doesn't preach to the reader or tell him what to think.

Who Might Like This Book This novel is on the short side, but I listed it in this chapter because of the weighty subject.

It will appeal to boys and girls, but boys should be especially drawn to it because of the male protagonist. Any readers who like straightforward stories that make them think will get something from this book. The open-ended nature of the ending allows readers to draw their own conclusions.

Notes to Parents This book can inspire some lively family discussions. It won a Newbery Honor in 1987.

If Your Child Liked This Book, Then Try . . . *The Wild Kid* by Harry Mazer (Simon & Schuster); *Bridge to Terabithia* by Katherine Paterson, illustrated by Donna Diamond (Newbery Medal winner, HarperTrophy).

The Kid Who Only Hit Homers

by

MATT CHRISTOPHER

Illustrator HARVEY KIDDER

Genre: Sports Fiction

Publisher: Little, Brown, $4.50 (p)

Page Length: 151

Type of Illustrations: Black and white, about one per chapter

Reluctant Reader Appeal: Fast-Paced Plot, Concise Chapters, Suitable Text, Kid Relevance

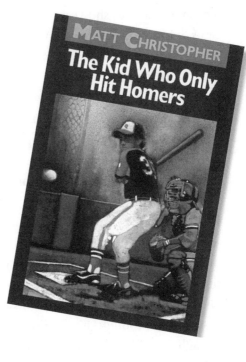

Suggested reading level: Ages 9–12

Sylvester found a bat he liked and stepped in front of the backstop screen. Rick Wilson walked out to the temporary pitching box, waited for Sylvester to get ready, then blazed one in.

Smack! Sylvester laid into it and blasted it over the left field fence.

"Jumping codfish!" cried Coach Corbin. "Look at that blast! Pitch another, Rick!"

Synopsis Sylvester Coddmyer III loves baseball more than anything and dreams of playing on his junior high team, the Hooper Redbirds. The only trouble is, Sylvester's a terrible player. But one day a stranger shows up at the practice field: a man named George Baruth, who looks a bit like Sylvester's idol, Babe Ruth. The man says he can help Sylvester become a better player.

Sylvester and Mr. Baruth practice together that evening, and Sylvester does seem to suddenly hit every pitch thrown his way. The next day, he showcases his new talent for the coach, who signs Sylvester up for the team. As the season progresses, Sylvester becomes a legend in his town and eventually in New York state: Every time he hits the ball, it's out of the park. He's also turned into an amazing right fielder with the speed of a track star and a glove that's a magnet for the ball.

But Sylvester has some nagging questions: Why does Mr. Baruth always disappear immediately after each game? How come no one in town knows this guy? Sylvester tries to brush these thoughts aside and enjoy being part of the team until Snooky Malone, a pesky neighborhood kid with an interest in astrology and the occult, begins drilling Sylvester about his unprecedented hitting streak and his mysterious coach. When the day comes for Mr. Baruth to say good-bye, Sylvester must play for the first time without his coach in the stands. He discovers that, though his hitting streak is over, he's improved enough to still be a valuable member of the team.

Why This Book Appeals to Reluctant Readers

Though the author attempts to infuse the story with a subtle moral lesson about greed and the fleeting nature of fame, this is really a book about playing baseball. The bulk of the story is made up of fast-paced, play-by-play accounts of individual games and Sylvester's superhuman hitting and catching abilities. What child who loves baseball but lacks natural athletic talent hasn't dreamed of suddenly being able to play like Babe Ruth, even for one season? For baseball fans, this book is pure immediate gratification.

Who Might Like This Book For pure entertainment and sports-centered action, Matt Christopher is the perfect choice for reluctant readers. I have a friend who, at age 40, is a successful business owner but hated to read when he was in sixth and seventh grade. "The only books I'd ever pick up," he told me recently, "were Matt Christopher books. I read everything he wrote."

Notes to Parents Matt Christopher has been writing for decades, and some of his older books have minor details that may seem dated to your kids and might trigger some questions. However, these are minor plot points and don't detract from the overall timeless nature of the story.

If Your Child Liked This Book, Then Try . . . Matt Christopher has written many novels centered around different sports. Some include *Tough to Tackle, Dirt Bike Racer, The Basket Counts, Ice Magic,* and *Return of the Home Run Kid* (all published by Little, Brown).

Little House on the Prairie

by

LAURA INGALLS WILDER

Illustrator GARTH WILLIAMS

Genre: Historical Fiction

Publisher: HarperCollins, $5.95 (p)

Page Length: 335

Type of Illustrations: Black and white, about three per chapter

Reluctant Reader Appeal: Well-Defined Characters, Concise Chapters, Suitable Text, Unique Presentation

Suggested reading level: Ages 8–12

"He's awful big," Laura whispered.

"Yes, and see how his coat shines," Pa whispered into her hair. The moonlight made little glitters in the edges of the shaggy fur, all around the big wolf.

"They are in a ring clear around the house," Pa whispered. Laura pattered beside him to the other window. He leaned his gun against that wall and lifted her up again. There, sure enough, was the other half of the circle of wolves. All their eyes glittered green in the shadow of the house. Laura could hear

their breathing. When they saw Pa and Laura looking out, the middle of the circle moved back a little way.

Synopsis It is the mid-1870s, and according to Charles "Pa" Ingalls, the woods in Wisconsin are getting too crowded. So he packs up his family in a covered wagon and heads to the wide-open prairies of Oklahoma.

The story is told from the point of view of Laura, the middle daughter, and is based on the real-life experiences of the author when she was about 5 or 6 years old. In language as spare and vivid as the prairie itself, the text depicts the Ingalls family on their long and often dangerous journey until they find the perfect spot for their new homestead. Over the course of a year, they build a house, meet their far-flung neighbors, encounter wolves and a panther, endure fires and malaria, and become acquainted with both friendly and hostile Indians. One day, as Pa is plowing the fields for their first planting, a neighbor stops by to tell him that his homestead is built three miles inside Indian territory and that the government is on its way to force him to move. Immediately Pa decides to leave, and the next day the Ingalls are in their wagon again, moving on to their next home.

Why This Book Appeals to Reluctant Readers The Little House books have been considered American classics since they were first published in the 1930s. Their appeal is more than the story of a pioneer family traveling through the West in the 1870s and 1880s; it's the immediacy that comes with a story told by someone who was there. Because Laura Ingalls Wilder writes the story through the eyes of her own childhood, she focuses on the details children find fascinating and important. Aspects of a child's life at the time creep naturally into the text (children should be seen and not heard, parents are to be obeyed without question), and Laura often displays the timeless emotions of a young girl with an older sibling whom she sees as perfect. The book is written in episodic chapters, each of which stands alone as a short story. So, if kids don't want to read about how Pa and Laura built a door to the cabin to keep the wolves out, they can skip to when the Indians paid a visit or the chimney caught on fire.

Who Might Like This Book Though this book revolves around the experiences of a girl, there's enough danger and adventure to entice boys as well, at least on the younger end of the intended age-group. Children who appreciate biographies, books about the settling of the West, or who live in the areas mentioned in this series should find the LITTLE HOUSE books compelling.

Notes to Parents *Little House on the Prairie* is probably the best-known book in this series, but if your child wants to read the series in order, start with *Little House in the Big Woods* and read the books as listed below.

It may be tempting to get the shorter LITTLE HOUSE editions that have come out recently (some in picture book form), but I suggest you wait until your child can read the longer, original versions. The abbreviated stories lose much of Wilder's descriptive language, which makes these texts so memorable.

If Your Child Liked This Book, Then Try . . . The entire LITTLE HOUSE series, published by HarperCollins, which goes in this order: *Little House in the Big Woods, Little House on the Prairie, Farmer Boy, On the Banks of Plum Creek, By the Shores of Silver Lake, The Long Winter, Little Town on the Prairie,* and *These Happy Golden Years: The First Four Years.*

Dear Mrs. Ryan, You're Ruining My Life

by

JENNIFER B. JONES

Genre: Contemporary Fiction

Publisher: Walker &
Company, $15.95 (h)

Page Length: 122

Type of Illustrations: None

Reluctant Reader Appeal:
Humor, Well-Defined
Characters, Fast-Paced Plot,
Concise Chapters, Suitable
Text, Kid Relevance

**Suggested
reading level:**
Ages 8–12

"*My best ideas come from real life, from things that happen to
me, or to people close to me.*"

*I couldn't believe she said it. But she did it every time. See,
the main characters in all Mom's books are always boys my age.
It only takes a bear with very little brains to figure out which
people close to her give her the best ideas. I could feel the kids
turning to look at me.*

*Bethany was grinning as if she'd just sold a best-seller herself.
"Do you ever put things that Harvey has done in your books?"*

Synopsis Fifth-grader Harvey Ryan dreads the day every year that his mother, a popular children's author, comes to speak to his class. It's bad enough that embarrassing things Harvey does always end up in his mother's books, but having to sit there while his mother talks about him in front of his classmates is even worse. Then Harvey's best friend, Cecilia "Seal" Spicer, comes up with an idea: If they can find Harvey's mom a boyfriend, she'll stop paying so much attention to Harvey's life. And she's got the perfect man: Rob Stevens, the school principal.

Harvey and Seal conspire to get Mrs. Ryan and Mr. Stevens together, and at first things seem to be working. Then the kids at school catch on that Harvey's mom is dating the principal, and Harvey is more embarrassed than ever. To top it off, Harvey's dad, a former minor-league baseball player, had promised to coach Harvey's team that summer, then backed out when he and his new wife bought a business. Harvey's parents are ruining his life.

Why This Book Appeals to Reluctant Readers The funny, fast plot of this book revolves around two things of paramount concern to many children: being embarrassed by their parents and conflicting feelings about their parents' divorce and ensuing relationships. The author weaves these two themes together seamlessly and throws in enough baseball action to keep the book from getting heavy. The prickly embarrassment Harvey feels when his mother forces him to be the center of attention will get a laugh from any adolescent who has been caught in public with her parents.

Who Might Like This Book The book's lighthearted tone and multiple themes will appeal to boys and girls alike. Kids who like real situations written with humor will appreciate this book.

If Your Child Liked This Book, Then Try . . . *The Agony of Alice* by Phyllis Reynolds Naylor (Atheneum); *The Best School Year Ever* by Barbara Robinson (HarperCollins).

Peppermints in the Parlor

by

BARBARA BROOKS WALLACE

Genre: Historical
Mystery/Suspense

Publisher: Aladdin
Paperbacks, $4.99 (p)

Page Length: 198

Type of Illustrations: None

Reluctant Reader Appeal:
Well-Defined Characters,
Fast-Paced Plot, Concise
Chapters, Suitable Text

**Suggested
reading level:**
Ages 8–12

*"Emily, my dear child, don't you know me? This is your Aunt
Twice!"*

*Was it? Emily wondered with a sharp stab of fright. If so,
where were the flyaway shining curls and dancing green eyes?
Where was the fashionable coat with the nipped-in waist, and
where the feathered Paris bonnet? And most important, where
was the pink-cheeked face, as pretty as her own Mama's had
been? How could this thin, sunken person be the Aunt Twice she
had once known?*

Synopsis Emily Luccock, a recently orphaned 11-year-old, has
come to live with her wealthy Aunt and Uncle Twice at Sugar Hill
Hall, their grand, white-pillared mansion. But when a pale,

frightened Aunt Twice picks her up, Emily knows something's horribly wrong. When she gets to Sugar Hill Hall, Emily learns that Aunt Twice is kept a virtual prisoner by the evil Mrs. Meeching, who has taken over the mansion and converted it into a home for the aged whom no one wants. Emily is expected to be a servant and live in the dark, damp cellar. And what's more, Uncle Twice has disappeared.

In the midst of this bleak existence, the only bright spot is a bowl of peppermints prominently displayed at the foot of the staircase, but anyone who so much as touches them gets sent to the terrifying Remembrance Room. Emily soon decides to get to the bottom of the mystery of Sugar Hill Hall, even though dangerous eyes and ears lurk around every shadowy corner.

Why This Book Appeals to Reluctant Readers The book has all the elements of a classic mystery written in the style and time period of Charles Dickens, including a smart, spunky, orphaned protagonist and a creepy villain dressed in black who seems to ooze evil from every pore. The setting, characters, and plot all create a level of suspense that doesn't let up until the last page. Emily's situation is dire, but she's such a sympathetic character that the reader can't help but stick with her until she solves the mystery of Sugar Hill Hall.

Who Might Like This Book Mystery lovers for certain, especially readers who like period mysteries. Because of the female protagonist, this book is more likely to be read by girls, though boys may find it compelling as well.

Notes to Parents This book also makes a terrific read-aloud story for kids in third through sixth grades.

If Your Child Liked This Book, Then Try . . . Other mysteries by Barbara Brooks Wallace, including *Cousins in the Castle* and *The Twin in the Tavern* (Aladdin Paperbacks).

The Trolls

by

POLLY HORVATH

Genre: Humorous Fiction

Publisher: Farrar, Straus &
Giroux, $4.95 (p)

Page Length: 136

Type of Illustrations: None

Reluctant Reader Appeal:
Humor, Well-Defined
Characters, Fast-Paced Plot,
Concise Chapters

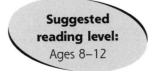

**Suggested
reading level:**
Ages 8–12

*At first the children thought Aunt Sally was a giant. Then
Melissa looked down and realized that Aunt Sally was wearing
very high heels. The shoes were thick and clunky and had laces
that wound around Aunt Sally's legs almost up to her knees.
That was the bottom half of her. The top half was mostly very
yellow hair that was piled way way up on top of her head like a
tower. In between the top and the bottom was the gist of Aunt
Sally. The gist was impressive enough. She had large, solid bones
and more cheek space than most people. Her lips were thick and
full. Her nose was a formidable entity and her eyes had more
sparkles than normal sparkly eyes. There just seemed to be more
altogether of Aunt Sally.*

Synopsis When their parents go to Paris for a week, Melissa, Amanda, and Pee Wee are left in the care of their father's sister from Canada, an eccentric aunt they've never met. Aunt Sally builds Pee Wee a tree house, doesn't make them eat green beans, and is full of fascinating stories about her and their father's childhood on Vancouver Island. The children are enthralled by Aunt Sally's renditions of characters such as Mrs. Gunderson the dog, Fat Little Mean Girl, and Great-Uncle Louis, a health nut who came for two weeks and stayed for six years. She also gives Pee Wee, who lives "the life of a worm" at the hands of his two older sisters, some much-needed respect. When Aunt Sally tells the children about the time she tried to give her own little brother, their father, to the trolls, the girls begin to understand that they shouldn't repeat the same mistakes as their family's previous generation.

Why This Book Appeals to Reluctant Readers Aunt Sally's yarns are spun with the straight-faced delivery of a master storyteller. The kids themselves are well drawn and interact like ordinary siblings; their dialogue is especially true to life. This is really two stories: the childhood adventures of Aunt Sally and her brother and the relationships of the present-day children. Both plots are intricately connected, and there are enough unexpected twists and turns to keep the reader wondering until the last page how each scenario will play out.

Who Might Like This Book The wild, weird, and wonderful characters in this book will appeal to both boys and girls. Kids who like clever humor, bigger-than-life people, or good storytelling will get a kick out of this story.

If Your Child Liked This Book, Then Try . . . Other stories by Polly Horvath, published by FSG, including *When the Circus Came to Town* and *Everything on a Waffle*.

Tuck Everlasting

by

NATALIE BABBITT

Genre: Adventure/Fantasy

Publisher: Farrar, Straus &
Giroux, $4.95 (p)

Page Length: 136

Type of Illustrations: None

Reluctant Reader Appeal:
Well-Defined Characters,
Fast-Paced Plot, Concise
Chapters, Kid Relevance

**Suggested
reading level:**
Ages 8–12

"*That was the first time we figured there was something peculiar,*" *said Mae.* "*Jesse fell out of a tree . . .*"

"*I was way up in the middle,*" *Jesse interrupted,* "*trying to saw off some of the big branches before we cut her down. I lost my balance and I fell . . .*"

"*He landed plum on his head,*" *said Mae with a shudder.* "*We thought for sure he'd broke his neck. But come to find out, it didn't hurt him a bit!*"

"*Then Pa got snake bite . . .*"

"*And Jesse ate the poison toadstool . . .*"

"*And I cut myself,*" *said Mae.* "*Remember? Slicing bread.*"

But it was the passage of time that worried them the most. They had worked the farm, settled down, made friends. But after ten years, then twenty, they had to face the fact that there was something terribly wrong. None of them was getting any older.

Synopsis This richly told tale is actually two stories in one: It's about 10-year-old Winnie Foster, who runs away from home and becomes embroiled in an adventure involving a mysterious stranger, kidnapping, jailbreak, and murder. It's also about the Tuck family, who many years ago accidentally drank from a magical spring that gives eternal life, and now they never grow older, never change. The stories cross paths when Winnie kneels down to unsuspectingly sip from the spring, and Jesse Tuck grabs her and carries her off. Once Jesse introduces Winnie to his kind and lonely family, Winnie vows that the spring will remain a secret. But the stranger has other plans, and Winnie has to fight to help the Tucks keep their peaceful lives without becoming some sort of circus sideshow or, worse, without people everywhere flocking to the spring to achieve their own immortality. And Winnie must grapple with the notion of living forever herself and decide if such a gift would be a blessing or a curse.

Why This Book Appeals to Reluctant Readers This is truly a beautifully written book, a classic that has opened children up to the magic of language and literature for many years. The strands of the plot start out separately, gradually coming together as the tension mounts. Besides being a fast-paced adventure, *Tuck Everlasting* raises sophisticated philosophical ideas rarely found in books for this age-group. The characters themselves present both sides of the issues, and it's up to the reader to decide who is right.

Who Might Like This Book Girls who like fairy-tale kinds of adventure stories or those who appreciate books with interesting characters and thoughtful themes. Boys may like it too.

If Your Child Liked This Book, Then Try . . . Other novels by Natalie Babbitt, published by FSG, including *Knee-Knock Rise, Goody Hall,* and *The Search for Delicious.* Also try *Because of Winn-Dixie* by Kate DiCamillo (Candlewick).

The Boys Start the War

by

PHYLLIS REYNOLDS NAYLOR

Genre: Contemporary Fiction

Publisher: Yearling, $5.99 (p)

Page Length: 133

Type of Illustrations: None

Reluctant Reader Appeal:
Humor, Well-Defined Characters, Fast-Paced Plot, Concise Chapters, Kid Relevance

Suggested reading level:
Ages 8–12

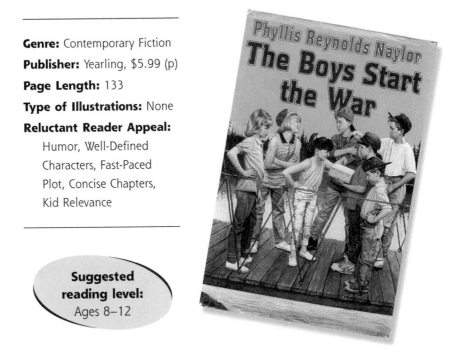

Wally was miserable. *"I just declared war,"* he said, and told them what had happened.

"Hoo boy!" Josh whistled.

"Wow!" said Peter.

For the rest of the way home Jake and Josh talked about what they would do if the Malloys tried to get even with Wally for bumping Caroline's nose. They were in the same class with Eddie.

"That Eddie would try anything," said Jake. *"If she'd dump her tray on me in front of teachers and everybody, you can imagine what she'd do when no one was looking."*

"Did you watch her pitch at recess? Whomp! The ball comes at you before you can look at it cross-eyed," Josh went on.

"Who's the other sister?" Peter asked, walking fast to keep up.

"Beth," Josh told him. "She's weird. Sits on the steps at recess and reads a book."

"A Whomper, a Weirdo, and a Crazie," said Jake, and sighed. . . .

Synopsis The Hatford brothers are hoping boys will move into the house across the river where their best friends, the Bensons, used to live. But the Malloys, a family with three girls, arrive instead. Wally and his brothers Jake, Josh, and Peter decide to make life so miserable for Caroline, Eddie, and Beth that they'll move back to Ohio. Wally declares war on the first day of school, but the boys don't count on the girls fighting back. The plot ricochets back and forth as the boys play tricks on the girls and the girls up the ante to get even. The fun-filled, inventive contests—which include dead fish, floating heads, and finally taking someone prisoner—are chronicled in chapters that alternate viewpoints between Wally and Caroline. By the end of the book, the sides are fairly even, but the war—more one of wits than mean-spirited attacks—is still on.

Why This Book Appeals to Reluctant Readers The author deftly captures the humor, imagination, and banter of middle-grade kids. The characters, ranging in age from 7 to 11, are unique and realistically show how creative kids can be when living in a small town with lots of time on their hands. The Hatfords and Malloys pull stunts that are within the range of ordinary children—not too elaborate but very inventive. Both genders are equally represented in this fast-paced account of a classic contest of the boys against the girls.

Who Might Like This Book Since the viewpoint shifts from male to female in alternating chapters, boys and girls alike should appreciate this story. Kids who like fun, action-packed contemporary plots about how boys and girls relate (but not on a romantic level) will find this a light, entertaining read.

Notes to Parents Phyllis Reynolds Naylor is best known for writing award-winning books like *Shiloh* (1992 Newbery Medal winner). If your child likes this author, try browsing through her many titles in the middle-grade fiction section.

If Your Child Liked This Book, Then Try . . . Other books featuring the Hatfords and Malloys, including *The Girls Get Even* and *The Boys Against the Girls* (Delacorte). Also try *The Boy Trap* by Nancy Matson (Front Street/Cricket Books).

Charlotte's Web

by

E. B. WHITE

Illustrator GARTH WILLIAMS

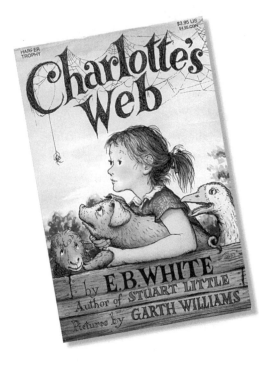

Genre: Fiction/Animal Characters

Publisher: HarperTrophy, $5.95 (p)

Page Length: 184

Type of Illustrations: Black and white

Reluctant Reader Appeal: Humor, Well-Defined Characters, Concise Chapters, Kid Relevance

Suggested reading level: Ages 8–12

Darkness settled over everything. Soon there were only shadows and the noises of the sheep chewing their cuds, and occasionally the rattle of a cow-chain up overhead. You can imagine Wilbur's surprise when, out of the darkness, came a small voice he had never heard before. It sounded rather thin, but pleasant. "Do you want a friend, Wilbur?" it said. "I'll be a friend to you. I've watched you all day and I like you."

"But I can't see you," said Wilbur, jumping to his feet. "Where are you? And who are you?"

"I'm right up here," said the voice. "Go to sleep. You'll see me in the morning."

Synopsis Wilbur the pig is born the runt of the litter and saved from death by 8-year-old Fern Arable. When he moves to Fern's uncle's farm, Wilbur meets a host of barnyard animals: geese, sheep, cows, and a greedy rat. But no one is Wilbur's special friend, and he's sure he'll die of loneliness. Then he meets Charlotte.

Charlotte is a beautiful spider who lives in the doorway of the barn. She is refined and intelligent and has a way with words. Charlotte teaches Wilbur about life and loving himself. Then Wilbur learns that he is to be fattened up and eventually slaughtered. The sensitive Wilbur panics, but Charlotte vows to save him. During the night, she spins a message into her web, and the next morning everyone knows Wilbur is "Some pig." As Charlotte creates more messages over the coming weeks, word spreads around the county that Wilbur is not an ordinary pig.

By the end of the summer, Wilbur's future is secure, but Charlotte knows her short life is almost over. While at the county fair with Wilbur, Charlotte lays her egg sac and dies. Distraught, Wilbur returns home without his friend but with her egg sac intact, and the next spring the cycle of life continues.

Why This Book Appeals to Reluctant Readers
Middle graders experience intense friendships themselves and so love to see this reflected in their books. The animal characters, especially Wilbur, mirror the feelings of a middle-grade child, ranging from loneliness to embarrassment to sheer joy. E. B. White does not write down to his readers; the sentences are sometimes longer, and the vocabulary occasionally more sophisticated, than in modern books for this age-group. There are many moments of quiet conversation; it's not entirely action packed. But the story has enough emotion, tension, and well-placed climaxes to keep the pages turning. And the plot is one the readers have never seen before.

Who Might Like This Book Any child who loves animals, interesting characters, and smart, funny dialogue. This story does have a strong emotional element, but the author simply presents these events as facts of life on the farm (and Charlotte is very matter-of-fact about her own impending death). The story ends on a happy note, with the continuation of life assured. The force of true friendship, and the lasting impact that it has on all involved, is what the reader takes from this book.

Notes to Parents Sometimes parents are afraid to expose their children to books that might make them sad. If you have a very sensitive child and haven't read *Charlotte's Web* yourself, read the book before giving it to your child. Or read it together and talk about friendship, sacrifice, and the cycle of life. Ultimately, use your own judgment if you feel your child isn't ready for a book about the death of a friend.

If Your Child Liked This Book, Then Try . . . *Stuart Little* by E. B. White, illustrated by Garth Williams (Harper-Trophy); *The Incredible Journey* by Sheila Burnford, illustrated by Carl Burger (Laurel Leaf); *Poppy* by Avi (Avon).

The Doll People

by

ANN M. MARTIN AND

LAURA GODWIN

Illustrator BRIAN SELZNICK

Genre: Fiction/Dolls

Publisher: Hyperion Books for Children, $15.99 (h)

Page Length: 256

Type of Illustrations: Black and white, on almost every page

Reluctant Reader Appeal: Humor, Well-Defined Characters, Concise Chapters, Fast-Paced Plot, Kid Relevance

Suggested reading level:
Ages 8–12

Annabelle looked out the side window of the dollhouse and saw the round yellow eye of a cat staring back at her. She sighed. Why couldn't The Captain take a nap?

Annabelle flopped on her bed. She tried to remember where Kate had left her that morning. It had been somewhere in the nursery. On her bed? Sitting on the floor playing with Baby Betsy? Calling to Nanny from the doorway? Annabelle got to her

feet again and peered through the window. The Captain was still standing on the shelf on which the dollhouse sat, staring in at the Dolls. When he saw Annabelle he licked his lips. Annabelle stuck her tongue out at him.

"Scat!" she called in her tiny doll voice.

Synopsis For the past 100 years, 8-year-old Annabelle Doll has lived in her dollhouse on the same shelf in the same room. The only ripple in this routine was when Annabelle's Auntie Sarah disappeared 45 years ago without a trace.

Then one day, Annabelle finds Auntie Sarah's diary and realizes that she had left the dollhouse on many occasions to explore and maybe even go Outside. Annabelle wants to explore as well, thinking she might find Auntie Sarah. Finally, her parents reluctantly agree, as long as Uncle Doll goes along.

On that first night away from the dollhouse, Annabelle and Uncle Doll discover a box filled with the Funcrafts, the "Real Pink Plastic" family who is moving into the room next door. Annabelle and Tiffany, the girl Funcraft, become friends and form a club to search for Auntie Sarah. As they read Sarah's diary each night, the mystery deepens—someone else has written in the diary and wants them to search the attic!

This is part friendship story, part suspenseful adventure. The contrast between the prim Dolls and the loud, fun-loving Funcrafts provides humor and diversity of characters not always found in books about toys. The Palmer's cat and the ever-present threat of being turned into Permanent Doll State (in which dolls cease to become alive if humans see them moving or talking) offer enough tension and danger to keep readers turning the pages.

Why This Book Appeals to Reluctant Readers If this book had been published when I was 9, it would have ranked among my favorites. The authors have created a completely believable world in which dolls are alive but can permit themselves to move or talk only when the humans aren't home. How the dolls navigate through the Palmer's house, what they think about when they're being played with, and how their personalities fit the time in which they were made are all details the authors have covered with great care. The mystery of Auntie Sarah's disappearance is credible, and Annabelle and Tiffany solve it in a plausible way. The smallest details (such as the Funcrafts pretending to eat their plastic food at a barbecue) make this story delightful to read. Be sure to check out the book's end pages, designed to look like catalog order forms for each dollhouse.

Who Might Like This Book This book is a must for girls who play with dolls or who have recently given them up but may still secretly believe that dolls could be alive.

If Your Child Liked This Book, Then Try . . . *The Borrowers* by Mary Norton, illustrated by Beth Krush and Joe Krush (Harcourt Brace).

From the Mixed-Up Files of Mrs. Basil E. Frankweiler

by

E. L. KONIGSBURG

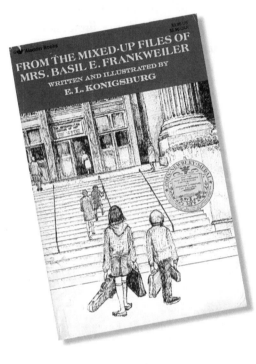

Genre: Mystery/Fiction

Publisher: Atheneum, $16.00 (h); Aladdin, $5.50 (p)

Page Length: 176

Type of Illustrations: Black and white, one every few chapters

Reluctant Reader Appeal: Humor, Well-Defined Characters, Fast-Paced Plot, Suitable Text, Kid Relevance

Suggested reading level: Ages 9–12

Claudia knew that she could never pull off the old-fashioned kind of running away. That is, running away in the heat of anger with a knapsack on her back. She didn't like discomfort; even picnics were untidy and inconvenient: all those insects and the sun melting the icing on the cupcakes. Therefore, she decided that her leaving home would not be just running from somewhere but would be running to somewhere. To a large place, a comfortable place, an indoor place, and preferably a beautiful place. And that's why she decided upon the Metropolitan Museum of Art in New York City.

Synopsis Claudia is the oldest child and the only girl in her family and, in her opinion at least, subject to a lot of injustice. So she decides to run away from her boring Greenwich, Connecticut, life—not for long, just enough to earn some appreciation from her parents. She plans carefully: She wants to be comfortable, and she wants to go somewhere important. She chooses her brother Jamie as her traveling companion (he could be counted on to be quiet, and he saves all his allowance). Then, a month before Claudia's twelfth birthday, she and Jamie run away to the Metropolitan Museum of Art in New York City.

For a while, Claudia and Jamie love their new home. They sleep in historic beds, blend into school groups during the day, and take baths in the museum fountain at night. Then one day, Claudia stumbles on an amazing statue, and even the experts don't seem to know who the artist is. Claudia becomes obsessed with solving the mystery, hoping that somehow finding the answer will make her more important. Her quest brings her to the wealthy, formidable Mrs. Basil E. Frankweiler, the former owner of the statue. Within her files lies the answer Claudia seeks.

Why This Book Appeals to Reluctant Readers This was my favorite book when I was in fifth grade. Not only did I admire Claudia's organizational and planning skills, but I wholeheartedly agreed with her desire to run away to somewhere elegant and grand. And I completely identified with her need to *become* someone. In reading the book again as an adult, I'm still struck by the illicit thrill of seeing Claudia and Jamie dodge the security guards and hide in the bathrooms during the museum's opening and closing hours. Claudia approaches her adventure as an opportunity to improve herself; the mystery is an added bonus. This book is funny, original, and populated with very real characters. The story is told by Mrs. Frankweiler in a file to her lawyer, and her matter-of-fact, sometimes stern tone can't conceal her empathy and admiration for Claudia. Her asides to her lawyer (who turns out to be the children's grandfather) sound like a schoolmarm admonishing a wayward pupil.

Who Might Like This Book Girls in particular will love this book, especially those who are entering adolescence and dream of becoming an individual who stands out from the crowd.

If Your Child Liked This Book, Then Try . . . *The View from Saturday* by E. L. Konigsburg (1997 Newbery Medal winner, published by Atheneum).

The Journal of Wong Ming-Chung: A Chinese Miner, California, 1852

(MY NAME IS AMERICA series)

by

LAURENCE YEP

Genre: Historical Fiction

Publisher: Scholastic, $10.95 (h)

Page Length: 219

Type of Illustrations: Black-and-white historical photographs and drawings in the historical note at the end of the book

Reluctant Reader Appeal: Well-Defined Characters, Concise Chapters, Suitable Text, Unique Presentation

Suggested reading level: Ages 9–12

July 16
Big Bend
I'm scared.

At first, I didn't pay any attention to the American when he walked into camp. However, all around me the other miners jerked their heads around like a flock of startled birds.

Uncle got hold of me and told me to be careful because the tax man was here.

Uncle explained that the Americans tax foreign miners. They had started it last year. The price was very high at twenty dollars a month. The purpose was to drive a lot of the Australians and

*the South Americans from the gold fields. And it had. So they
had stopped the tax.*

*But recently, the Americans had passed another law. This
time mainly against the Chinese.*

Synopsis Eleven-year-old Wong Ming-Chung (which means
"Bright Intelligence," though he's better known as "Runt"), starts
a journal in 1851 to chronicle his family's struggle to survive in
their war-ravaged Chinese village and his Uncle Stone's journey
to America to strike it rich on the "Golden Mountain" in
California. Uncle Stone does find gold, and soon Runt joins him
in America. After a difficult and dangerous journey across the
ocean, Runt finds his uncle and discovers that the Golden
Mountain consists mainly of flecks of gold dust, mud, bitter cold,
and countless hours of backbreaking labor in return for wages
that are hardly prosperous. Runt also finds that California is a
land of few laws and violent prejudice against foreigners, but
especially the Chinese. Despite these setbacks, Runt does forge
some strong friendships with miners of all races and cleverly
devises a way for him and his uncle to eventually strike it rich.
The historical note at the end gives the reader a factual background of China and America during this time and includes period photographs and drawings.

Why This Book Appeals to Reluctant Readers The
action unfolds quickly in the text's diary format. Through Runt's
eyes, the reader sees the customs of village life in China, the inhu-
mane conditions of his ocean crossing, and the excitement of
booming San Francisco and the rough mining camps. The reader
understands the perspective of the indomitable spirit of those
who came for gold because they had no other options. Well-
researched settings and characters from both countries provide
fascinating details sometimes overlooked in history books. Runt's
first-person account helps the reader empathize with his struggle:

a young boy attempting to achieve independence while feeling the weight of intense family and cultural obligations.

Who Might Like This Book The MY NAME IS AMERICA series features young male protagonists from different ethnic backgrounds during pivotal periods in American history, so this book will be especially appealing to boys. The diary format is perfect for readers who like history but don't want to wade through dense texts full of dates and broad events. Those interested in the California gold rush or kids who want to know more about Chinese American history will find Runt's story intriguing.

Notes to Parents MY NAME IS AMERICA is part of the DEAR AMERICA line from Scholastic. The DEAR AMERICA books feature young female protagonists and are written in the same diary format. Both series use well-known writers to chronicle the lives of fictional characters in America's past.

If Your Child Liked This Book, Then Try . . . There are many other books in the MY NAME IS AMERICA series, covering a variety of time periods. Some include *The Journal of Sean Sullivan: A Transcontinental Railroad Worker* by William Durbin, *The Journal of Joshua Loper: A Black Cowboy* by Walter Dean Myers, *The Journal of Scott Pendleton Collins: A World War II Soldier* by Walter Dean Myers, and *The Journal of Jasper Jonathan Pierce: A Pilgrim Boy* by Ann Rinaldi (all from Scholastic).

A Long Way from Chicago:
A Novel in Stories

by

RICHARD PECK

Genre: Historical Fiction

Publisher: Dial Books for
Young Readers, $5.99 (p)

Page Length: 148

Type of Illustrations: None

Reluctant Reader Appeal:
Humor, Well-Defined
Characters, Fast-Paced Plot,
Concise Chapters

**Suggested
reading level:**
Ages 9–12

*He was a big, tall galoot of a kid with narrow eyes. . . . The
uniform he had on was all white with a cap to match. In his
hand was a wire holder for milk bottles. He was ready to make
his escape, but Grandma was saying, "I hope I have better luck
with your milk today than the last batch. I found a dead mouse
in your delivery yesterday."*

The kid's eyes widened. "Naw you never," he said.

*"Be real careful about calling a customer a liar," she
remarked. "I had to feed that milk to the cat. And the mouse
too, of course."*

"Naw," the kid said, reaching around for the knob on the screen door behind him.

Grandma was telling one of her whoppers. If she'd found a mouse in the milk, she'd have exploded like the mailbox. She was telling a whopper, and I wondered why.

Synopsis Joey and his sister Mary Alice lived in Chicago in the bad old days of Al Capone and Bugs Moran. Starting in 1929, when Joey was 9 years old, his parents decided to send the kids to visit their grandmother for a week every August. Grandma Dowdel canned tomatoes, made her own soap, and her house had an outdoor "privy." Joey and Mary Alice were sure visiting Grandma would be dull.

Their opinion slowly changed as, over the course of seven years, they got to know their grandmother and the eccentricities of small-town life. Crusty and unaffectionate, Grandma was not above telling a lie or tall tale to get what she wanted. But Joey soon learned that Grandma had a soft spot for the poor and meek, and her lies ultimately benefited someone else. Whether it was making a war hero out of a pauper so he could get a decent burial or putting the bullying Cowgill boys in their place with a mouse and a bottle of milk, Grandma provided enough drama for Joey and Mary Alice to forget all about the big city.

Why This Book Appeals to Reluctant Readers Joey never quite knows what to make of Grandma Dowdel, and yet he admires her ability to get what she wants without anyone being the wiser. Grandma Dowdel is a wonderfully quirky, complex character who continues to surprise Joey, Mary Alice, and the reader. The dialogue and period details are so seamlessly interwoven into the plot that the reader is easily transported back to the 1930s. Each chapter stands alone as a short story, so this book can be read in several sittings without losing the flow of the narrative.

Who Might Like This Book Boys and girls, especially those who like historical fiction or stories about small-town life, or who are simply drawn to funny, eccentric characters.

Notes to Parents Though Grandma concocts lies and occasionally wields a shotgun, she's really not violent or mean. And once in a while her lies do backfire. All in all, this is a very wholesome, lighthearted book. *A Long Way from Chicago: A Novel in Stories* won a Newbery Honor in 1999 and was a National Book Award Finalist.

If Your Child Liked This Book, Then Try . . . *A Year Down Yonder* by Richard Peck (Dial Books; the sequel to *Chicago* and the 2001 Newbery Medal winner), *Love Among the Walnuts* by Jean Ferris (Harcourt Brace), and *Bat 6* by Virginia Euwer Wolff (Scholastic).

Lily's Crossing
by
PATRICIA REILLY GIFF

Genre: Historical Fiction

Publisher: Delacorte Press,
$5.50 (p)

Page Length: 181

Type of Illustrations: None

Reluctant Reader Appeal:
Well-Defined Characters,
Fast-Paced Plot, Concise
Chapters, Kid Relevance

**Suggested
reading level:**
Ages 8–12

*"I have to tell you . . ." Poppy's eyes were open now, blue with
paler flecks of gray, his face suddenly serious.*

*"The Dillons left for Detroit," she said quickly. "Mr. Dillon's
going to be a foreman in a factory in charge of making planes.
Top secret, Margaret says."*

*Poppy grinned. "It won't be top secret for long, not if
Margaret knows about it."*

Lily swallowed, watching him smile.

*He reached out, put his hand on the oars. "I have to go too.
I came tonight to tell you."*

*She didn't look at him. "To a factory like the Dillons? When
would we leave?"*

She looked out across the water, seeing him shake his head from the corner of her eye.

"The army needs engineers," Poppy said.

For a moment she felt as if she couldn't breathe. "Who's going to take care of me?"

Synopsis It's 1944, and Lily Mollahan is excitedly planning her yearly summer exodus from sticky New York City to her family's beach house in Rockaway. But this year's different: There's a war on, her summer friend, Margaret, is moving to Detroit, and Lily's father is joining the U.S. Army Corps of Engineers to fight in Europe. Lily is so hurt and furious that she refuses to even say good-bye.

But then Albert, an orphaned Hungarian refugee, comes to stay with his relatives down the street, and Lily learns that the war has touched people all over the world. Albert had to leave his younger sister, Ruth, in France, and gradually Lily opens up to the awkward, needy boy.

Lily is a complex, believable child—she's an unenthusiastic student who tells elaborate lies to make herself seem important or to get out of trouble. She lost her mother at an early age and is now under the care of her strict grandmother, which helps her understand Albert's losses even more. But Lily's growing insight into herself and her new empathy for others almost comes too late—one of her lies nearly costs Albert his life. The plot's heart-stopping climax is closely followed by touching, tearful family reunions at the end of the book.

Why This Book Appeals to Reluctant Readers Lily and Albert are both very real, appealing characters. The wryly humorous text presents their relationship's tentative beginning and its ups and downs before they become best friends. Their respective losses give the story poignancy and emotional depth that middle-grade readers appreciate. Patricia Reilly Giff's trademark tight sentences and quick plot are underlined by the building tension from the war, Poppy's absence, and Lily's mounting lies. The backdrop of the time period gives readers a perspective on this time in American history when a war overseas deeply affected the lives of those at home and when children savored every moment of summers free of appointments and prepackaged entertainment.

Who Might Like This Book Lily has enough spunk, courage, and athletic ability to appeal to many boys, but because of the book's title, cover illustration, and female protagonist, it will most likely find favor with girls. Readers who love stories about friendship or historical fiction will appreciate this book.

Notes to Parents *Lily's Crossing* won a Newbery Honor in 1998.

If Your Child Liked This Book, Then Try . . . *Nory Ryan's Song* by Patricia Reilly Giff (Bantam Doubleday Dell); *Out of the Dust* by Karen Hesse (Scholastic, 1998 Newbery Medal winner).

For YOUR Eyes Only!

by

JOANNE ROCKLIN

Illustrator MARK TODD

Genre: Contemporary Fiction

Publisher: Scholastic, $3.99 (p)

Page Length: 136

Type of Illustrations: Black and white

Reluctant Reader Appeal: Humor, Well-Defined Characters, Concise Chapters, Suitable Text, Kid Relevance

Suggested reading level: Ages 9–12

Monday, February 5

    I didn't know writing a poem was so hard. I'm sorry, Mr. M., but mine are so STUPID I can't show them to you. If I try to make a beautiful rhyme like that poem on the chalkboard, I end up with the wrong poem. . . .

    Maybe it's because I don't have a haven of privacy to do my thinking in. If I lived with my father and Matilda in their big house in San Francisco, then I could have my CHOICE of havens. . . .

Synopsis When Lucy Keane's teacher breaks her ankle, the class gets a substitute. Mr. Moffat puts a new poem on the chalkboard every Monday and urges Lucy's class to record their own thoughts and poems in journals. Lucy takes this assignment to heart, using Mr. Moffat as a sounding board for her troubles and experimenting with her own poetic voice. She asks Mr. Moffat to be her mentor and pleads that he keep the journal "for your eyes only (FYEO)."

Through Lucy's journal entries and her poems, the reader learns that her parents are divorced, and Lucy, her mother, and her younger twin brothers live in a cramped apartment in Los Angeles. Lucy can't seem to get along with her mother, who refuses to understand her. Beatrice has been Lucy's best friend forever, but suddenly the two seem to be growing apart. And to top it off, Lucy's window faces the apartment of Andy Cooper, a boy in Lucy's class whom she hates with a vengeance.

Gradually, Andy's journal entries pop up as well, first in the form of drawings and then as words. Andy has a secret he can't share with anybody, and this makes him very angry.

Then one day, something magical happens: Wild ducks inhabit the swimming pool of the apartment complex where Lucy and Andy live. Observing the ducks and keeping them safe from Andy's violent stepfather (who is the building superintendent) forges a bond between Lucy and Andy and allows them to see each other in a new light.

Why This Book Appeals to Reluctant Readers This book is made up entirely of journal entries and poems, so the story is easily read in short segments. The author exposes the reader to some wonderful poetry in a very entertaining format, and through Lucy's interpretation of those poems the reader can see how words evoke emotions. Lucy and Andy are seeking creative outlets for their pent-up feelings and feel safe to do so only when they find an adult who will listen without passing judgment.

Who Might Like This Book Girls especially, but boys as well who are sensitive or creative, and readers who are drawn to issue-driven stories (involving relationships, emotions, and personal growth) more than action-oriented plots. Preteens who are growing out of their old family/friendship roles and coming into their own identities will also relate to this story.

Notes to Parents *For YOUR Eyes Only!* is an excellent way to expose your child to poetry and perhaps inspire her to write her own.

If Your Child Liked This Book, Then Try . . . *Dear Mr. Henshaw* by Beverly Cleary, illustrated by Paul O. Zelinsky (Avon).

Revenge of the Snob Squad

(THE SNOB SQUAD series)

by

JULIE ANNE PETERS

Genre: Contemporary Fiction

Publisher: Little, Brown,
$4.99 (p)

Page Length: 120

Type of Illustrations: None

Reluctant Reader Appeal:
Humor, Well-Defined
Characters, Fast-Paced Plot,
Kid Relevance

**Suggested
reading level:**
Ages 9–12

*As usual, the elite cliques immediately separated themselves from
the rest of us pond scum. Mr. Dietz blew his whistle, hoping, I
guess, to cut through the comas. Good luck.*

"Okay, folks, let's choose up teams."

*To make myself invisible (which is a laugh if you could see
me), I slouched against the tumbling mats in the back. Why
delude myself? I always have been, and always will be, the last
one picked for any team—sports or academic. Lydia Beals may
be called Bealsqueal behind her back, but they call me Lardo
Legs to my face.*

Synopsis When the sixth-grade gym class is divided into relay race teams, Jenny Solano knows her team—the self-named Snob Squad—has no chance of winning. Jenny is a compulsive overeater and far from athletic. Lydia Beals, the team captain, is a despised whiner and overprotected daughter of a child psychologist. Maxine McFarland is a tall, tough outsider who rarely participates in gym class. Rounding out the team is the physically challenged, unfortunately named Prairie Cactus.

The only thing the girls have in common is their hatred of the popular Neon Nikes, the relay team led by the principal's daughter Ashley Krupps. Each member of the Snob Squad has been humiliated by Ashley and her friends in the past. As they get to know each other, the girls form a friendship and decide to band together to get revenge on the popular crowd. Their efforts backfire miserably—and often hilariously. But despite the Squad's failures, Jenny gets the strength from her friends to face her "void" and makes the decision to take control of her life and not act like the popular kids.

Why This Book Appeals to Reluctant Readers Jenny, the queen of glib self-mockery and shrewd observation, provides an absolutely authentic voice to the fast-paced narration. The author doesn't pull any punches—the sixth graders who taunt the Snob Squad do so with the malicious confidence that comes from being part of a protected clique. Jenny's brutal honesty about how it feels to be scorned by the "in crowd" will touch any reader who's ever been there. The book's ending is believable because the author didn't solve all Jenny's problems but allowed her to glimpse the light at the end of the tunnel.

Who Might Like This Book Middle school girls (or those approaching middle school) who appreciate sharp, witty dialogue and commentary on adolescent social behavior. Any child who has ever felt like an outcast will relate to this story. Even readers who have always been on top of the social pyramid might gain a new perspective from this book.

Notes to Parents You might be taken aback by some of the remarks the sixth-grade characters make to one another. But before you dismiss this book as being over the top, try to remember what middle school was really like. If your child is encountering classmates like these, books that realistically reflect your child's experience can be a great starting point for conversation. If your child doesn't talk about school (as many middle schoolers won't), then a book can at least let her know she's not alone.

If Your Child Liked This Book, Then Try . . . Other books in the series: *Romance of the Snob Squad* and *A Snitch in the Snob Squad.* Also try *How Do You Spell Geek?* by Julie Anne Peters (all from Little, Brown).

The Lion, the Witch and the Wardrobe

(THE CHRONICLES OF NARNIA)

by

C. S. LEWIS

Illustrator PAULINE BAYNES

Genre: Fantasy

Publisher: HarperCollins, $7.95 (p)

Page Length: About 200, depending on the edition

Type of Illustrations: Black and white, on chapter openings

Reluctant Reader Appeal: Well-Defined Characters, Fast-Paced Plot, Concise Chapters, Kid Relevance

Suggested reading level: Ages 8–12

"Narnia? What's that?" said Lucy.

"This is the land of Narnia," said the Faun, "where we are now; all that lies between the lamp-post and the great castle of Cair Paravel on the eastern sea. And you—you have come from the wild woods of the west?"

"I—I got in through the wardrobe in the spare room," said Lucy.

"Ah!" said Mr. Tumnus in a rather melancholy voice, "if only I had worked harder at geography when I was a little Faun, I should no doubt know all about those strange countries. It is too late now."

Synopsis Lucy, Edmund, Susan, and Peter are sent away from their London home during World War II to stay with a family friend in the country. One day while playing hide-and-seek, Lucy (the youngest) slips into a wardrobe filled with fur coats. She pushes farther back into the wardrobe and suddenly finds herself standing in a snowy wood under a lamppost. She meets a Faun, who tells her she's in the land of Narnia, now under the rule of the White Witch and in a state of perpetual winter. Lucy returns to collect her siblings, and together they embark on an extraordinary adventure.

Narnia, they learn, was once populated by all sorts of mythical creatures: talking animals, dwarfs, giants, unicorns, satyrs, and fauns. But the White Witch has turned many of them to stone, and the rest live in terror. Legend has it that four children (two Sons of Adam and two Daughters of Eve) will come one day and then Aslan, the Great Lion, will return and restore springtime to Narnia. The children become swept up in fulfilling this prophecy, helping Aslan battle the Witch and bring peace to the land.

Why This Book Appeals to Reluctant Readers THE CHRONICLES OF NARNIA is a classic fantasy series, read and reread by children and adults. What make this first story so alluring are the deft characterizations of classic mythical creatures and their blending of animal and human attributes. The swiftly moving story line is underwritten by the age-old clash of good versus evil. Battles, magic, feasts, and celebrations abound.

Who Might Like This Book Children who are drawn to fantasy and mythology and even those who like fast-paced adventure stories.

Notes to Parents This is an excellent book to read aloud to children of various ages. The plot and themes will hold the attention of kids from about 8 years old through early teens. It's also a good book for older readers who want an absorbing story written at a middle-grade reading level. Because the author is British, some of the words (especially in the children's dialogue) may look a bit strange to American kids, but they are easy to understand within context and add to the charm of the story.

If Your Child Liked This Book, Then Try . . . THE CHRONICLES OF NARNIA is a seven-volume series that tells the history of Narnia from its creation to the exodus of its people to a new paradise. The titles can be found separately or as a boxed set. They are *The Lion, the Witch and the Wardrobe, Prince Caspian, The Voyage of the "Dawn Treader," The Silver Chair, The Horse and His Boy, The Magician's Nephew,* and *The Last Battle.*

Maniac Magee

by

JERRY SPINELLI

Genre: Contemporary Fiction

Publisher: Little, Brown,
$5.95 (p)

Page Length: 184

Type of Illustrations: None

Reluctant Reader Appeal:
Humor, Well-Defined
Characters, Fast-Paced
Plot, Suitable Text, Kid
Relevance

**Suggested
reading level:**
Ages 9–12

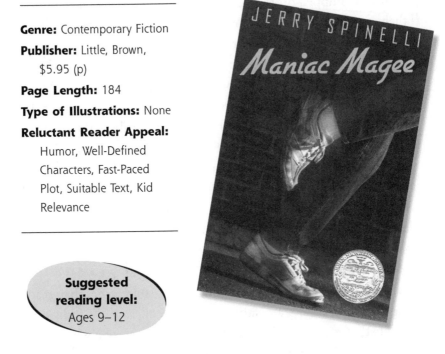

*Everyone knows that Maniac Magee (then Jeffrey) started out in
Hollidaysburg and wound up in Two Mills. The question is:
What took him so long? And what did he do along the way?*

*Sure, two hundred miles is a long way, especially on foot,
but the year that it took him to cover it was about fifty-one
weeks more than he needed—figuring the way he could run,
even then.*

*The legend doesn't have the answer. That's why this period is
known as The Lost Year.*

*And another question: Why did he stay here? Why Two
Mills? . . .*

Some say he just got tired of running. Some say it was the butterscotch Krimpets. And some say he only intended to pause here but that he stayed because he was so happy to make a friend.

Synopsis Jeffrey Lionel Magee was orphaned when he was 3 years old. Shipped off to live with his aunt and uncle, he endured their stony silence toward each other for eight years until he couldn't take it anymore. He ran out into the night and didn't stop running for a year. And the legend of Maniac Magee was born.

Much of the legend was built on Maniac's supposed athletic prowess: He could outrun dogs, he could hit a home run off the best Little League pitcher, and he could sprint along the steel rail of the railroad tracks. But there are some known facts: Like no one had ever done before, Maniac crossed the boundary between the white West End and the black East End and confronted racism and prejudice head-on. In doing so, Maniac finally found a home in an unexpected place.

Why This Book Appeals to Reluctant Readers The reader almost feels as if he's listening to this story rather than reading it. The chapters are short, colorful renderings of individual events that are gradually pieced together to form the whole plot. Like all good legends, this is told with humor and drama, and the moral of the story is one readers will take with them long after the book is finished.

Who Might Like This Book Maniac will appeal to boys, and the plot's reliance on action and exaggeration will hold the interest of readers who become bored quickly with novels.

Notes to Parents *Maniac Magee* has won many awards and honors, including the Newbery Medal in 1991.

If Your Child Liked This Book, Then Try . . . Other novels by Jerry Spinelli, including *Stargirl* and *Crash* (Knopf).

The Invasion

(ANIMORPHS series)

by

K. A. APPLEGATE

Genre: Science Fiction

Publisher: Scholastic,
$4.99 (p)

Page Length: 184

Type of Illustrations: None

Reluctant Reader Appeal:
Well-Defined Characters,
Fast-Paced Plot, Concise
Chapters, Suitable Text

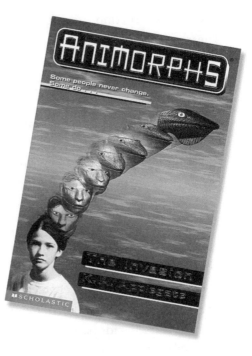

**Suggested
reading level:**
Ages 9–12

I took a deep breath. I closed my eyes. I recalled the picture of Homer I'd formed in my mind. I thought about becoming Homer.

I opened my eyes. "Bow wow," I said, laughing. "Guess it didn't work for me, Tobias."

The back of my hand itched and I scratched it.

"Jake?" Tobias said.

"What?"

"Look at your hand."

I looked at my hand. It was covered with orange fur. . . .

"My hand!" I said. "Fur!"

"Yeah, and your ears . . ." Tobias said.

I ran to the mirror over my dresser. My ears had moved. They had slid up the side of my head, and were definitely larger than they should be.

Synopsis Jake and his friends are walking through an abandoned construction site one night when they see a spaceship land nearby. A blue creature emerges, part deer, part scorpion, part something else. It communicates with the teenagers by thought, and it's friendly. It's also dying.

The creature—called an Andalite—had come to help protect earth from the invasion of parasite-like creatures called Yeerks. The Yeerks are invading every planet in the universe, infesting host bodies and controlling their brains, and they had already landed on earth. More Andalite forces are on their way, but it could take a year for them to arrive.

Just before the Yeerk spaceship lands at the construction site, the Andalite gives Jake and his friends a gift: the ability to "morph" into any animal simply by touching that animal and acquiring its DNA. This, he says, will enable them to fight the Yeerks until more help arrives. Minutes later, the Andalite is destroyed by Yeerk forces, and the kids barely escape with their lives.

What follows is a suspenseful, tension-filled, and fascinating story of how the five teenagers learn to use their morphing skills and begin to identify and take on the Controllers in their midst, some much closer than they could have imagined. The Animorphs (as the kids now call themselves) must keep their identities a secret and try to thwart the Yeerks's power plays until help eventually arrives.

Why This Book Appeals to Reluctant Readers This story moves along at a breakneck speed from page one, throwing nail-biting twists and turns at the reader in every chapter. The aliens—creepy and terrifying—are vividly described. The combination of aliens and animals makes for a distinctive story line; one of the most fascinating aspects of this book is how carefully the author conveys how it *feels* to be an animal, both physically and mentally. The unsettling ending will have readers eagerly reaching for the next book in the series.

Who Might Like This Book Many boys who won't read anything else will pick up science fiction, and this plot is fairly straightforward and easy to follow for fans of the genre. Boys and girls who love action, suspense, or creatures from outer space will be drawn to this series.

If Your Child Liked This Book, Then Try . . . There are over 30 books in the ANIMORPHS series, which has a continuing story line, so the books are best read in sequence (each story is told by a different character). They are all shelved together in the children's fiction section of a bookstore or library.

Ella Enchanted

by

GAIL CARSON LEVINE

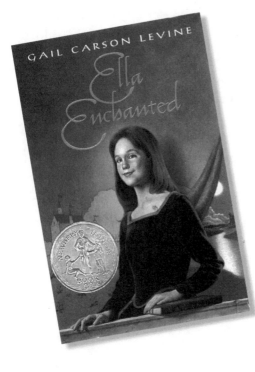

Genre: Fantasy

Publisher: HarperCollins,
$5.95 (p)

Page Length: 240

Type of Illustrations: None

Reluctant Reader Appeal:
Humor, Well-Defined
Characters, Fast-Paced
Plot, Kid Relevance

**Suggested
reading level:**
Age 8 and up

That fool of a fairy Lucinda did not intend to lay a curse on me. She meant to bestow a gift. When I cried inconsolably through my first hour of life, my tears were her inspiration. Shaking her head sympathetically at Mother, the fairy touched my nose. "My gift is obedience. Ella will always be obedient. Now stop crying, child."

I stopped.

Synopsis Ella is an intelligent, strong-willed girl who is cursed from birth: She must obey any direct order or suffer a strong physical reaction. Only her mother, their cook Mandy, and Lucinda the fairy know of Ella's curse, and for most of her childhood Ella manages to avoid any truly unpleasant orders. But when Ella is 14, her beloved mother dies. Ella is befriended by the charismatic Prince Charmont at her mother's funeral, but they barely get to know each other before her father (a traveling trader who is rarely around) sends Ella to finishing school with the daughters of Lady Olga. Hattie, the oldest daughter, discovers Ella's curse and uses it to make Ella her servant. Finally, Ella runs away from finishing school, determined to find Lucinda and convince her to reverse the curse. She tracks down Lucinda at a giant's wedding but never gets to speak with the fairy. After Ella returns home, her father marries Lady Olga, making Hattie and her younger sister, Olive, Ella's stepsisters.

During this time, Prince Charmont and Ella have been corresponding, and he proposes marriage. But Ella must break it off because her curse would be a horrible liability for a future king, and so she is forced to do so in a way that will keep the prince from ever contacting her again.

Once the prince returns from his travels, the king holds three balls in the hopes that the prince will find a wife. Ella attends in disguise, just to be near the prince. In the end, she is discovered and finds a way to break the curse on her own.

Why This Book Appeals to Reluctant Readers The above synopsis only scratches the surface of this complex and magical story. Ella is a very likable heroine: She's smart, brave, and completely herself. Ogres, elves, centaurs, giants, and gnomes populate the book, complete with their own cultures and languages. The romance between Ella and Prince Chamont is sweet and innocent. The story moves quickly, and the unique characters keep the reader involved in the mounting tension. Ella deals with issues relevant to any adolescent (discovering one's own strengths, achieving independence) with charm and humor.

Who Might Like This Book This book is great for girls who love fantasy or strong heroines. The parallels to the Cinderella story are subtle at first, getting stronger in the second half of the book. It will certainly hold the attention of older girls, but it's also a wonderful story to read out loud to girls in third or fourth grade.

Notes to Parents *Ella Enchanted* won a Newbery Honor in 1998.

If Your Child Liked This Book, Then Try . . . *The Last of the Really Great Whangdoodles* by Julie Andrews Edwards (HarperTrophy); *Spinners* by Donna Jo Napoli (Dutton).

Harry Potter and the Sorcerer's Stone

(HARRY POTTER series)

by

J. K. ROWLING

Illustrator MARY GRANDPRÉ

Genre: Fantasy

Publisher: Scholastic,
$6.99 (p)

Page Length: 309

Type of Illustrations: Black
and white, on chapter
openings

Reluctant Reader Appeal:
Humor, Well-Defined
Characters, Fast-Paced Plot,
Kid Relevance

**Suggested
reading level:**
Ages 8–13

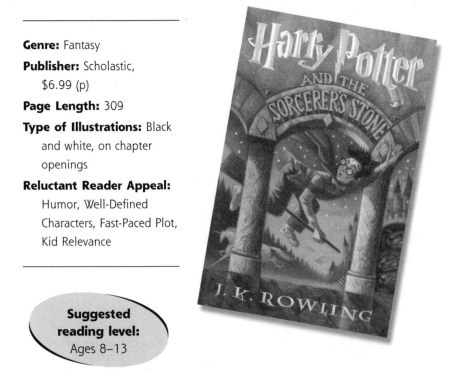

Synopsis Orphaned as a baby when his parents were killed by
the evil sorcerer Voldemort, Harry Potter has grown up in the
home of his aunt and uncle, where he's forced to sleep in a broom
closet under the stairs. On his eleventh birthday, Harry receives
strange messages that culminate with the arrival of a giant named
Hagrid. Harry finds out that he's destined to be a great wizard (he
has the lightning bolt–shaped scar on his forehead to prove it),

and Hagrid is there to escort him to the Hogwarts School of Witchcraft and Wizardry. Harry, who is astonished to learn that his parents were a famous witch and wizard, goes on a magical shopping trip to buy supplies for school (robes, cauldron, broomstick, wand, and an owl) and then takes the train to Hogwarts. There Harry (already a celebrity in the world of magic) busies himself with his studies and sports and finds he excels in Quidditch (a complicated game played with four different balls while riding a broomstick). He also makes friends and enemies and becomes embroiled in a mystery/adventure that ultimately brings him face-to-face with Voldemort.

But this book is so much more than a fast-paced plot with an endearing main character. The author has based Hogwarts on traditional English boarding schools and the competitions between Houses in academics (Transfiguration, Herbology, Defense Against the Dark Arts) and sports meld beautifully with the otherworldly nature of the setting. Quirky, humorous details abound from jellybeans thaat taste like strawberries, sardines, or ear wax to the Nimbus Two Thousand, the Ferrari of broomsticks. And yet, the magical world exists within a logical, believable framework, made all the more real because it's separate from the world of Muggles, ordinary human beings. This is a world the reader can get lost in and will continue to inhabit long after the book is finished.

Why This Book Appeals to Reluctant Readers Aside from the plot that moves along at lightning speed and the fantastic world in which this novel is set, Harry is a charming main character. He's struggling with many things an ordinary kid in a new school would face, and he's also worried about living up to his legacy. But he rises to the occasion through decency, hard work, and humility. This is a longer book than most middle graders are used to reading, but that doesn't seem to deter fans of the HARRY POTTER series (later books are even longer). A classic story of good versus evil, with the bad guys clearly drawn, gives this book timeless appeal.

Who Might Like This Book Boys and girls (and their parents!) all over the world seem to be equally enchanted with Harry Potter. In fact, kids who have never read an entire book before are devouring this series. Lovers of fantasy, adventure, mysteries, and humor will all enjoy this book.

Notes to Parents I know many younger children who have loved hearing this book read out loud. Though the plot does involve witches and wizards, the magic is of the hocus-pocus, witches' brew variety, not summoning up evil spirits. J. K. Rowling continues to write another installment of the series about once a year, with Harry growing older with each book. As a result, the problems he faces will also get more complex, so you might want to preview later books in the series for readers at the younger end of the age range.

If Your Child Liked This Book, Then Try . . . *Harry Potter and the Chamber of Secrets, Harry Potter and the Prisoner of Azkaban,* and *Harry Potter and the Goblet of Fire* (Scholastic).

It's Disgusting and We Ate It! True Food Facts from Around the World

by

JAMES SOLHEIM

Illustrator ERIC BRACE

Genre: Nonfiction/World History and Food

Publisher: Simon & Schuster, $6.99 (p)

Page Length: 40

Type of Illustrations: Color, on every page

Reluctant Reader Appeal: Humor, Concise Chapters, Kid Relevance, Unique Presentation, Visual Appeal

---

Suggested reading level:
Ages 7–12

A Bowl of Hot, Tasty Garbage from the Sewer
One fancy soup served at royal feasts was called "garbage." It was made with birds' heads, feet, livers, necks, and gizzards. Soup was often called "sewe" and the server was called the "sewer."

Just think how often kings must have shouted to their servants, "Get some garbage from the sewer and bring it for my dinner!"

Synopsis This book takes a facetious look at what people have considered gourmet food throughout the ages. Chapters with titles like "From Mammoth Meatballs to Squirrel Stew" and "If You Think That's Sick, Look in Your Fridge" explore the different exotic, strange, and unappetizing foods people all over the world have used for everything from feasts to medicinal purposes. Poems, recipes, fascinating facts, and jokes are interspersed throughout the text. The hip, edgy artwork gives the book a very modern, irreverent look. A recommended reading list urges kids to find out more about the history of food.

Why This Book Appeals to Reluctant Readers Never has food been so deliciously disgusting, something middle-grade readers will find very amusing. The solid information, combined with the humorous presentation, gives readers a unique perspective on world history and cultures. The text's accessible language and lighthearted style keep the reading easy; a new food is introduced every two pages, so the reader never gets bored.

Who Might Like This Book Both genders should find this book interesting and entertaining, though many of the jokes will appeal especially to the male sense of humor. Kids who like to cook, readers who prefer to get their social studies with a dose of comedy, or kids who relish getting grossed out will love this book.

If Your Child Liked This Book, Then Try . . . *Good Morning, Let's Eat* (A WORLD OF DIFFERENCE series) by Karin Luisa Badt (Children's Press).

My Pony Book

by

LOUISE PRITCHARD

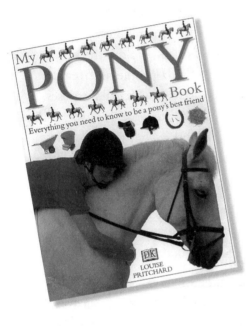

Genre: Nonfiction/Ponies

Publisher: DK Publishing Inc., $15.95 (h)

Page Length: 61

Type of Illustrations: Color photographs, throughout

Reluctant Reader Appeal: Concise Chapters, Kid Relevance, Unique Presentation, Visual Appeal

Suggested reading level: Ages 8–12

Looking after a pony is a responsible job and takes a lot of time. Domestic ponies rely on humans for their food and shelter, so it is important that they are looked after properly. There is much more to stable management than feeding a pony a few carrots and throwing on a saddle. Loving care will be rewarded by a pony's trust and a special relationship between pony and rider.

Morning

If you are looking after a pony you will need to check it at least twice a day. Be prepared for hard work and an early start, especially during the school year when you will have to fit the pony

in with school. Ponies are much happier with a routine. A pony will soon learn to expect feeding, grooming, and exercise at roughly the same time every day.

Synopsis This book was designed with young female pony lovers in mind. Each two-page spread covers a different topic, such as the history of ponies, identifying colors and markings, ponies' natural behavior, caring for a pony, tack and riding equipment, proper riding and jumping postures, and taking your pony to a show or on a trail. Most of the information is presented in one-paragraph captions to the numerous, detailed color photographs. The result is a visually dynamic book packed with information.

Why This Book Appeals to Reluctant Readers This book provides just what fans of ponies and horses want: lots of pictures and a good overview of what is involved in owning a pony. The information is direct and to the point, and the book is organized so the reader can easily flip to the section she needs.

Who Might Like This Book Boys who want a pony will like this book, but it's clearly designed for girls (the models in the pictures are all female). Any girl who dreams of getting her own pony—or has the opportunity to get one and wants a general, easy-to-use resource—will love this book.

Notes to Parents The wealth of illustrations make this a wonderful book to read with a younger child or one who can't yet read all the text herself.

If Your Child Liked This Book, Then Try . . . Also from DK Publishing: *The Ultimate Horse Book, The Young Rider, The Complete Horse Care Manual,* and *The Encyclopedia of the Horse.*

Find the Constellations

by

H . A . R E Y

Illustrator H . A . R E Y

Genre: Nonfiction/Astronomy

Publisher: Houghton Mifflin, $9.95 (p)

Page Length: 72

Type of Illustrations: Color, on every page

Reluctant Reader Appeal: Concise Chapters, Suitable Text, Unique Presentation, Visual Appeal

Suggested reading level: Ages 9–12

Light is the fastest thing there is. It travels 186,000 miles a second, and in a year almost six million million miles. In numbers this would read 6,000,000,000,000 miles. So many zeros would get anyone mixed up. It is easier to say or write "1 light-year" than to use all those millions of millions of miles.

Now if we say the star Rigel is 545 light-years away, it means that its light took 545 years to get here. It left Rigel before Columbus discovered America and traveled all those years through space to reach us. And it would take us 545 years to get from the Earth to the star Rigel if we had space ships which had the speed of light.

Synopsis H. A. Rey (cocreator of the classic *Curious George* books) obviously finds stargazing to be a fun and exciting hobby, and he easily conveys this feeling through his informal, chatty text. The reader is introduced to the major constellations, sky views during the four seasons, planets in our solar system, and basic scientific principles, such as the speed of light and how planets' orbits would affect space travel. The text is sprinkled with interesting star trivia and pop quizzes that test the reader's knowledge. Precise yet understandable illustrations break up the text on every page, and tiny cartoon characters direct the reader to related information in other parts of the book. The revised edition includes a sky chart that's accurate through 2006.

Why This Book Appeals to Reluctant Readers The author's sheer delight for the topic is infectious, and readers will quickly find themselves identifying stars in the night sky. Each short chapter concentrates on one constellation or concept, allowing the book to be read a chapter at a time and then put to instant use. The illustrations are straightforward and easy to interpret. This is one of those hands-on books that shows how the right kind of information can open the door to a whole new world.

Who Might Like This Book Boys or girls who are interested in astronomy, space travel, or science in general. This book is also good for a parent to read with a younger child because the information can be instantly used when looking at the stars.

Notes to Parents Books like *Find the Constellations* make a great basis for family activities. Stargazing also leads to other skills, such as learning how to read a compass.

If Your Child Liked This Book, Then Try . . . *Do Stars Have Points? Questions and Answers About Stars and Planets* by Melvin and Gilda Berger, illustrated by Vincent Di Fate (Scholastic QUESTIONS & ANSWERS series).

. . . If You Lived at the Time of the American Revolution

by

KAY MOORE

Illustrator DANIEL O'LEARY

Genre: Nonfiction/American History

Publisher: Scholastic, $5.99 (p)

Page Length: 80

Type of Illustrations: Color, on almost every page

Reluctant Reader Appeal: Concise Chapters, Suitable Text, Kid Relevance, Unique Presentation, Visual Appeal

Suggested reading level:
Ages 7–11

What Started the Revolution?

The first settlers in the colonies liked having British help and protection. British soldiers were there to help them fight Native American enemies and to keep other countries, such as France and Spain, from invading. It was like your mother watching over you. However, as you grow older, you will want more freedom to make your own decisions. That is how many of the colonists felt.

The colonists grew tired of following British rules. England controlled trade and told people where they could settle. They forced the colonists to provide housing and food for the British soldiers sent to protect them. . . .

Synopsis This book places the reader back at the time of the American Revolution and shows what everyday life would have been like. Constructed as a series of questions and answers, the book uses uncomplicated explanations for the causes and results of the Revolution, the difference between patriots and loyalists, how the average family lived during wartime, and how the country changed after the war. The questions have a very childlike tone; the answers, ranging from one to five illustrated pages, are often written in the second person to draw the reader into the book (*To wash your hands and face, you poured water into a bowl.*). The illustrations, most of which are oil paintings, have an old-fashioned quality and yet still convey great emotion and detail.

Why This Book Appeals to Reluctant Readers This book puts the American Revolution into a very personal, human context. The details of daily life are given as much weight as the larger political events, which in turn make the war more understandable and accessible to young readers. The table of contents lists every question, so readers can look up specific information as needed, though reading the questions and answers in order will make the later events more comprehensible. The tone of the text is light and direct without being condescending, making this a good choice for older readers as well.

Who Might Like This Book Readers interested in American history, battles, or colonial times; children who live in one of the 13 original states and want to know more about their area's history or those studying the American Revolution in school and need something more inspiring to read than a textbook.

Notes to Parents If this format but not the subject is appealing to your child, try one of the other books in the series listed below.

If Your Child Liked This Book, Then Try . . . Other books in this series, all from Scholastic (various illustrators): *If Your Name Was Changed at Ellis Island, If You Traveled West in a Covered Wagon, If You Traveled on the Underground Railroad, If You Lived at the Time of Martin Luther King* (all by Ellen Levine), *If You Lived in Colonial Times, If You Sailed on the Mayflower in 1620* (both by Ann McGovern), *If You Lived at the Time of the Civil War* by Kay Moore, *If You Lived with the Hopi* by Anne Kamma, and *If You Were There When They Signed the Constitution* by Elizabeth Levy.

Brain Surgery for Beginners and Other Major Operations for Minors: A Scalpel-Free Guide to Your Insides

by

STEVE PARKER

Illustrator DAVID WEST

Genre: Nonfiction/Brain
Function

Publisher: The Millbrook
Press, $21.90 (h)

Page Length: 62

Type of Illustrations: Color,
on every page

Reluctant Reader Appeal:
Humor, Suitable Text,
Kid Relevance, Unique
Presentation, Visual Appeal

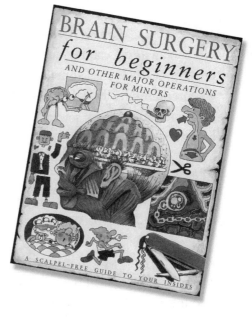

**Suggested
reading level:**
Ages 8–12

The Talking Brain

*People open their mouths and speak without thinking. They say
the most stupid things! Actually, even the simplest "Hello there!"*

needs a great deal of brain power. The brain assesses the situation, chooses the right words from the memory banks, puts them in the correct order, and sends nerve signals to dozens of muscles in the neck, throat and mouth, so that the words come out clearly.

Synopsis This book takes a look the human brain and how it controls the entire body. Broken into six chapters, the major functions of the brain are explained as they relate to the body's senses, motor functions, thought, and automatic actions such as breathing. The information is broken into one-paragraph, subtitled chunks on each heavily illustrated, large-format page. Facts are interlaced with humor; the main illustrations of body-part cross sections are well detailed, but funny cartoon-type characters also romp across the pages.

Why This Book Appeals to Reluctant Readers Human anatomy can be interesting but complex; this book takes one aspect of physical function and yet covers the whole body in an entertaining way. The information is presented in small, easily identifiable pieces, so readers can skim each page to find the facts they want or read an entire two-page spread to go in-depth on one particular topic. The illustrations greatly enhance the text and add humor as well. A glossary and index at the end of the book help the reader look up specific information they might need for school reports or to help them study for tests.

Who Might Like This Book Kids interested in anatomy or who are studying it in school. This is also a good book to read to a younger child who has questions about how her body works.

If Your Child Liked This Book, Then Try . . . *Big Head!* by Peter Rowan, illustrated by John Temperton (Knopf); *The Brain: Our Nervous System* by Seymour Simon (Morrow).

Lives of the Presidents: Fame, Shame (and What the Neighbors Thought)

by

KATHLEEN KRULL

Illustrator KATHRYN HEWITT

Genre: Nonfiction/Biography

Publisher: Harcourt Brace, $20.00 (h)

Page Length: 96

Type of Illustrations: Color, one per chapter

Reluctant Reader Appeal: Well-Defined Characters, Concise Chapters, Suitable Text, Unique Presentation

Suggested reading level: Ages 9–12

John F. Kennedy

Although he presented an image of athletic vigor and energy in public, John Kennedy often spent more than half the day in bed and sometimes had to use crutches to get about. With a potentially fatal adrenal gland failure, he suffered frequent infections and fevers of up to 106 degrees. One leg was shorter than the other, and his chronic back pain, aggravated by a World War II injury, required him to wear a back brace and to get up to five shots a day deep in his muscles. He found that sitting in a rocking chair eased the pain and had a chair available wherever he went. He used a sunlamp daily to get his healthy glow, and the way he looked—tan, handsome, with thick, glossy hair—helped him win the closest presidential election in American history.

Synopsis Many books chronicle the accomplishments of American presidents. In *Lives of the Presidents,* however, Kathleen Krull takes an offbeat look at the men who held the office. What did they like to eat? Who threw the best parties? Which president's wife was addicted to soap operas? In entries ranging from one paragraph to three pages, each president is objectively presented as a human being first, politician second. Readers learn about their strengths, their idiosyncrasies, their embarrassing habits, and their dreams. The upbeat text is paired with lively caricatures of each president and his wife, and the cover illustration provides a glimpse into each president's personality and whom he admired from previous administrations.

Why This Book Appeals to Reluctant Readers It's always fun to deconstruct a celebrity (even a political one) to see how he's really not that different from anyone else. The compact entries give an interesting, down-to-earth perspective on these historical figures and may help the reader better understand the presidents' accomplishments—and failures—while in office. This book makes easy background reading for an American history class or as supplemental research for school reports. But it's also fun to learn how eccentric you can be and still get elected president.

Who Might Like This Book Trivia buffs will love the little-known and unusual information about the subjects. Kids interested in politics or American history will also enjoy this book.

Notes to Parents This book is a terrific basis for discussion because parents will learn from it as well. Published in 1998, it doesn't contain some of the more recent, juicier information on President Clinton (though, because the text never stoops to muckraking, even President Kennedy's extramarital affairs are mentioned only in passing), nor does it include anything on the 2000 presidential election. But the real value of this book is all the quirky details of presidents who served at a time when the media didn't monitor their every move.

If Your Child Liked This Book, Then Try . . . Other books in this series by Kathleen Krull, illustrated by Kathryn Hewitt: *Lives of the Musicians: Good Times, Bad Times (and What the Neighbors Thought)*, *Lives of the Writers: Comedies, Tragedies (and What the Neighbors Thought)*, *Lives of the Artists: Masterpieces, Messes (and What the Neighbors Thought)*, and *Lives of the Athletes: Thrills, Spills (and What the Neighbors Thought)*, all from Harcourt Brace.

In the Huddle with . . . John Elway

by

MATT CHRISTOPHER

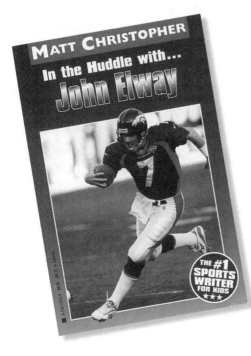

Genre: Sports Biography

Publisher: Little, Brown,
$4.95 (p)

Page Length: 109

Type of Illustrations:
Insert of black-and-white
photographs

Reluctant Reader Appeal:
Fast-Paced Plot, Concise
Chapters, Kid Relevance

**Suggested
reading level:**
Ages 9–13

*After only a few exhibition games, Denver coach Dan Reeves
named Elway the starting quarterback. John responded by playing like a rookie.*

*In the season opener against Pittsburgh, the Steelers' vaunted
defense went after Elway with a vengeance. It seemed they shared
the Broncos' feelings of animosity against the young highly paid star.*

*The first three times the Broncos had the ball, Elway failed
to complete a pass as Pittsburgh forced him to rush every play.
The fourth time Denver got the ball, John finally completed a
pass, but it was an interception by Pittsburgh. The next time, he
was sacked, and later he fumbled while being sacked again.*

Synopsis The life of Denver Broncos famed quarterback John Elway is chronicled from his birth to his first Super Bowl win in 1998, at age 37. Each chapter spans an important period in Elway's life, covering his athletic accomplishments in school; his rise to quarterback at Stanford; his stint with the New York Yankees minor league baseball team; and his sometimes-rocky career with the Broncos. The author gives evenhanded treatment to Elway's successes and failures and touches on his close ties to family, his propensity for hard work, and his innate love for playing ball.

Why This Book Appeals to Reluctant Readers This book is loaded with the facts, events, and dates that make up a sports hero's life. The text is active and fast paced; the author describes Elway's feelings about his athletic accomplishments and failures without sentimentalizing. Play-by-play descriptions of crucial games will engross sports fans. The complex sentences and longer paragraphs may be more difficult than some readers are used to, but if they have an interest in the subject, they'll keep reading.

Who Might Like This Book Many middle school boys will read sports biographies after they've given up everything else. Football fans of either gender will like this book, especially if they're very interested in the details of the game.

Notes to Parents If your child wants to learn about different athletes, try another biography by Matt Christopher, some of which are listed below.

If Your Child Liked This Book, Then Try . . . In the Huddle with . . . Steve Young, On the Field with . . . Emmitt Smith, On the Court with . . . Michael Jordan, On the Court with . . . Lisa Leslie, On the Ice with . . . Tara Lipinski, and *On the Course with . . . Tiger Woods* (all by Matt Christopher, published by Little, Brown).

Dr. Fred's Weather Watch: Create and Run Your Own Weather Station

by

FRED BORTZ, PH.D., WITH

J. MARSHALL SHEPHERD, PH.D.

Illustrator INGRID OLSEN

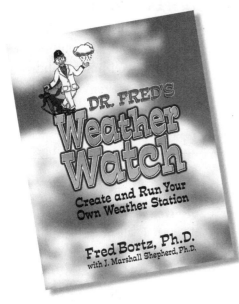

Genre: Nonfiction/
Meteorology

Publisher: McGraw-Hill,
$11.95 (p)

Page Length: 98

Type of Illustrations: Black
and white, on every page

Reluctant Reader Appeal:
Concise Chapters, Suitable
Text, Kid Relevance,
Unique Presentation

**Suggested
reading level:**
Ages 9–13

*If you want to predict the weather in your neighborhood, you
need to understand not only the air movement in a small area,
or the local wind, but also air movements all around the world.
Winds are driven by pressure gradients. One kind of pressure
gradient is known as a "front." Fronts are boundary lines in the*

air between regions with different weather conditions. They form when high and low pressure air masses move toward each other. As a front passes your neighborhood, you can expect strong local winds.

Synopsis Part introduction to meteorology, part biography of J. Marshall Shepherd (a young meteorologist with NASA who built his own neighborhood weather station when he was in sixth grade), and part science project, *Dr. Fred's Weather Watch* shows readers how to accurately predict the weather in their own neighborhoods using simple materials. Each chapter covers one broad concept, such as air pressure, beginning with a clear explanation of the topic and introducing scientific terms. Then step-by-step instructions are given for building an instrument to match the concept presented, such as a barometer, followed by experiments or activities to read the weather. Chapters also include interesting weather facts and phenomena and questions that urge readers to compare their weather findings with official forecasts.

Why This Book Appeals to Reluctant Readers Learning to predict the weather brings instant gratification; it's a force that affects our everyday lives and provides an opportunity to witness scientific principles at work. Dr. Fred gives just enough information in each chapter so the reader can understand the purpose of each instrument and how it works but isn't weighed down with unnecessary facts and figures. The result is a book that's very process-oriented—the learning is in the doing.

Who Might Like This Book Teachers have told me that the weather is perennially a favorite subject in elementary and middle school science classes. Boys and girls who show an interest in physics will appreciate the practical applications of the experiments. Kids who are struggling with science can also gain a better understanding of broad concepts because the activities demonstrate physics at work in concrete, visual ways. Children who need a project for science fairs or those who enjoy working in groups will find many ideas in this book. Finally, building a weather station is an ideal family project or experiment for older and younger siblings to do together.

If Your Child Liked This Book, Then Try . . . THE SCIENCE FUNDAMENTALS series by Robert W. Wood (McGraw-Hill); *Catastrophe! Great Engineering Failure—and Success* by Fred Bortz, Ph.D. (W. H. Freeman).

Chapter Eight

Ready for Anything

Novels and nonfiction with more sophisticated themes to hold the interest of readers in upper elementary grades and middle school.

FICTION

Anastasia Krupnik by Lois Lowry · page 265

Bloomability by Sharon Creech · page 268

Weirdo's War by Michael Coleman · page 271

If You Only Knew (THE FRIENDSHIP RING series) by Rachel Vail · page 274

The Phantom Tollbooth by Norton Juster · page 277

A Is for AARRGH! by William J. Brooke · page 279

Holes by Louis Sachar · page 282

Julie of the Wolves by Jean Craighead George · page 285

Hatchet by Gary Paulsen · page 288

Owl in Love by Patrice Kindl · page 290

The Great Gilly Hopkins by Katherine Paterson · page 292

Nothing but the Truth: A Documentary Novel by Avi · page 295

The Giver by Lois Lowry · page 298

The Goats by Brock Cole · page 301

The Smugglers by Iain Lawrence · page 304

Athletic Shorts: 6 Short Stories by Chris Crutcher · page 306

NONFICTION

Cool Women: The Thinking Girl's Guide to the Hippest Women in History edited by Pam Nelson, written by Dawn Chipman, Mari Florence, and Naomi Wax · page 309

The Deep Time Diaries (As Recorded by Neesha and Jon Olifee) by Gary Raham · page 312

Light Shining Through the Mist: A Photobiography of Dian Fossey by Tom L. Matthews · page 315

No Pretty Pictures: A Child of War by Anita Lobel · page 317

The Boys' War: Confederate and Union Soldiers Talk About the Civil War by Jim Murphy · page 320

No More Strangers Now: Young Voices from a New South Africa Interviews by Tim McKee · page 323

The New Way Things Work by David Macaulay · page 326

Martian Fossils on Earth? The Story of Meteorite ALH 84001 by Fred Bortz · page 329

It Is a Good Day to Die: Indian Eyewitnesses Tell the Story of the Battle of Little Bighorn by Herman J. Viola · page 331

At Her Majesty's Request: An African Princess in Victorian England by Walter Dean Myers · page 334

Go for the Goal: A Champion's Guide to Winning in Soccer and Life by Mia Hamm, with Aaron Heifetz · page 337

Kids at Work: Lewis Hine and the Crusade Against Child Labor by Russell Freedman · page 339

Chinese Cinderella: The True Story of an Unwanted Daughter by Adeline Yen Mah · page 342

Anastasia Krupnik

by

LOIS LOWRY

Genre: Contemporary Fiction

Publisher: Houghton Mifflin,
$1.99 (p)

Page Length: 113

Type of Illustrations: None

Reluctant Reader Appeal:
Humor, Well-Defined
Characters, Fast-Paced
Plot, Kid Relevance

**Suggested
reading level:**
Ages 9–12

"Nothing interesting ever, ever *happens to me," said Anastasia
gloomily. "No wonder I don't have any memories yet."*

"What on earth do you mean? I can think of lots of interesting things that have happened to you," said her mother.

"Name three."

*"When you were two years old you ate ant poison and had to
have your stomach pumped."*

"That's one. And I don't even remember it."

*"Well, when you were four you wandered off when we were
in Harvard Square. And finally I called the police, and when
they finally found you, you were way down on Green Street,
walking with an old lady who was wearing army boots and had
a Tupperware bowl on her head."*

Synopsis A lot happens to Anastasia Krupnik the year she's 10, and she begins to keep a journal of all her loves and hates. But between falling in and out of love with Washburn Cummings, getting to know her 92-year-old grandmother who lives in a nursing home and can't remember her name, and hating her teacher who doesn't appreciate her poetry, Anastasia finds out something that's definitely on her "hate" list: Her parents are having a baby. Her poet father calls her "mercurial," and it does seem that the things on Anastasia's list keep changing sides. To top it all off, Anastasia's worried that she hasn't lived enough to have an "inward eye," or memories, like her grandmother does. But when her grandmother dies, Anastasia realizes she does have memories, and when her brother Sam is born, Anastasia decides that she can love him after all.

Why This Book Appeals to Reluctant Readers It's nice to see a family in middle-grade fiction who is interesting not because it's dysfunctional but because it's made up of smart, unique, well-drawn characters. Anastasia's poet/professor father is wise and down to earth and has a dry sense of humor. Her mother, an artist, has a sunny, sensitive disposition, though she's susceptible to the hormonal mood swings of pregnancy. They obviously care very much about Anastasia, who's trying to form a clear identity for herself before her baby brother is born. Their dialogue is sharp, funny, and convincing and portrays Anastasia's realistic feelings toward her parents, which range from exasperation to love. The chapters have an episodic feel, almost like a series of short stories, making it easy to read this book in several sittings. The story flows quickly, and the author never condescends to the reader. Instead, she respects that even small changes can seem catastrophic to a 10-year-old.

Who Might Like This Book The story gets its forward movement more from Anastasia's emotions than from dramatic plot developments, and so it will probably appeal to girls more than boys. Readers who like books that explore the feelings inherent in everyday events or books that revolve around realistic, quirky characters with a bit of an edge will love this book. The story, written in 1979, has a few dated details, but they don't distract from the plot and might even lure kids who are into retro.

Notes to Parents Because the characters are very real, they do a few things not found in more sterile novels for this age-group. A few swear words appear in the dialogue (uttered by adults), and Anastasia's father lets her slurp the foam off his beer. When Anastasia's given the job of naming her future brother, she first chooses the worst name she knows (One-Ball Reilly, which Anastasia heard in a song some boys were singing). It's not dwelt on, and Anastasia soon decides to name her brother after her grandfather. These small touches make the characters more authentic, but if you have any doubts about giving this book to your child, read it yourself first.

If Your Child Liked This Book, Then Try . . . Other books by Lois Lowry featuring Anastasia Krupnik, including *All About Sam; Anastasia, Absolutely; Anastasia, Ask Your Analyst;* and *Anastasia on Her Own* (in paperback from Dell Yearling).

Bloomability

by

SHARON CREECH

Genre: Contemporary Fiction
Publisher: HarperCollins,
$5.95 (p)
Page Length: 273
Type of Illustrations: None
Reluctant Reader Appeal:
Humor, Well-Defined
Characters, Concise
Chapters, Kid Relevance,
Suitable Text

**Suggested
reading level:**
Ages 8–12

This is the place that Mrs. Stirling had chosen to set up an American school for students from all over the world. This is the place where I'd go to school. I wouldn't be alone, like the boarding students would be, Uncle Max said. I'd be living with him and Aunt Sandy.

I still thought they might be luring me to a prison, and I still didn't understand why I was here, why I couldn't be with my mother and father and Crick and Stella and the new baby. I thought it was because I'd done something wrong, and this was my punishment. Or maybe they had to make room for the new baby and one of us had to go. Me.

Synopsis Thirteen-year-old Dinnie has never lived more than a year in the same place. Her father (a jack-of-all-trades) moves her family from state to state in search of "opportunities." While they're living in New Mexico, Dinnie's brother Crick ends up in jail, and her sister Stella runs off to marry a Marine and then comes home pregnant. One night Dinnie's Aunt Sandy and Uncle Max arrive at her home and stay up all night talking to Dinnie's mother. The next morning Dinnie is "kidnapped": swept off to the airport with her relatives and flown to Switzerland, where Uncle Max has a new job as headmaster of an American school.

At first, Dinnie isn't comfortable with her "second life," as she calls it. She's homesick, confused as to why her parents sent her away, and tired of being a stranger yet again. But as the students return to school after summer break, Dinnie realizes that they're all strangers. She makes friends from all over the world and gradually opens up to the beauty of Switzerland and the "bloomabilities" available to her if she has the courage to embrace them.

Why This Book Appeals to Reluctant Readers Being 13—and desperately trying to fit in while discovering what's special and unique about yourself—is a hard age for any adolescent. Any reader who has ever felt unsure of herself or out of place will identify with Dinnie's fears. Dinnie's imaginary protective bubble, through which she lets only select streams of information, is the perfect metaphor for the tough yet transparent shield teens erect to protect their fragile egos. The short chapters and vivid descriptions of the idyllic setting quickly pull the reader through Dinnie's emotional journey, perhaps giving the reader some direction for taking a journey of her own.

Who Might Like This Book Girls who are crossing the threshold from childhood to young adulthood and feel lost at times; readers who have traveled (or dream of traveling) to

Switzerland or Italy; kids who like coming-of-age stories told with humor and set in interesting locations.

Notes to Parents Sharon Creech is a very talented author whose middle-grade novels have gained a large following, especially among girls. Her books often deal with a female protagonist taking a physical and/or emotional journey to find herself. I had trouble deciding which of her titles to include here and chose *Bloomability* because of its interesting setting. If your child likes this author, try more of her books, listed below. They are also excellent choices for mothers and daughters to read together.

If Your Child Liked This Book, Then Try . . . *Walk Two Moons* (1995 Newbery Medal winner), *Absolutely Normal Chaos, Chasing Redbird,* and *The Wanderer* (all by Sharon Creech, published by HarperCollins).

Weirdo's War
by
MICHAEL COLEMAN

Genre: Contemporary Fiction/
Adventure
Publisher: Orchard Books,
$16.95 (h)
Page Length: 184
Type of Illustrations: None
Reluctant Reader Appeal:
Well-Defined Characters,
Fast-Paced Plot, Concise
Chapters, Kid Relevance

**Suggested
reading level:**
Ages 9–13

*From the moment the ground gave way beneath our feet, it
couldn't have taken more than a couple of seconds. But it seemed
to go on forever, a nightmare in slow motion.*

"Watch out. It's slippery in here."

*I followed him into the cave, the entrance just a thin slit in
the rock.*

*Out of the wet and into the dry. Out of the warm and into
the cool. Out of the light and into the dark.*

*That's when it happened. I heard the groan of the earth. A
shout. The sound of him falling. And then it was as if somebody
had pulled the ground from beneath my feet and I was falling too.*

I didn't scream.

Synopsis Daniel Edwards is an intelligent loner who has earned the nickname "Weirdo" from his classmates. Daniel thinks he's weird too because he can't stop seeing the world as a series of mathematical equations. He doesn't want any part of the popular group of boys who have taunted him since elementary school, including Tosh Tozer, a large, athletic, and rather dim-witted classmate.

During spring break in his first year of high school, Daniel's parents send him on a class wilderness trip led by Mr. Axelmann, the physical education teacher who has made Daniel and Tozer's lives miserable all year. While on a complicated scavenger hunt, Daniel and Tozer become trapped in an underground cavern along with Axelmann, who is gravely injured. Though the main story all takes place in the cavern, the reader learns of the events leading up to the characters' present situation through a series of flashbacks told from Daniel's point of view. The book ends with an exciting, tension-filled climax as the boys rescue themselves and Axelmann from certain death.

Why This Book Appeals to Reluctant Readers If I had to choose one word to describe this book, it would be "suspense." From the opening paragraphs, the author continually plunges the characters into deeper and deeper danger and then pulls back at a climactic moment to give the reader more clues as to how the characters got there in the first place. The drama has a strong psychological element as well; Daniel reveals more about himself and Tozer with each chapter, and the reader comes to understand each boy and why he behaves as he does. The characters are surprising: Tozer is not a stock bully, which Daniel eventually learns. And Daniel is able to finally admit that Tozer's way of dealing with the world sometimes works. Though this is a highly emotional story, the emotions are conveyed through quick actions and a series of dramatic plot twists.

Who Might Like This Book Anyone who likes adventure stories, but especially boys. It's a rare "relationship" story with male protagonists—not a romantic relationship but a book about how boys relate to each other and establish their complex social pecking order. Readers come to understand two very different types of people, but the lessons unfold subtly and naturally within the story. This is not a didactic book but rather suspense with substance.

Notes to Parents *Weirdo's War* was short-listed for the prestigious Carnegie Medal in Great Britain, where it was originally published.

If Your Child Liked This Book, Then Try . . . *Maze* by Will Hobbs (Avon); *Downriver* by Will Hobbs (Dell).

If You Only Knew

(THE FRIENDSHIP RING series)

by

RACHEL VAIL

Genre: Contemporary Fiction

Publisher: Scholastic,
$4.99 (p)

Page Length: 151

Type of Illustrations: None

Reluctant Reader Appeal:
Humor, Well-Defined
Characters, Concise
Chapters, Suitable Text,
Kid Relevance

**Suggested
reading level:**
Ages 9–13

"Seventh grade is the most horrible year," Devin confided, plunging her hand into the soapsuds to open the drain. It was our turn to do the dishes.

"Really? How come?" I can always trust Devin out of all my sisters to tell me the truth and not baby me.

"And you're gonna be all alone," she continued. "At least Colette was around for me. I mean, it was Colette, but still, once I had to go to the girls' room and cry? She cut English and stayed with me the whole period."

"Well, I don't cry in school." I dried my hands on the bottom half of her towel.

She smiled. "Just wait till the hormones kick in."

Synopsis Zoe is the youngest of five sisters, and she's never had anything that's completely her own. Her clothes are hand-me-downs, she shares a room, and she even looks like pieces of the other people in her family. But Zoe's an easygoing, happy 12-year-old who is friends with everyone in her grade. She's never had a best friend, but that's okay. At least it has been until now.

When Zoe enters seventh grade, everything changes. She desperately wants CJ Hurley to be her best friend, but CJ and Morgan Miller have been best friends since fourth grade. Tommy Levit has been her buddy for years, but now she can't hit tennis balls with him without wondering when he got so cute. But of course, Tommy doesn't like her *like that*—he thinks she's one of the guys, right? And why does Zoe, who has always felt so comfortable in her body, keep bumping into things? How come she never noticed that her hair is so flat, and why can't she wear a T-shirt to school without everyone staring at her breasts?

By the end of the first week of school, Zoe's crying in the bathroom, wondering how she'll hold it all together until the hormones work themselves out.

Why This Book Appeals to Reluctant Readers This is a book about how it *feels* to be a girl in middle school, and it's as if the author transported herself back to seventh grade and took copious notes. It's not a typical "problem novel" in which something dramatic happens to the character—Zoe gets along with her family, she's always had lots of friends, she's good at sports—but rather about those momentous inner changes that come with puberty and make you feel like you don't know yourself anymore. Any reader who's been blindsided by her hormones and is desperately trying to hold it all together will relate to Zoe.

Who Might Like This Book This is absolutely a girl book. Though the story is character driven and emotional rather than focused on a fast-paced plot, it should appeal to most girls in the throes of puberty, especially those who might feel that no one understands what they're going through.

If Your Child Liked This Book, Then Try . . . Other books in THE FRIENDSHIP RING series, each focusing on a different kid in the group: *please, please, please* (CJ's story), *not that i care* (Morgan's story), *what are friends for?* (Olivia's story), *popularity contest* (Zoe's story), and *fill in the blank* (Tommy's story), all by Rachel Vail and published by Scholastic. Also try *Are You There God? It's Me, Margaret* by Judy Blume (Dell Yearling) and *All Alone in the Universe* by Lynne Rae Perkins (Greenwillow).

The Phantom Tollbooth

by

NORTON JUSTER

Illustrator JULES FEIFFER

Genre: Fantasy/Humor

Publisher: Random House, $5.99 (p)

Page Length: 256

Type of Illustrations: Black and white, every few pages

Reluctant Reader Appeal: Humor, Well-Defined Characters, Fast-Paced Plot, Unique Presentation

Suggested reading level: Ages 8–12

Synopsis Milo is terminally bored, with nothing but time on his hands. Then one day, a mysterious package appears in his room: It's a kit to assemble a tollbooth, complete with map and road signs. Milo grudgingly puts the tollbooth together, then climbs into his electric toy car and drives through. Suddenly, Milo finds himself speeding along an unfamiliar highway. It's the beginning of an adventure that will change Milo's life forever.

As Milo journeys through the strange land, he comes across places like Dictionopolis (where words rule) and Digitopolis (a city governed by numbers), the Foothills of Confusion, and the

Island of Conclusions (you get there by jumping). He meets Tock the watchdog and Humbug, who join him on his travels. Ultimately, Milo and his companions travel to the Mountains of Ignorance, where they rescue the princesses Rhyme and Reason and restore prosperity to the Kingdom of Wisdom.

This fantastic novel, compared to *Alice in Wonderland* when it was first published in 1961, is a celebration of language and numbers. Wordplay and puns abound, and the reader will be inspired to take a new, playful look at the meaning of words and their ability to unlock the imagination.

Why This Book Appeals to Reluctant Readers This is a one-of-a-kind book, the type of story that sticks with you long after the last page. The characters are trapped within their very literal personalities, creating humorous problems for Milo when he tries to converse with them. This book challenges the reader to think about the specific and broader meanings of words and numbers—the building blocks of communication—and how those meanings apply to life in general. The story moves quickly and is so unexpected that the reader has to keep going just to see who is around the next curve of the road.

Who Might Like This Book Boys and girls who might be bored with reading because they need a challenging book. This story isn't hard to read, but it requires some concentration to uncover the layers of meaning. A great choice for kids with active imaginations or those who show some interest in linguistics and wordplay.

If Your Child Liked This Book, Then Try . . . *The House with a Clock in Its Walls* by John Bellairs, illustrated by Edward Gorey (Puffin).

A Is for AARRGH!
by

WILLIAM J. BROOKE

Genre: Humorous Fiction

Publisher: Joanna Cotler Books/HarperCollins, $5.95 (p)

Page Length: 249

Type of Illustrations: None

Reluctant Reader Appeal: Humor, Well-Defined Characters, Fast-Paced Plot, Kid Relevance, Suitable Text

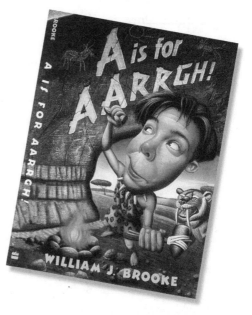

Suggested reading level: Age 10 and up

Around the caves, the only need for communication was if some-one had something you wanted, like a nice haunch of meat. Then you'd tap him with your club to indicate direct address and point and grunt and maybe drool a bit to make it absolute-ly clear. If he didn't get the message, you'd repeat the process: tap, point, grunt, drool. And so on, each tap being a little more emphatic, with the first one being none too timid itself. Even-tually, you would bring him to a state of either understanding or unconsciousness.

Synopsis Long, long ago, cavemen managed to communicate with grunts, finger-pointing, and the liberal use of clubs. It wasn't a perfect system, but it was all they had. Then one day, Mog, the son of Tribe leader Brog, pointed to the sky and uttered humanity's first word: "sun." Mog soon went around naming everything in sight. Once the Tribe caught on to what he was doing, they understood how these nouns could be useful—so useful, in fact, that Brog's hunters could actually work together to kill an antelope instead of just relying on dumb luck.

One day a strange girl arrived out of nowhere. She didn't speak, but her silence inspired Mog to invent adjectives, verbs, adverbs, modifiers, past and future tense, and prepositions. The Tribe was thrilled, Brog was proud, and even Drog—the laziest member of the group—contributed by inventing contractions. One night around the fire, the girl stood up and used Mog's words to tell the most wonderful stories the Tribe had ever heard. Mog, no longer the center of attention, decided to leave. As he walked over the hill and toward the sea, he realized the girl was following him. She seemed familiar with the coast and showed Mog where to find fresh water to drink and how to eat sea turtles. She even saved his life when she spoke directly to Mog for the first time ("Mog, look out!") just as he was about to be attacked by a saber-toothed tiger.

Meanwhile, back home, lazy Drog had used Mog's words to gain power over the Tribe, inventing money and proclaiming himself Mayor. When Mog returned home for a visit, he immediately understood how Drog had used language to manipulate everyone else, including Brog. In a funny, fast-paced climax, Mog returned the power of words to the Tribe and taught them a bit of tolerance at the same time.

Why This Book Appeals to Reluctant Readers It's just plain funny. The tone of the narrative is that of a story being told aloud around a campfire. This book isn't just a study of linguistics—every part of speech is put to hilarious use before it earns a place in the Tribe's vocabulary.

This book also has some thoughtful, relevant subtexts. Mog is trying desperately to find his place in the Tribe. He wants to make his father proud, but when he finally does achieve status, his ego gets the better of him. Ego is also Drog's downfall (coupled with laziness). This story cleverly points out that it's the listener, not the speaker, who really gives words their power. These are interesting points for the reader to ponder, but if it's just a fun story the reader wants, he'll get that here too.

Who Might Like This Book Boys or girls who like funny, slightly absurd stories. The humor has a physical/visual element as well as an intellectual component, which makes it a good book to read aloud to children of various ages.

Notes to Parents This story takes gentle pokes at social classes, government, and religious institutions, but in a very general way. There is no profanity or violence (except for some cartoon-like caveman clubbing as a way of communicating) and so it can be read aloud to children as young as third grade if they can focus on a longer story.

If Your Child Liked This Book, Then Try . . . *Frindle* by Andrew Clements (Simon & Schuster); *Orwell's Luck* by Richard W. Jennings (Walter Lorraine Books/Houghton Mifflin).

Holes

by

LOUIS SACHAR

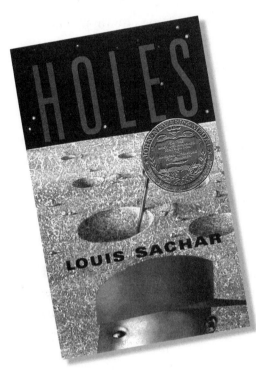

Genre: Humorous Fiction

Publisher: Farrar, Straus & Giroux, $5.99 (p)

Page Length: 233

Type of Illustrations: None

Reluctant Reader Appeal: Humor, Well-Defined Characters, Fast-Paced Plot, Concise Chapters, Kid Relevance

Suggested reading level: Age 10 and up

"You want to run away?" Mr. Sir asked him.

Stanley looked back at him, unsure what he meant.

"If you want to run away, go ahead, start running. I'm not going to stop you."

Stanley didn't know what kind of game Mr. Sir was playing.

"I see you're looking at my gun. Don't worry. I'm not going to shoot you." He tapped his holster. "This is for yellow-spotted lizards. I wouldn't waste a bullet on you."

"I'm not going to run away," Stanley said.

"Good thinking," said Mr. Sir. "Nobody runs away from here. We don't need a fence. Know why? Because we've got the only water for a hundred miles. You want to run away? You'll be buzzard food in three days."

Synopsis Stanley Yelnats's family is cursed with bad luck, which can all be traced back to his no-good-dirty-rotten-pig-stealing-great-great-grandfather, and Stanley is no exception. When he's wrongly accused of stealing a pair of shoes that once belonged to baseball great Clyde Livingston, Stanley is sent to Camp Green Lake (where the lake has dried up and the "camp" is a detention center for boys). As punishment, the boys must dig a hole each day—5 feet deep, 5 feet across—in the hot, hard earth. It doesn't take Stanley long to realize that the digging does more than "build character"; the camp warden is looking for something. Stanley eventually digs up the truth and in the process unearths the reason fate has been so unkind to the Yelnats clan.

This story starts out like a complicated puzzle with pieces that can't possibly fit together. Stanley's great-great grandfather; Kissing Kate Barlow (who became a ruthless outlaw and whose recipe for spiced peaches plays an important role in the plot); Sam, the Onion Man; Zero (Stanley's friend at camp who was so named because that's exactly what the world found him to be and with whom Stanley escapes); the Warden, Ms. Walker, who has something more on her mind than disciplining troubled boys; and even a lullaby that's been sung for generations about the Yelnats family. All these seemingly unconnected elements are woven tighter together until—surprisingly—the whole thing makes sense at the end. The complex plot is highly entertaining; the unsentimental, darkly humorous tone of the book only serves to emphasize the theme that, eventually, everyone gets what he deserves.

Why This Book Appeals to Reluctant Readers On the surface, this book reads like a tall tale, but the deadpan tone and brilliantly intricate plot imply that somewhere these eccentric characters just might exist. The short chapters throw unexpected twists and turns at the reader on every page. Stanley feels like a real kid who's been horribly misunderstood; the reader can't help rooting for him. The sophisticated humor appeals to older readers, but the book still has enough silliness to be just plain fun.

Who Might Like This Book *Holes* is a hit with both boys and girls, but its dark humor and suspense is an especially big draw for boys who wouldn't otherwise read fiction.

Notes to Parents *Holes* has won many prestigious awards, including the 1999 Newbery Medal, the 1998 National Book Award for Young People's Literature, and an ALA Best Book for Young Adults.

If Your Child Liked This Book, Then Try . . . *There's a Boy in the Girls' Bathroom* by Louis Sachar (Random House).

Julie of the Wolves

by

JEAN CRAIGHEAD GEORGE

Illustrator JOHN SCHOENHERR

Genre: Contemporary
Fiction/Adventure

Publisher: HarperCollins,
$5.95 (p)

Page Length: 170

Type of Illustrations: Black
and white, about one per
chapter

Reluctant Reader Appeal:
Well-Defined Characters,
Fast-Paced Plot, Suitable
Text, Kid Relevance

**Suggested
reading level:**
Age 10 and up

*. . . Miyax was lost. She had been lost without food for many
sleeps on the North Slope of Alaska. The barren slope stretches for
three hundred miles from the Brooks Range to the Arctic Ocean,
and for more than eight hundred miles from the Chukchi to the
Beaufort Sea. No roads cross it; ponds and lakes freckle its immen-
sity. Winds scream across it, and the view in every direction is
exactly the same. Somewhere in this cosmos was Miyax; and the
very life in her body, its spark and warmth, depended upon these
wolves for survival. And she was not so sure they would help.*

Synopsis Miyax lived a traditional Eskimo life with her father on the Alaskan coast. When Miyax was 9 years old, her aunt Martha arrived from the town of Mekoryuk and demanded that the girl come live with her and attend school. Miyax moved to town and began to take on the *gussak* (white people) ways; she was called Julie and learned to speak and write in English. A few months later, Miyax got word that her father had died while seal hunting. But he had left Miyax one escape route: When she was 13, she could go to Barrow and marry Daniel, the son of her father's hunting partner. As soon as she turned 13, Miyax left her domineering aunt and journeyed to Barrow to become a bride.

But Daniel turned out to be simpleminded and cruel, and after a few months in Barrow, Miyax decided to run away to San Francisco to live with her pen pal Amy, who had been inviting Miyax to come visit for years. Miyax packed her gear and started walking through the Northern Wilderness to Point Hope, where she would catch a ship to San Francisco. But the landscape was unfamiliar to Miyax, and soon she was lost and out of food.

Miyax had learned the ways of the wolf from her father and knew that if she observed the wolves long enough, she could eventually communicate with them. Gradually, Miyax gained the trust of the wolves, who fed her and became her companions for many months. Eventually, Miyax learned that her father was actually alive and married to a white woman. Miyax tracked him down, but soon left when she saw how he had abandoned the Eskimo ways. Encroaching civilization and the death of one of her beloved wolves forced Miyax to call herself Julie once more and head back to her father.

Why This Book Appeals to Reluctant Readers This is a rare adventure story for girls, in which the heroine is brave, smart, and resourceful. Unlike some other adventure stories in which the character is thrown into the wilderness with no knowledge of how to survive, Miyax has experience with hunting, tracking, and building shelters from earth and snow. However, she's also smart enough to realize that she didn't bring the right tools with her to hunt large game and so must depend on the wolves for survival. Though this story deals with many substantial emotional issues, they are conveyed through action and suspense. The intricate details of the Alaskan landscape, the ways of the animals, and the physical and mental steps Miyax takes each time she hunts, traps, builds a shelter, or constructs a sled are fascinating. The reader is quickly drawn into a world that operates on another clock and a different set of rules from her own.

Who Might Like This Book Anyone who loves the outdoors, is interested in Alaska or wolves, or appreciates stories about the bond between animals and humans might like this book. The story has some sad moments, but it also raises thought-provoking issues, especially for those readers concerned about the environment.

Notes to Parents *Julie of the Wolves* won the Newbery Medal in 1973.

If Your Child Liked This Book, Then Try . . . Other adventure stories by this same author, including *My Side of the Mountain* (Puffin Books) and *The Summer of the Falcon* (Harper).

Hatchet

by

GARY PAULSEN

Genre: Fiction/Adventure

Publisher: Simon & Schuster, $16.95 (h); Puffin Books, $4.99 (p)

Page Length: 195

Type of Illustrations: None

Reluctant Reader Appeal: Well-Defined Characters, Fast-Paced Plot, Concise Chapters, Suitable Text

Suggested reading level: Age 12 and up

Stopped.

Seconds passed, seconds that became all of his life, and he began to know what he was seeing, began to understand what he saw and that was worse, so much worse that he wanted to make his mind freeze again.

He was sitting in a bushplane roaring seven thousand feet above the northern wilderness with a pilot who had suffered a massive heart attack and who was either dead or in something close to a coma.

He was alone.

In the roaring plane with no pilot he was alone.

Alone.

Synopsis Thirteen-year-old Brian Robeson is filled with thoughts of his parents' divorce as he flies in a single-engine plane to visit his father in the Canadian wilderness. When the pilot suffers a massive heart attack and dies, Brian must land the plane by himself and then somehow stay alive until he is rescued. Armed only with the clothes on his back and a hatchet he received from his mother as a parting gift, Brian must put the nagging memories of his parents' breakup behind him and focus on the basic needs he has always taken for granted: food, clothing, warmth, and shelter. During his 54-day stint alone in the wilderness, Brian gradually turns inward and becomes a stripped-down version of his old self, shedding emotional luxuries like pity and self-doubt to build a stronger, tougher, and more introspective personality who is forced to live one day at a time.

Why This Book Appeals to Reluctant Readers Brian Robeson is an ordinary kid with no special skills or tools, and because of this the reader can sympathize with him and also put himself in Brian's place. Brian's transformation is remarkable mainly because it's so believable. Though this is a one-character novel, there is no lull in the action. Brian—and the reader—never forget that death could be just around the corner.

Who Might Like This Book Boys especially love Gary Paulsen's books. Fans of adventure stories will appreciate the climactic chapter endings and the classic man-against-nature struggle of the protagonist.

Notes to Parents Though most of Gary Paulsen's books are outdoor adventure stories, they have more depth than some other adventure books, especially those aimed at boys. *Hatchet* won a Newbery Honor in 1988.

If Your Child Liked This Book, Then Try . . . Other books by Gary Paulsen, including *Dogsong* (Aladdin), *River* (Yearling), and *Tracker* (Puffin).

Owl in Love

by

PATRICE KINDL

Genre: Fiction/Supernatural

Publisher: Houghton Mifflin, $5.99 (p)

Page Length: 204

Type of Illustrations: None

Reluctant Reader Appeal: Humor, Well-Defined Characters, Fast-Paced Plot, Kid Relevance

Suggested reading level:
Age 10 and up

Sometimes I would not like to be what I am.

As a child I was teased by the other children and pestered by the grownups for never bringing a lunch of my own to school or eating the hot lunch provided. My coloring in health is naturally gray rather than rosy, and this convinced them all that I was at death's door, entirely owing to my refusal to eat the "nice ravioli" or pizza or whatever disgusting messes the school kitchen produced.

My diet is largely composed of small rodents and insects. I can hardly lunch on grasshoppers before the eyes of several hundred ninth-graders, so I prefer not to eat lunch at all. Besides, it is unnatural for an owl to be awake at noon (though not so un-

usual as some people imagine), and a heavy meal makes it all the harder to concentrate upon my studies.

Synopsis Every few generations of Owl Tycho's family produces a shape-shifter: an outwardly normal human who can transform herself into an owl at will. Owl exhibits many of the ordinary behaviors of a 14-year-old, including consulting teen magazines for advice on how to handle her secret love for her science teacher. But she acts on these feelings in decidedly birdlike ways, such as perching on a tree outside Mr. Lindstrom's bedroom at night to watch him sleep. Then, during one nightly vigil, Owl discovers that an insane owl and a wild boy haunt the woods near Mr. Lindstrom's home. As she tries to protect her chosen mate, Owl uncovers the identity of the other owl and gives up her schoolgirl crush for a more realistic romance.

Why This Book Appeals to Reluctant Readers First and foremost, this book is offbeat and funny. The first-person narration provides Owl with a wise, wry, and keenly self-aware voice that embodies the passion and confusion of an adolescent girl. The author does a fine job of blending Owl's human and bird natures into one, so the reader never loses track of her dual makeup. Owl's parents—gentle, quirky witches who sell herbal remedies—are devoted to Owl and fully support her nightly vigils. Short scenes featuring the mysterious boy pop up from the beginning, adding an element of suspense to the book.

Who Might Like This Book Girls who like unusual fantasy and humorous looks at first love.

If Your Child Liked This Book, Then Try . . . *The Woman in the Wall* by Patrice Kindl (Houghton Mifflin).

The Great Gilly Hopkins

by

KATHERINE PATERSON

Genre: Contemporary Fiction

Publisher: HarperCollins, $5.95 (p)

Page Length: 192

Type of Illustrations: None

Reluctant Reader Appeal: Humor, Well-Defined Characters, Fast-Paced Plot, Suitable Text, Kid Relevance

Suggested reading level: Age 10 and up

Mrs. Trotter glanced down at the hand on the knob. "Well, make yourself at home. You hear now?"

Gilly slammed the door after her. God! Listening to that woman was like licking melted ice cream off the carton. She tested the dust on the top of the bureau, and then, standing on the bed, wrote in huge cursive curlicues, "Ms. Galadriel Hopkins." She stared at the lovely letters she had made for a moment before slapping down her open palm in the middle of them and rubbing them all away.

Synopsis Gilly Hopkins is a smart, tough 11-year-old who has been in and out of foster homes for most of her life. She's learned not to care too much about anyone and makes a game out of being as unpleasant as possible. Her rationale for her behavior is that one day she'll return to her mother (whom she imagines to be perfect), a longing that's strengthened every time her mother writes an occasional brief letter. Gilly's determination to reunite with the parent she barely knows comes to a head when she's placed with Maime Trotter ("a huge hippopotamus of a woman") who is also foster parent to William Ernest Teague, a shy, nervous 7-year-old whom Gilly thinks is "retarded." The final addition to this unconventional family is Trotter's next door neighbor Mr. Randolph, a blind black man who dines with them every night.

Gilly hates Trotter's dusty, cramped house from the start, and she soon fires off a letter to her mother, pleading that she be rescued from her desperate situation. In the meantime, Gilly starts stealing money from Mr. Randolph toward a bus ticket to San Francisco.

But despite her best efforts, Trotter, William Ernest, and Mr. Randolph begin to get under Gilly's skin. By the time Gilly's grandmother arrives (having just learned she has a granddaughter), Gilly realizes that sometimes a wished-for happy ending turns out to be bittersweet.

Why This Book Appeals to Reluctant Readers Gilly could easily have become a very unsympathetic character, but her intelligence, stinging wit, and ultimately her heart make the reader cheer for her. This is a story of crossing the threshold from childhood innocence to adulthood: In one fell swoop, Gilly learns about loss, the unfairness of life, living with the consequences of one's actions, the destructive force of anger, and the true meaning of family, commitment, and love. It's a lot to take, but upper-middle-grade readers who long for intense emotion and a dose of reality in their books will cross the threshold with Gilly and come out stronger on the other side.

Who Might Like This Book Readers who like real, emotional characters and situations in their books. Kids who themselves have felt rejected or who have developed a tough persona to avoid getting hurt will identify strongly with Gilly's behavior.

Notes to Parents Gilly's prejudices are a result of her shaky self-esteem and gradually dissolve as the story progresses. A book like this might be a good way to open up discussion with your child on the topic of racism. Gilly does swear (she says "hell" and an occasional "damn"), but it's part of her rough-edged character and not condoned by the adults around her. This book won numerous awards, including a Newbery Honor.

If Your Child Liked This Book, Then Try . . . Other books by Katherine Paterson, including *Bridge to Terabithia* (1978 Newbery Medal award winner), *Jacob Have I Loved* (1981 Newbery winner), and *Lyddie*. Also try *Homecoming* by Cynthia Voight (Fawcett Juniper).

Nothing but the Truth: A Documentary Novel

by

AVI

Genre: Contemporary Fiction

Publisher: Orchard Books, $4.99 (p)

Page Length: 177

Type of Illustrations: None

Reluctant Reader Appeal:
Fast-Paced Plot, Concise Chapters, Kid Relevance, Unique Presentation

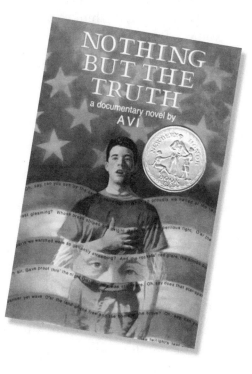

Suggested reading level:
Age 11 and up

10:30 P.M.

FROM THE DIARY OF PHILIP MALLOY

Got my term grades. Math, an A. Awesome wicked. B– in biology. That's OK too. And I got a C in history, which is cool. All of that stuff is dead anyway. A straight B in health. But then I got a D in English!!! Narwin is so dumb she didn't get the joke.

I'll have to try something different with her. Maybe I should tell her how boring she is. Bad combo—boring teaching and stupid books. What she really wants us to do is put down the things she *thinks. She wrote that on my exam paper too. Wish I hadn't thrown it out. It was funny. Bet Allison would have laughed. And now I'm going to get Narwin for a homeroom teacher too.* Not me.

Synopsis Philip Malloy is a ninth grader whose bad grade in English is keeping him off the track team. When Philip jokingly hums along with the national anthem played over the intercom at the beginning of each school day, his homeroom teacher, Miss Narwin, sends him to the vice principal's office. The incident escalates to a two-day suspension followed by national media attention based on the theory that Philip has been denied the right to express his patriotism. Eventually, Philip transfers to a school that doesn't have a track team, and Miss Narwin is forced to take a leave from teaching, a job she's loved for 21 years.

This story is told through school memos, news clips, excerpts from Philip's diary, letters Miss Narwin writes to her sister, and transcripts of conversations. The result is that the reader gets a shockingly clear picture of how well-intentioned people can misinterpret the facts by listening only to what they want to hear, by bending the truth to fit their own needs, or by being unwilling to look at the complete picture. In the end, only the reader knows the whole truth and understands that when people rely on their preconceptions to search for answers, nobody wins.

Why This Book Appeals to Reluctant Readers This is an incredibly eye-opening book. The spare, straightforward text—stripped of description, setting, or narrative—reads very quickly, and the reader is astounded at how fast the misconceptions build on each other. And yet the author provides a very real, detailed portrait of the principal characters, showing the reader how their views of themselves and their situations affect their judgment. The conversations between Philip and his parents are extremely believable and will hit a nerve with many readers. The unexpected ending—tragic, unnerving, and a bit scary in today's media-driven society—will have readers thinking about this book long after the last page. But probably the most appealing aspect of *Nothing but the Truth* is that the author trusts and respects readers enough to allow them to draw their own conclusions about right and wrong without an ounce of preaching—something adolescent readers will appreciate.

Who Might Like This Book Readers who enjoy heated discussions, who like to ponder weighty issues, or who keep up with current events and the news will find this book interesting.

Notes to Parents This is a great book to read with your child (or read yourself after your child has read it on his own), especially if you want to engage in book discussions as a family. Some readers might be put off by the format at first, but encourage them to stick with it for a couple of chapters. Once the child understands that every bit of information is relevant, then reading school memos makes sense. *Nothing but the Truth* won numerous prestigious awards, including a Newbery Honor.

If Your Child Liked This Book, Then Try... *Monster* by Walter Dean Myers, illustrated by Christopher Myers (HarperCollins, age 12 and up; also written in a documentary style, though for slightly older readers). Also by Avi: *The True Confessions of Charlotte Doyle* (Avon, ages 8–12, historical fiction with a female protagonist).

The Giver

by

LOIS LOWRY

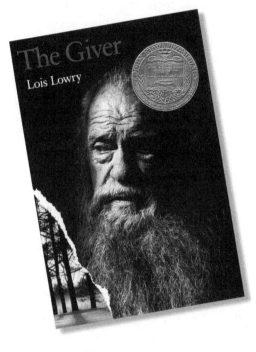

Genre: Science Fiction

Publisher: Houghton Mifflin, $15.00 (h); Laurel-Leaf, $6.50 (p)

Page Length: 180

Type of Illustrations: None

Reluctant Reader Appeal: Well-Defined Characters, Fast-Paced Plot, Concise Chapters, Kid Relevance

Suggested reading level: Age 12 and up

"Jonas," she said, speaking not to him alone but to the entire community of which he was a part, "you will be trained to be our next Receiver of Memory. We thank you for your childhood."

Then she turned and left the stage, left him there alone, standing and facing the crowd, which began spontaneously the collective murmur of his name.

"Jonas." It was a whisper at first: hushed, barely audible. "Jonas. Jonas."

Then louder, faster. "JONAS. JONAS. JONAS."

With the chant, Jonas knew, the community was accepting him and his new role, giving him life, the way they had given it to the newchild Caleb. His heart swelled with gratitude and pride.

But at the same time he was filled with fear. He did not know what his selection meant. He did not know what he was to become. Or what would become of him.

Synopsis Jonas lives in a Utopian community of the future, an orderly, safe world organized into what is known as Sameness. There are no colors, people live in assigned family units, and each year of childhood has special obligations and privileges. Everyone is content and cared for, and when they grow old, they are "released." When Jonas is 12, he is given his Life Assignment, and is shocked to learn that he has been chosen to be the Receiver of Memories and trained by the Giver, an old man who now holds the memories of the community's past that go back for generations. As Jonas begins to receive memories from the Giver, he experiences intense emotions for the first time: pain, loneliness, suffering, and sorrow but also joy, contentment, and love. Once Jonas has these memories, he realizes he'll never again feel part of a community of rigid rules and conformity; he wants to make his own decisions and think like an individual. He also senses that a carefully controlled world may not be the best answer for his community—when he finds out that sickly infants and the elderly are murdered when they're "released," he's sure he has to escape to the mysterious Elsewhere and start a new life.

Why This Book Appeals to Reluctant Readers This is a tightly plotted, riveting story that will keep readers spellbound until the last page. From the very beginning, Jonas's world is chillingly real to the reader. As his memories grow, along with the ability to see colors and feel sensations such as sunlight, wind, and cold, Jonas starts to grapple with issues like security versus freedom and safety versus risk. This is a coming-of-age story in the strictest sense, in which the character's eyes are fully opened to the world for the first time. Lowry's vivid descriptions and direct style of writing will compel the reader to ponder the deep meaning of this story long after the book is finished.

Who Might Like This Book This book works on so many levels that it will appeal to all kinds of readers. Those who like futuristic adventure stories, those who appreciate books that raise thought-provoking issues, and those who are drawn to coming-of-age stories with timeless, relevant themes will find this book fascinating.

Notes to Parents *The Giver* won numerous awards, including the Newbery Medal in 1994. The author has said in interviews that she deliberately left the ending ambiguous and won't comment on what some say is the story's religious symbolism because she wants each reader to apply his or her own interpretation to the themes. This opens the door for interesting discussions if you read the book along with your child.

If Your Child Liked This Book, Then Try . . . Other novels by Lois Lowry, including *Gathering Blue, Number the Stars* (both from Houghton Mifflin; *Number the Stars* won the 1990 Newbery Medal); and *The Ear, the Eye and the Arm* by Nancy Farmer (Orchard).

The Goats

by

BROCK COLE

Genre: Contemporary Fiction

Publisher: Farrar, Straus &
Giroux, $4.95 (p)

Page Length: 184

Type of Illustrations: None

Reluctant Reader Appeal:
Well-Defined Characters,
Fast-Paced Plot, Suitable
Text, Kid Relevance

**Suggested
reading level:**
Ages 9–12

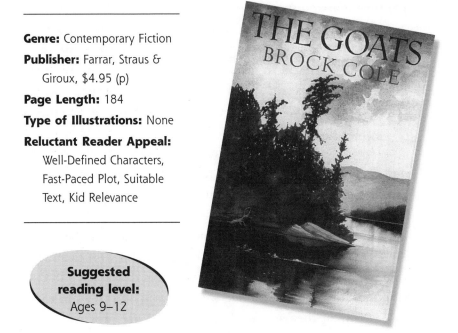

At the top of the island was an old tent platform. It had a canvas roof and sides of wood and screening. He stood at the edge of the clearing and looked at the tent platform and listened, but he couldn't hear anything except leaves rubbing against one another and the little slapping noises the waves made on the shore below. He crossed the clearing quickly and fumbled with the latch of the screen door. He was suddenly anxious to have the four walls around him.

He wasn't ready when someone inside said, "Go away."

Synopsis As per camp tradition, a boy and girl are chosen to be the "goats" and are stripped and marooned on a small island overnight. The other campers think this is a big joke, but the boy and girl don't see it that way. Instead of waiting to be rescued in the morning, they decide to disappear. They swim to shore during the night and spend three days on the run. The boy and girl aren't criminals: They keep careful track of the food and clothes they're forced to steal, leaving IOUs when they can. Some of the people they meet try to help them; others think they're juvenile delinquents and want to call the police. But the boy and girl refuse to get caught—their lives have changed forever, and they're never going back to the camp.

The boy and girl do have names—Howie and Laura—but the author rarely uses them, as if to remind the reader that the other campers see these two as anonymous geeks. It takes only a few hours for these "helpless" 13-year-olds to band together and discover a strength in themselves and each other that they never knew existed. When Laura and Howie do finally allow themselves to be found at the end of the book, they've developed a level of emotional intimacy and appreciation for each other that makes up for everything they've missed all their lives and will bind them together forever.

Why This Book Appeals to Reluctant Readers This is a book of literary substance that works on two levels: the exciting, sometimes tension-filled plot of how Howie and Laura elude capture and survive on their own for three days and the symbolic story of being stripped of one's dignity and rebuilding a sense of self on a firmer foundation. Howie and Laura are multidimensional characters caught at the brink of young adulthood but not quite ready to leave childhood behind. The author has poignantly presented that phase of life when the way others expect you to act is very different from how you feel inside.

Who Might Like This Book The publisher's age designation for *The Goats* is 9 to 12, but I feel it's more appropriate for age 12 and up or perhaps a very mature 11-year-old. Younger readers might get distracted (or be made uncomfortable) by the nakedness of the characters at the beginning of the story (though Howie and Laura take great pains to hide their bodies from each other) and miss the story's deeper meaning. Any child who has ever been made a "goat" by his or her peers will derive inspiration from Howie and Laura's journey.

Notes to Parents The characters' nakedness is not sexual in nature but representative of being emotionally exposed and vulnerable. However, if you have any doubts, read this book yourself before giving it to your child.

If Your Child Liked This Book, Then Try . . . *Homecoming* by Cynthia Voigt (Fawcett Juniper).

The Smugglers

by

IAIN LAWRENCE

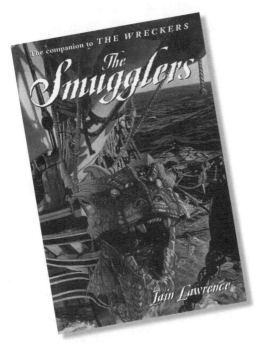

Genre: Historical
Fiction/Adventure

Publisher: Delacorte, $15.95
(h); Dell, $4.99 (p)

Page Length: 184

Type of Illustrations: None

Reluctant Reader Appeal:
Well-Defined Characters,
Fast-Paced Plot, Concise
Chapters, Suitable Text

**Suggested
reading level:**
Ages 10–14

*"A word of advice," said he. "You stay clear of that ship. The
Dragon."*

*I heard Father snort, a sound I knew well. I had seen his
clerks cringe at that noise, whole rows of them turning their
heads.*

*"She's bad luck," Larson continued. "No, she's worse than
that. She's evil."*

"How can a ship be evil?" I asked.

"I don't know," said he. "I'm only aware of the one that is."

Synopsis Despite a stranger's dire warning, 16-year-old John Spencer takes the responsibility for overseeing the voyage of his father's new ship, the *Dragon,* up the English coast to London with a cargo of wool. But the captain John's father first hires is killed, and he's forced to hire a substitute—the volatile Scottish Captain Crowe. Once at sea, John learns of a smuggling ship headed to France to bring stolen loot back to England and tells the captain he wants to try to head off the smugglers. Captain Crowe is happy to oblige. Along the way, John realizes that Crowe and his questionable crew are really the pirates John had read about, and he'd been set up from the beginning. Now, with the help of a mysterious stowaway, John must save his father's ship and himself from the murderous lot.

Why This Book Appeals to Reluctant Readers This book is bursting with vivid characters who practically leap off the page; a sympathetic, believable hero; and nonstop action propelled by situations that are never quite what they seem. The historical details add to the rich setting, and all the essential elements for a good pirate tale are here, from storms at sea to ghostly legends. Taut suspense, cliffhanger scenes, and a thrilling finale all keep readers turning the pages.

Who Might Like This Book Boys who like action/adventure stories, historical fiction, or anything to do with pirates will love this book. The text is ripe with sailing terms and pirate vernacular. Some of the more technical scenes may be a bit difficult (though not impossible) for readers with no knowledge of sailing.

If Your Child Liked This Book, Then Try . . . Two companion volumes by Iain Lawrence, published by Delacorte: *The Wreckers* (the first book chronologically, though the stories don't have to be read in sequence) and *The Buccaneers* (the third book in this series).

Athletic Shorts:
6 Short Stories

by

CHRIS CRUTCHER

Genre: Contemporary
   Fiction/Sports
Publisher: Greenwillow,
   $4.99 (p)
Page Length: 154
Type of Illustrations: None
Reluctant Reader Appeal:
   Humor, Well-Defined
   Characters, Fast-Paced
   Plot, Concise Chapters,
   Kid Relevance

**Suggested
reading level:**
Age 12 and up

*My father is the Great Cecil B. Rivers. Three-year three-sport
letterman at Coho High School in the mid-1950's and number
two wrestler at 177 at the University of Oklahoma after that.
Number two is mysteriously absent from his version. Dad and
I don't always see eye to eye—to the extent that at times we see
eye to black eye. Dad thinks I'm too frivolous to grow up in the
world as he knows it, and he's right. I wouldn't want to grow up
in the world as he knows it. Dad wants to toughen me up.*

Synopsis Five of these six short stories feature characters from Crutcher's young adult novels, but the reader needn't be familiar with the characters to enjoy this book. All involve high school boys and sports, but the real theme of each story is growth. The plots—some humorous, some serious—range from a huge football player being elected Senior Winter Ball King as a joke (he can't dance, and the kids all tease him anyway because both his parents are gay) to a swimmer who tries to forgive the boy who caused his parents' and brother's deaths. Racism, bigotry, love, humiliation, the baggage sons inherit from their fathers—it's all here. And while each story contains the raw emotions and realistic situations endured by the main characters, this is not a depressing collection. Rather, it's a tribute to the resilience, strength, and sheer determination of these teens to face their problems and try to change them—or, at the very least, to look them in the eye and not blink.

Why This Book Appeals to Reluctant Readers Chris Crutcher is known as an author who writes stories teenage boys will read. The characters in his books are all heavily into sports, but his novels involve so much more than athletics. He acknowledges the complex problems many junior high and high school boys face from family, peers, or themselves, and he writes about them with honesty and compassion. This book is a good introduction to Crutcher's work for readers who might not be ready to tackle a whole novel or who might want to meet some of the characters before committing to a longer book. Crutcher writes about the mental and physical challenges of high school sports from the inside, as one who has played the games and suffered through grueling physical workouts. His characters all have a deep commitment to athletics, often because of—or in spite of—whatever's going on in the rest of their lives. The stories in this collection are on the long side—they average about 25 pages—

but they are concise in that each features a full-blown character, a problem, and a story arc with a beginning, middle, and end.

Who Might Like This Book Mature boys from eighth grade on up who want books that are written specifically for them, that give them action but also acknowledge the complex emotions teens face as they grow from boys to men.

Notes to Parents These stories, as all of Crutcher's work, present characters with realism. Racists use racial epithets, abused boys talk about getting black eyes from their fathers, and the characters swear when they're angry. None of this is gratuitous, and it's balanced with a lot of team camaraderie, courage, and pride in one's accomplishments. But if you have any doubts about whether your child is mature enough for such a book, please read it yourself first.

If Your Child Liked This Book, Then Try . . . Young adult novels by Chris Crutcher, including *The Crazy Horse Electric Game, Stotan!,* and *Running Loose* (Greenwillow).

Cool Women:
The Thinking Girl's
Guide to the Hippest
Women in History

Edited by PAM NELSON

Written by DAWN CHIPMAN, MARI
FLORENCE, AND NAOMI WAX

Design by AMY INOUYOE

Genre: Nonfiction/Women's
Studies

Publisher: Girl Press,
$19.95 (h)

Page Length: 128

Type of Illustrations: Color
and black-and-white pho-
tos and drawings

Reluctant Reader Appeal:
Humor, Concise Chapters,
Kid Relevance, Unique
Presentation, Visual Appeal

**Suggested
reading level:**
Age 10 and up

In 1891, Marie Curie walked into the boys club of the science world and basically tore the place apart. Not that she really meant to—Marie didn't want to cause trouble, but she was so brilliant that she couldn't help but smash through cozy stereotypes with every new breakthrough discovery. Since most fields of science were closed to women at the turn of the century, Marie started by discovering her own—radiology. When they wouldn't let her into the prestigious Academy of Science, she won the Nobel Prize in physics just to press the point. And after there was some talk about the first one being a fluke, she won another Nobel (in chemistry) just to set the record straight.

Synopsis Make no mistake: The women in this book are *cool*. From Josephine Baker to Mae West, Calamity Jane to Rosie the Riveter, Cool Goddesses to Righteous Queens, *Cool Women* provides high-energy snapshots of the lives of notable women throughout history. But rather than relying on straight biographical information and lists of accomplishments, *Cool Women* looks at the human aspect of heroines—fictional and real, dead and alive—who have helped shape modern young women's place in the world. Their fears, inspirations, and problems all shed light on how these women were, at their core not all that different from the girls reading their stories. The eye-popping layout gives each woman a two-page spread that dramatically combines photographs, illustrations, and design to match the subject. The writing style is hip and entertaining, and the text is broken up by catchy subheadings, allowing the reader to easily absorb the information.

Why This Book Appeals to Reluctant Readers *Cool Women* is like MTV-meets-*Encyclopaedia Britannica*. The information is not in-depth enough to write a school report on each subject but can be very inspiring. This book gives the reader a peek into the lives of fascinating women in politics, literature, civil rights, science, sports, and the arts. It whets the appetite without overwhelming and in many instances provides resources for further reading. Most significant, this book can open a young woman's eyes to role models she's never heard of before and get her excited about finding out more.

Who Might Like This Book Girls who are at the stage in their adolescence when they're starting to ask "Who am I?" and "Who will I become?" Also, girls interested in women's studies or history in general.

If Your Child Liked This Book, Then Try . . . *Her Story: Women Who Changed the World,* edited by Ruth Ashby and Deborah Gore Ohrn (Viking); *The American Women's Almanac: An Inspiring and Irreverent Women's History* by Louise Bernikow (Berkley Publishing).

The Deep Time Diaries
As Recorded by Neesha
and Jon Olifee

by

GARY RAHAM

Genre: Nonfiction/Geology-
Paleontology

Publisher: Fulcrum
Publishing, $17.95 (h)

Page Length: 82

Type of Illustrations: Color
and black and white, on
every page

Reluctant Reader Appeal:
Humor, Concise Chapters,
Fast-Paced Plot, Unique
Presentation, Visual Appeal

**Suggested
reading level:**
Ages 9–12

Jump 3: Late Cretaceous, 68 million years B.P.
Day 1: Entry by Jon Olifee

*Be it here recorded: Today I became the first person ever to touch
a living <u>Triceratops</u>! Smelled 'em too. They clear their bowels
real fast when they're scared.*

*We saw thousands of them from the air as the shuttle cruised
over rolling, tree-speckled plains. The herds raised clouds of dust*

when they ran away from our passing shadow. We saw armored, knob-tailed ankylosaurs and speedy ostrich dinos too. The shuttle landed on high ground not far from a pair of sixty-foot-tall hadrosaurs munching pine boughs at the edge of a small forest. . . .

Synopsis According to the "Transcriber's" introduction, this book is based on diaries kept by Jon and Neesha Olifee, a brother and sister from the future. During a research assignment conducted by the children's scientist parents, the family is accidentally trapped inside a time machine created by a mysterious race of Builders. The time machine hurls the Olifees through a space-time wormhole to some unknown point in the earth's distant past. The family lands in each place just long enough to look around and gather data and then is whisked off again on another "jump." Unable to control the ship or determine where they'll end up, the family is sent further back in time with each journey, ending with the Precambrian period.

"Transcriber" Gary Raham occasionally adds his own interpretation of what the children must be encountering and includes activities, resources, maps, a glossary, and illustrated time line to put the information in an understandable context. The detailed, vibrant illustrations round out a book loaded with action, danger, and scientific facts.

Why This Book Appeals to Reluctant Readers This book has it all: time travel, technology, dinosaurs, and two narrators who sound remarkably like modern-day siblings. The diary entries are funny and action packed, and each chapter slips in a tremendous amount of information about the dinosaurs and landscape during that period of time. The story also has a mystery/suspense element: Who were the Builders, and where will the Olifees end up? The color illustrations are stunning; the black-and-white spot art is charming and funny. This is a book that can easily be read several times, especially by dinosaur lovers.

Who Might Like This Book Boys or girls who like dinosaurs and/or science fiction and even those who enjoy suspense-filled time travel. It will be especially appealing to would-be paleontologists or geologists. This book could also work as a read-aloud story for younger children (age 8 and up) who are already fascinated by dinosaurs.

Notes to Parents Though the diary entries are fictional, I've classified this book as nonfiction because of the predominance of facts about dinosaurs and the earth's history. Books that mix fiction and nonfiction but are primarily intended to teach about a subject are generally considered nonfiction by bookstores and libraries.

If Your Child Liked This Book, Then Try . . . *Dino Trekking: The Ultimate Dinosaur Lover's Travel Guide* by Kelly Milner Halls (John Wiley & Sons), *Dinosaurs* by Michael J. Benton (Dorling Kindersley), and the DINOTOPIA series (middle-grade fiction) by Donald F. Glut (Random House).

Light Shining Through the Mist: A Photobiography of Dian Fossey

by

TOM L. MATTHEWS

Genre: Biography

Publisher: National Geographic Society, $17.95 (h)

Page Length: 64

Type of Illustrations: Color and black-and-white photographs, on every page

Reluctant Reader Appeal: Well-Defined Characters, Suitable Text, Unique Presentation, Visual Appeal

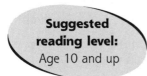

Suggested reading level: Age 10 and up

She wanted to know about their social interaction—how they acted together when they weren't being observed. And the only way to see how gorillas acted when they weren't being watched was to be accepted as a gorilla.

She aped, or imitated, gorilla behavior. Dian would crouch in the soaking-wet vegetation for hours in plain sight of a group. She would knuckle-walk around them, but keep her eyes turned *away, never staring. She groomed herself and made day nests to rest in and pretended to munch on gorilla delicacies like wild celery and bamboo. Sometimes, sensing distrust in the gorillas' eyes, she really chewed and swallowed the food!*

Synopsis Dian Fossey's dream of becoming a veterinarian was dashed when she failed physics and chemistry. She went to Africa, met Dr. Louis Leakey, and was given an opportunity that changed her life. In 1967, Fossey founded the Karisoke Research Center in Volcanoes National Park, Rwanda, and spent many years observing the behavior and social patterns of gorillas, defending them from hunters, and sometimes interacting with them. The author objectively examines Fossey's work as well as the extreme measures she used to protect the gorillas, which probably led to her mysterious death in 1985. Extraordinary photographs of Fossey and the gorillas she loved, liberal use of quotes from her writings, and detailed captions all give the reader an intimate, personal look at the woman who introduced mountain gorillas to the world and saved them from extinction.

Why This Book Appeals to Reluctant Readers The abundant photographs, lengthy captions, and quotes from Fossey's writings on each page give this biography the feeling of a photo-essay. Fossey's life is compelling in itself, but the up-close look at gorilla behavior and the strained political climate of Rwanda add emotional depth and tension to her story.

Who Might Like This Book Animal lovers, kids interested in preserving the environment or endangered species, or readers who also appreciate fine nature photography.

If Your Child Liked This Book, Then Try . . .
Walking with the Great Apes: Jane Goodall, Dian Fossey, Birute Galdikas by Sy Montgomery (Houghton Mifflin).

No Pretty Pictures: A Child of War

by

ANITA LOBEL

Genre: Nonfiction/Memoir

Publisher: Greenwillow,
$16.00 (h); Avon, $4.99 (p)

Page Length: 190

Type of Illustrations:
Insert of black-and-white
photographs

Reluctant Reader Appeal:
Well-Defined Characters,
Fast-Paced Plot, Kid
Relevance, Unique
Presentation

**Suggested
reading level:**
Age 10 and up

As the war went on, we were no longer able to find the flat navy blue envelopes of powder that had pictures of very pretty ladies on them. . . . Nainia used to buy the blond shampoo for herself and my brother, the black for me. For a long time now we had washed our hair with coarse soap, if we could find even that. Or we just sloshed our hair around in a bucket of water. And we could never quite get rid of the lice. Just when we thought that we had managed to explode the last bug by pressing the nails of our thumbs together, Nainia found more white dots that looked like the tiniest of rosary beads clinging here and there to a strand of hair on all our heads.

Synopsis Told with matter-of-fact honesty and great attention to detail, Anita Lobel (a Caldecott-winning children's book illustrator) tells of her childhood beginning at age 5 when the Nazis first entered her home in Krakow, Poland. From that moment, Anita and her brother were forced to live in secret. They hid with their Christian nanny in the country (her brother dressed as a girl to hide his circumcision), with their mother in the ghetto, and finally with the nanny again at a convent until they were discovered and imprisoned in a series of concentration camps until the war ended. With vivid recall, she recounts her child's-eye view of the details of her existence, using direct language that doesn't attempt to sugarcoat. After the war, Lobel was sent by the Red Cross to Sweden to recuperate from tuberculosis, and her initial distrust and terror of the doctors gradually evolved into feeling safe for the first time in her memory. She still felt like the "ugly, obvious Jew girl" when she started school at age 12 (for the first time in her life) along with her blonde Swedish classmates. But then she discovered she could draw, and her world finally began to change.

Why This Book Appeals to Reluctant Readers As Lobel points out in her prologue, because she was so young when she lost everything, she didn't know she was a victim. There is such an immediacy and honesty about her recollections that the reader can't help but feel that only children could have endured such horrific conditions. Adults would have wasted a lot of time feeling sorry for themselves, but Lobel and her brother were focused simply on survival. This is how it *felt* to be a young Jew in Poland during the Holocaust. The visceral nature of Lobel's memoir, the startling facts of her childhood, and the admirable strength of will required just to stay alive are reasons enough for any reader to be drawn to this book.

Who Might Like This Book Children who have studied the Holocaust in school and want another source of information (it's common for middle school students to read *The Diary of Anne Frank*), kids who are interested in Jewish history, and girls who like biographies of ordinary kids in extraordinary circumstances.

Notes to Parents *No Pretty Pictures* was nominated for a 1998 National Book Award for Young People's Literature.

If Your Child Liked This Book, Then Try . . . *Anne Frank: A Hidden Life* by Mirjam Pressler, translated by Anthea Bell (Dutton); *Four Perfect Pebbles: A Holocaust Story* by Lila Perl and Marion Blumenthal Lazan (Greenwillow).

The Boys' War: Confederate and Union Soldiers Talk About the Civil War

by

JIM MURPHY

Genre: Nonfiction/Civil War

Publisher: Clarion Books, $7.95 (p)

Page Length: 110

Type of Illustrations: Historical black-and-white photographs

Reluctant Reader Appeal: Concise Chapters, Kid Relevance, Unique Presentation, Visual Appeal

Suggested reading level: Age 10 and up

Suddenly, the war that had been a romantic dream was all around them like angry bees. Elisha Stockwell found himself facedown on the ground, shells exploding all around and soldiers screaming for help: "I want to say, as we lay there and the shells were flying over us, my thoughts went back to my home, and I thought what a foolish boy I was to run away and get into such a mess as I was in. I would have been glad to have seen my father coming after me."

Synopsis In the Civil War, an estimated 10 to 20 percent of both armies—or 250,000 to 420,000 soldiers—were actually boys age 16 and younger. Most were uneducated farm boys who enlisted to seek adventure, either with their parents' permission or by running away and lying about their ages. *The Boys' War* tells their story, drawing heavily on diaries and letters home to describe the war in the boys' own words.

Though this book does provide a chronological account of the war from the first shots at Fort Sumter to the surviving boys' return home at the war's end, it is not the traditional rendition of dates and battles. Rather, it looks at the Civil War through the eyes of the youngest soldiers, focusing on the details that consumed them the most: homesickness, the long marches, the people they met, how food was prepared, the ill-fitting uniforms and outdated artillery, and the fighting itself. The writings of the boys, complete with misspellings and the colloquialisms of the time, bring a personal and human voice to a pivotal event in American history.

Why This Book Appeals to Reluctant Readers

Nothing brings history alive like looking at a face and reading the words of an ordinary boy thrust into the middle of the action. Most of the boys did not join the army to fight for a cause; they were simply bored with small-town life and wanted adventure. The author doesn't judge this age-old adolescent complaint, nor does he take sides on the battlefield. When historical texts move away from broad, sweeping accounts of events and focus on the details, they become much more meaningful to the reader. The Civil War can be placed within the context of real life lived by actual people, and the reader can begin to envision what he might have felt under the same circumstances.

Who Might Like This Book

Boys especially will feel a connection to the voices in the letters and diaries, but girls who are interested in history will also find this book fascinating. The text is not overly difficult—it's written at an average young adult reading level—but it is fairly substantial. Children reading well below grade level might want to read this book with an adult or tackle the book one chapter at a time. Students studying the Civil War at school will find this book is an excellent way to supplement textbooks or help reinforce and understand the sequence of events.

Notes to Parents This book does not sugarcoat the realities of a war fought face-to-face on a battlefield. The boys' writings sometimes describe grisly battle scenes, and the photographs do include dead and wounded soldiers (though the sepia tone softens the images somewhat). The glory—and the horror—of war are given equal time.

The Boys' War was chosen as an American Library Association Best Book for Young Adults and won the Golden Kite Award from the Society of Children's Book Writers.

If Your Child Liked This Book, Then Try... A *Separate Battle: Women and the Civil War* by Ina Chang (Puffin), *Behind the Blue and Gray: The Soldier's Life in the Civil War* by Delia Ray (Puffin), and *Blizzard! The Storm That Changed America* by Jim Murphy (Scholastic).

No More Strangers Now: Young Voices from a New South Africa

Interviews by TIM McKEE

Photography ANNE BLACKSHAW

Genre: Nonfiction/South
Africa/Race Relations

Publisher: DK Ink, $11.95 (p)

Page Length: 107

Type of Illustrations: Black-
and-white photographs
throughout

Reluctant Reader Appeal:
Well-Defined Characters,
Concise Chapters, Kid
Relevance, Unique
Presentation, Visual Appeal

**Suggested
reading level:**
Age 11 and up

*As a Coloured, apartheid taught me basically that I'm better
than blacks but that I can never be white. We were on the fence,
stuck in the middle. . . .*

*So I grew up thinking just like the apartheid government
wanted me to. Even though I had black relatives, I was always*

taught to curse my own blackness because it prevented me from being white. I was angry about my parts that were black; I grew my hair long and used a hair relaxer to make it thin, so that I would not look like a black person. And I saw whites as superior. Whenever I had contact with them, they were dressed well and drove nice cars. When I saw the way whites were portrayed on TV, I thought, That's the ideal way of living. I'd always say to myself, If only my hair was straight and I had blue eyes, I'd be white.

Synopsis Twelve South African teenagers from different racial and socioeconomic groups are brought together to tell of their upbringing during apartheid and their experiences since. Each teen speaks candidly about his or her family, school life, and how they have struggled to overcome the violence, poverty, and racial segregation of a bitterly divided country. Their messages of hope and forgiveness are testimony to their passionate belief that the new South Africa will be different from the land of their parents.

An introduction provides an overview of the history of apartheid and how this book came about. Each teen's story is prefaced by a brief explanation of a law or social convention that contributed to the teen's lifestyle and attitudes. The reader begins to understand how society can shape a person's opinions of himself and others and to appreciate how far these teens have come in changing their beliefs. Candid photos of the teens depict their families and homes and capture their optimistic outlook on the future.

Why This Book Appeals to Reluctant Readers What will probably strike readers the most is the similarity between the South African teens and themselves; the themes of poverty, racism, tolerance, and finding one's identity within society are issues that affect students all over the world.

Another appealing element of this book is how it explains apartheid in a way that no history textbook can. For middle school students who are becoming globally aware or those studying South Africa in school, this book will help them understand what apartheid was, how it devastated a country, and how a nation is beginning to rebuild.

Who Might Like This Book Students interested in politics or social issues or those wanting to read about South African history. Kids who might not like world politics but appreciate stories about people in other cultures may also find this book interesting. Teens dealing with issues like racism and intolerance in their own school might gain new perspective from the stories in *No More Strangers Now.*

If Your Child Liked This Book, Then Try . . . *Many Stones* by Carolyn Coman (Front Street Books, nonfiction), *South Africa: Coming of Age Under Apartheid* by Jason Laure and Ettagale Laure (Farrar, Straus & Giroux), and *Crocodile Burning* by Michael Williams (Dutton, fiction).

The New Way Things Work

by

DAVID MACAULAY

Illustrator DAVID MACAULAY

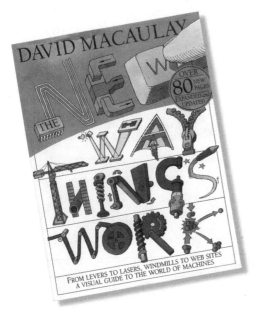

Genre: Nonfiction/Technology

Publisher: Houghton Mifflin, $35.00 (h)

Page Length: 400

Type of Illustrations: Color, on every page

Reluctant Reader Appeal: Concise Chapters, Kid Relevance, Unique Presentation, Visual Appeal

Suggested reading level: All ages

To any machine, work is a matter of principle, because everything a machine does is in accordance with a set of principles or scientific laws. To see the way a machine works, you can take the covers off and look inside. But to understand what goes on, you need to get to know the principles that govern its actions. The machines in this [book] are therefore grouped by their principles rather than by their uses. This produces some interesting neighbors: The plow rubs shoulders with the zipper, for example, and the hydroelectric power station with the dentist's drill. They may look different, be vastly different in scale, and have different purposes, but when seen in terms of principles, they work the same way.

Synopsis An updated edition of the wildly popular *The Way Things Work* (first published in 1988), *The New Way Things Work* takes the reader step-by-step through the evolution of technology, starting with the inclined plane and ending with computers. Along the way, the reader sees how one invention clearly paves the way for another. The book is divided into five sections: "The Mechanics of Movement," "Harnessing the Elements," "Working with Waves," "Electricity & Automation," and "The Digital Domain." A special chapter at the end ("Eureka! The Invention of Machines") gives the reader one-paragraph summaries of civilization's most influential machines.

Not only is this book organized so the reader understands the principles of machines and sees how one builds on the next, but each machine is carefully illustrated, cross-sectioned, and labeled. The concepts are imparted as much through the illustrations as the text. This strong visual component helps make machines understandable even for the technologically impaired and yet keeps the book interesting for the mechanically minded.

Why This Book Appeals to Reluctant Readers Individual concepts and machines are explained in one-half to two pages (including the illustrations), so the text is short and to the point. Whether it's a drinking straw or a nuclear reactor, if the reader wants to know how it works and why, it's in this book. Once readers see that even the simple, everyday tools we take for granted were painstakingly invented by someone, they can't help but be motivated to question, search, and discover more of the modern world on their own.

Who Might Like This Book Any child who is constantly taking apart your toaster, grandfather clock, or the television set to see how it works; kids who love shop class or tinkering with tools; even those inquisitive children who are curious about their surroundings and ask questions such as "Why does the car start when you turn the key?"

Notes to Parents I've listed this book for ages 10 and up because I feel that it will appeal to reluctant readers who can enjoy the book on their own. However, it's certainly appropriate for younger children when read with an adult. Also, it's great for those of you who don't know the answers to your kids' questions about technology and want to find out the information together.

The original *The Way Things Work* won many prestigious awards in the United States and England and spent several months on numerous bestseller lists.

If Your Child Liked This Book, Then Try . . . Other works by David Macaulay done in the same format, including *Unbuilding, Building Big, Castle, City, Underground,* and *Cathedral: The Story of Its Construction* (from Houghton Mifflin). Also check out the interactive CD-ROM version of *The New Way Things Work* from Dorling Kindersley.

Martian Fossils on Earth? The Story of Meteorite ALH 84001

by

FRED BORTZ

Genre: Nonfiction/Meteorites

Publisher: The Millbrook Press, $21.40 (h)

Page Length: 72

Type of Illustrations: Color and black-and-white photographs, on nearly every page

Reluctant Reader Appeal: Concise Chapters, Suitable Text, Unique Presentation, Visual Appeal

---

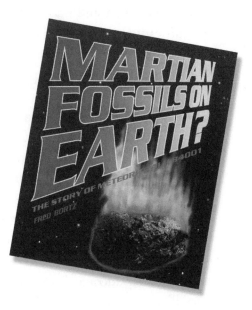

Suggested reading level:
Ages 8–13

Why Are Scientists So Excited About a Rock?

Because scientists love the excitement of discovery, they sometimes love the search for answers even more that the answers themselves. That is why they are so excited about a rock. Deep within this rock are structures and substances that will allow scientists to explore one of the most intriguing questions of all time: Is there life on other worlds?

The rock is known as meteorite ALH 84001. It is about the size and shape of a potato and weighs 1.94 kilograms (about 4 pounds). A meteorite is a rock that fell to Earth from space.

Meteorite ALH 84001 landed in the Allan Hills area of Antarctica about 13,000 years ago. It was discovered in December 1984 by the scientists of the Antarctic Search for Meteorites (ANSMET) project, led by William Cassidy.

Synopsis In short chapters that all begin with a question, the author leads the reader through the process of scientific inquiry and discovery surrounding a meteorite from Mars and its possible evidence for life on that planet. Along the way, readers learn background information about Mars, meteorites in general, and how scientists collect their data. Photographs greatly enhance the text, and an author's note and glossary round out the information. Readers will be inspired to continue asking questions and researching this topic—and related subjects—on their own.

Why This Book Appeals to Reluctant Readers Bortz has a knack for taking complicated scientific concepts and explaining them in a straightforward yet entertaining way. The short chapters adequately answer the opening questions without overwhelming the reader with excess information. Chapter openings are designed to have the look of an old science fiction movie, yet the photographs bring the reader up close to the real thing. The author is careful to distinguish between fact and theory, encouraging readers to think through the evidence themselves.

Who Might Like This Book Kids who are fascinated with astronomy, space exploration, fossils, and science in general.

If Your Child Liked This Book, Then Try . . .
Collision Course! Cosmic Impacts and Life on Earth by Fred Bortz (Millbrook).

It Is a Good Day to Die: Indian Eyewitnesses Tell the Story of the Battle of the Little Bighorn

by

HERMAN J. VIOLA

Genre: Nonfiction/Native American History

Publisher: Crown Publishers, $12.95 (p)

Page Length: 100

Type of Illustrations: Black-and-white historical photographs in introduction and epilogue

Reluctant Reader Appeal: Well-Defined Characters, Concise Chapters, Suitable Text, Unique Presentation

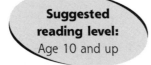

Suggested reading level: Age 10 and up

Wooden Leg

My brother and I ran to our camp and to our home lodge. I got my lariat and my six-shooter. I quickly emptied out my war bag and set myself at getting ready to go into battle. I jerked off my

ordinary clothing. I jerked on a pair of new breeches that had been given to me by a Hunkpapa Sioux. I had a good cloth shirt, and I put it on. My old moccasins were kicked off and a pair of beaded moccasins substituted for them. My father had caught my favorite horse, and he strapped on a blanket and arranged the rawhide lariat into a bridle. He stood holding my mount.

Synopsis The battle at the Little Bighorn River on June 25, 1876, was a defining moment in the Plains Indians' struggle to maintain their lifestyle and protect their homeland against the onslaught of white settlers. Since no U.S. Army soldiers survived the battle, the only eyewitness accounts come from the Indians who were there. *It Is a Good Day to Die* compiles these stories, collected by army investigators and historians in the years following the Battle of Little Bighorn, to try to piece together what happened that day and provide a picture of the conflict from the perspective of the Native Americans.

First-person narratives of one to two pages each make up the bulk of the book. The author prefaces these narratives with an introduction that provides a background to the conflict between the United States and Native American peoples and gives an overview of the battle to the best of historians' knowledge. An epilogue explains how the U.S. Army hunted down the Lakota and Cheyenne tribes after the battle and forced them into reservations. Biographical notes give thumbnail sketches of each of the Native Americans featured in the book.

Why This Book Appeals to Reluctant Readers This book gives readers a unique perspective to an infamous moment in U.S. history. The first-person accounts offer sensory details historians can't provide: the sound of screaming children, the smell of blood, and the clouds of dust from charging horses that made it hard to tell Indian from Army soldier. Because many of the narratives were recorded long after the battle, the Native Americans quoted were able to place the battle within the context of how their way of life had been changing and what it would mean to future generations. The honor of Indian soldiers comes through, from carefully dressing for battle (in order to look their best in death) to admiration for the bravery displayed by the vastly outnumbered U.S. Cavalry. This book gives the reader a lot to mull over but is not intimidating: The short accounts are vivid and compelling, and the generous leading (space between lines of text) makes the pages easy to read.

Who Might Like This Book Readers who are familiar with the Battle of Little Bighorn from school history classes and want more information, those interested in Native American history, and kids who have visited (or plan to visit) the battlefield in Montana.

If Your Child Liked This Book, Then Try . . . Black Elk Speaks from the University of Nebraska Press (found in the adult nonfiction section).

At Her Majesty's Request: An African Princess in Victorian England

by

WALTER DEAN MYERS

Genre: Nonfiction/Biography

Publisher: Scholastic,
$15.95 (h)

Page Length: 146

Type of Illustrations: Historical black-and-white photographs and drawings, about five per chapter.

Reluctant Reader Appeal: Well-Defined Characters, Concise Chapters, Suitable Text, Unique Presentation

Suggested reading level: Age 10–14

For the first time King Gezo hesitated. It was important for him to be respected as a great leader. He spoke to his ministers. The girl had been kept alive in captivity for two years. The King could not stop a practice that his people had carried on for so many years. But he also understood that it was not wise to anger the powerful British. When the conference with his ministers ended, it was announced that the killing of the adults would continue. The girl, however, would be given to Commander Forbes's queen. She would be a present from the King of the blacks to the Queen of the whites.

Synopsis In 1850, British naval officer Frederick E. Forbes saved the life of a 7-year-old African princess from a rival tribe's ritual sacrifice and brought the girl (whom he named Sarah Forbes Bonetta) back to England as a gift for Queen Victoria. Sarah became the queen's protégée, raised in a position of privilege, protection, and celebrity. She lived in a series of upper-middle-class British households, growing very fond of her adopted families. At one point in her life, she was sent back to Africa (the damp climate of England was thought to be bad for her health), where she attended the Female Institution in Freetown. Throughout the years, Sarah continued a steady correspondence with Queen Victoria and visited her when in London.

Though Sarah was often happy, she never felt that she really fit in anywhere. Since she was being groomed to take her place in British society, she had no choice but to marry a suitable man when she reached the proper age. Though Sarah resisted, she was eventually forced to marry a West African businessman, whom she swore she would never love. They moved back to Africa and named their first child Victoria (the queen was her godmother), and Sarah finally grew content with family life until she died of tuberculosis at age 37.

This story is all the more astounding because it's true. Walter Dean Myers discovered a packet of Sarah's letters in a rare-book bookshop in London and used them as a starting point to meticulously piece together her story. Excerpts from her letters, as well as correspondence from other people in Sarah's life, are sprinkled throughout the text. Reproductions of historical photographs and documents helps bring to life the subject as well as the time, attitudes, and society and offers insight into the relationship between England and Africa during this time.

Why This Book Appeals to Reluctant Readers Sarah herself is the most compelling reason to read this book. Though relatively little is known of her life, the information that survives all shows that Sarah was an extraordinary person. Readers will find much to admire about this young woman caught in a position for which she had no role models. Her life took huge swings between good luck and tragedy, and Myers keeps the story moving by chronicling a major phase of Sarah's life in each chapter. The details and customs of the time provide a backdrop for Sarah's story and also give the reader a painless history lesson.

Who Might Like This Book Because of the female protagonist and the focus on a young woman's place in Victorian England, girls will probably be drawn to this book more than boys. Those who have shown an interest in historical fiction will appreciate this true story. Readers who like history in general, especially British and African history, will like the unique viewpoint this book offers. Finally, readers who reach for biographies (or even kids who like to watch biographies on television) might be drawn to Sarah's unusual life.

Notes to Parents Walter Dean Myers is one of the most honored and respected children's book authors today. He has written many works of fiction, nonfiction, and poetry, mostly for middle-grade and young adult audiences. If your child likes his writing style, browse through his other works at the library to find another appealing subject.

If Your Child Liked This Book, Then Try . . . *Victoria's Daughters* by Jerrold M. Packard (St. Martin's Press, probably shelved with adult nonfiction). Another biography by Walter Dean Myers that will appeal to sports fans is *The Greatest: Muhammad Ali* (Scholastic).

Go for the Goal:
A Champion's Guide to Winning in Soccer and Life

by

MIA HAMM WITH AARON HEIFETZ

Genre: Autobiography/Soccer
Techniques

Publisher: HarperCollins,
$12.00 (p)

Page Length: 222

Type of Illustrations: Color
and black-and-white pho-
tographs throughout

Reluctant Reader Appeal:
Well-Defined Characters,
Fast-Paced Plot, Concise
Chapters, Kid Relevance,
Unique Presentation

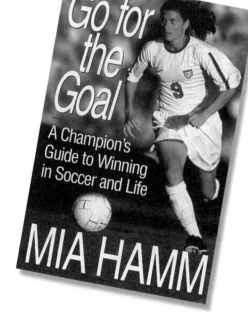

**Suggested
reading level:**
Age 10 and up

The ability to make your skills come through under pressure in a game situation, to be able to control the ball with your feet as if they were your hands, is the essence of soccer. You must love the feel of the ball as you touch it with every surface of your cleats, your legs, your chest and head. Strive to make your skills so sharp and clean that they will not break down in the high-pressure atmosphere of the game. The only way to achieve this is to make the ball your constant companion, which means it should be at your feet mornings, afternoons, before and after practice, most days of the off-season, and, for the hard-core and superstitious, even when you sleep.

Synopsis With humility and a friendly, down-to-earth voice, Mia Hamm—star of the U.S. National Soccer Team, Olympic Gold Medalist, World Cup champion, and five-time National Player of the Year—recounts her rise from suburban recreational league soccer star to breaking nearly every record in the sport. But this book is not just an autobiography; it's also a step-by-step guide on how to become a better soccer player. Personal anecdotes, practical advice, diagrams, and tips from Hamm's teammates mix to provide the reader with solid coaching on both the mental and the physical aspects of the game. Any girl who dreams of following in Hamm's footsteps will find inspiration from the text and the action-packed photographs. (Note: The paperback edition, published by Quill Press, has been updated to include the story of the 1999 Women's World Cup.)

Why This Book Appeals to Reluctant Readers Hamm focuses on soccer first and herself second, making the game the real focal point of the book. Her tone is never condescending; the reader senses that, with a lot of work and the right attitude, she has the chance of one day becoming a soccer star as well.

Who Might Like This Book Girls who love playing soccer or following the game. Boy soccer players might enjoy it as well.

If Your Child Liked This Book, Then Try . . . *On the Field with . . . Mia Hamm* by Matt Christopher (Little, Brown), *All-American Girls: The US Women's National Soccer Team* by Marla Miller (Econo-Clad Books), and *Gutsy Girls: Young Women Who Dare* by Tina Schwager and Michelle Schuerger (Free Spirit).

Kids at Work: Lewis Hine and the Crusade Against Child Labor

by

RUSSELL FREEDMAN

Photography LEWIS HINE

Genre: Nonfiction/Biography/
Social Reform

Publisher: Clarion Books,
$9.95 (p)

Page Length: 104

Type of Illustrations:
Full-page black-and-whie
photographs throughout

Reluctant Reader Appeal:
Concise Chapters, Suitable
Text, Kid Relevance,
Unique Presentation,
Visual Appeal

**Suggested
reading level:**
Age 10 and up

*Carrying a simple box camera like the one he used at Ellis
Island, Lewis Hine traveled back and forth across the country,
from the sardine canneries of Maine to the cotton fields of Texas.
He took pictures of kids at work, listened to their stories, and
reported on their lives.*

His goal was to open the public's eyes to the horrors of child labor. He wanted to move people into action.

Hine wasn't concerned with children who worked at odd jobs after school or did chores around the house or the family farm. He didn't object to youngsters working as trainees and apprentices, learning skills they would use for the rest of their lives. The campaign against child labor was not directed against them. It was aimed at the exploitation of boys and girls for cheap labor.

Synopsis In the early 20th century, children were regularly employed across the United States in backbreaking jobs in coal mines, factories, laundries, cotton mills, fields, and canneries. Lewis Hine, a schoolteacher and self-taught photographer, was so incensed by the use of children as low-wage workers that in 1908 he became an investigative reporter for the National Child Labor Committee, traveling around the United States and taking pictures of the kids at work. Hine felt that "seeing is believing" and that his heartbreaking, devastating photographs would spur the public to action.

It worked. Much of the public had until now refused to believe that children as young as 3 or 4 could be working in such conditions, but Hine's photographs left no doubt. In 1912, the government established the United States Children's Bureau to investigate working conditions, but it was still many years before child labor laws were put into effect.

This book focuses on Lewis Hine's life as an activist and his photographs of the step-by-step construction of the Empire State Building in New York City. Those photos are still heralded as a monument to the importance of human labor in the machine age. Today, Hine is considered a master American photographer whose work tells the story of early 20th-century laborers.

Why This Book Appeals to Reluctant Readers Lewis Hine is the perfect role model who used his art and passion to change children's lives in this country forever. Veteran biographer Russell Freedman steps back and lets Hine tell his story as much as possible, quoting from Hine's own writings, showing the conditions of factories and mines through Hine's eyes, and telling the individual stories of children Hine met and interviewed. Hine's photographs, each awarded a full page, are really the centerpieces of this book. Seeing the pictures of young laborers, many who look old beyond their years, will draw the reader inextricably into the text.

Who Might Like This Book Children who are interested in or concerned about civil rights and social issues or who like to read about early 20th-century U.S. history. Anyone interested in photography, especially documentary photography, will be fascinated by Hine's photos and how he used them to influence the country's social conscience.

If Your Child Liked This Book, Then Try . . . Russell Freedman has written many acclaimed biographies, including *Lincoln: A Photobiography* (Clarion Books, 1988 Newbery Medal winner); *The Wright Brothers: How They Invented the Airplane (with original photographs by Wilbur and Orville Wright)* (published by Holiday House, a Newbery Honor Book); and *Eleanor Roosevelt: A Life of Discovery* (Clarion Books, a Newbery Honor Book).

Chinese Cinderella: The True Story of an Unwanted Daughter

by

ADELINE YEN MAH

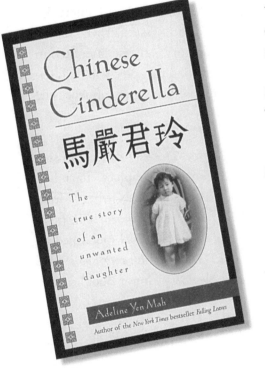

Genre: Nonfiction/Memoir

Publisher: Delacorte Press, $5.99 (p)

Page Length: 210

Type of Illustrations: Short insert of black-and-white photographs

Reluctant Reader Appeal: Well-Defined Characters, Concise Chapters, Kid Relevance, Unique Presentation

Suggested reading level: Age 12 and up

After school let out in the early afternoon, I waited with all the other first-graders by the school gate. One by one they were greeted and led away by their anxiously hovering mothers. Eventually, I was the only one left. Nobody had come for me. The metal gate slowly clanged shut behind me as I watched my classmates disperse, each clutching her mother's hand and eagerly recounting the adventures of her first day at school. After a long time, I peered through a crack into the deserted playground. Not a person was in sight. Cautiously, I pushed against the massive iron doorway. It was firmly locked. Trembling with fear, I realized that no one was coming to pick me up. Too embarrassed to knock or draw attention to myself, I walked tentatively out into the Shanghai streets. Surely, if I tried hard enough, I would remember the way home.

Synopsis As the author explains in her preface, she wrote this book in part for "those who were neglected and unloved as children." Adeline Yen Mah's story is all the more incredible because it's true. After her mother dies giving birth to her, Mah's affluent, powerful family considers her bad luck. Her father and siblings discriminate against her and make her feel unwanted. The only person who shows her love is her Aunt Baba, an unmarried woman who is financially dependent on Mah's father and so is given the task of raising Mah. The two share a bedroom and grow close.

Life doesn't get any easier for Mah when her father remarries a beautiful, cold woman and has two more children. The family later moves from Tianjin to Shanghai, and the children from Mah's father's first marriage are treated with disdain by their stepmother. But for Mah, it's even worse—despite her winning medals at school and doing her best to bring honor to the family, it's as if she doesn't exist. Mah eventually finds refuge in books and at age 14 wins an international playwriting contest. Her father finally acknowledges her and allows her to travel to England for college. In a postscript, the author explains that she went on to become a doctor and a writer. Though the story covers Mah's life from age 4 to 14, the reader gets a good sense of who Mah would become as a woman and how her strong spirit survived despite her miserable childhood.

Why This Book Appeals to Reluctant Readers Mah writes from her childhood viewpoint, so it's as if the reader is there with her, experiencing the feelings of sadness and abandonment firsthand. But this is not a depressing story; though Mah was treated deplorably by most of her family, her grandparents and aunt gave her love, and she found joy at school. Young adults who are developing an awareness of social issues will find Mah's story compelling and sympathetic.

Who Might Like This Book Children who are drawn to biographies of kids in tragic situations or readers who are interested in Chinese culture, especially in the mid-20th century. Girls in particular will be intrigued by Mah's memoir.

If Your Child Liked This Book, Then Try . . . *Ties That Bind, Ties That Break* by Lensey Namioka (fiction, Delacorte).

Further Recommended Reading

HERE'S A SHORT LIST of some other great books for reluctant readers. I've organized them by genre and listed the publisher's reading level after each title.

FICTION

General Fiction

Who's Afraid of the Dark? by Crosby Bonsall. Ages 6–9. (Harper I CAN READ series, Level 2)

Meet M & M by Pat Ross. Ages 7–9. (Puffin)

Class Clown by Johanna Hurwitz. Ages 7–10. (Morrow)

Help! My Life Is Going to the Dogs by Elizabeth Koehler-Pentacoff. Ages 7–10. (Troll)

Ramona Forever by Beverly Cleary. Ages 8–12. (Camelot)

Cody Unplugged by Betsy Duffey. Ages 8–12. (Viking)

Harriet the Spy by Louise Fitzhugh. Ages 8–12. (Harper)

The Wild Kid by Harry Mazer. Ages 8–12. (Simon & Schuster)

Almost Starring Skinnybones by Barbara Park. Ages 8–12. (Knopf)

Joey Pigza Swallowed the Key by Jack Gantos. Ages 9–12. (Farrar, Straus & Giroux)

Fade by Robert Cormier. Ages 10–14. (Dell)

The Cat Ate My Gymsuit by Paula Danziger. Age 10 and up. (Putnam)

The Outsiders by S. E. Hinton. Ages 10–14. (Viking)

Define "Normal" by Julie Anne Peters. Ages 10–14. (Little, Brown)

Historical

Sam the Minuteman by Nathaniel Benchley. Ages 7–9. (Harper I CAN READ series, Level 3)

The Josephina Story Quilt by Eleanor Coerr. Ages 7–9. (Harper I CAN READ series, Level 3)

Bud, Not Buddy by Christopher Paul Curtis. Ages 8–12. (Delacorte)

The Borning Room by Paul Fleischman. Ages 8–12. (HarperCollins)

In the Year of the Boar and Jackie Robinson by Bette Bao Lord. Ages 8–12. (HarperTrophy)

All-of-a-Kind Family by Sydney Taylor. Ages 8–12. (Yearling)

The Cay by Theodore Taylor. Ages 8–12. Historical/adventure. (Doubleday)

The Golden Goblet by Eloise Jarvis McGraw. Ages 9–12. Historical/adventure. (Puffin)

Catherine, Called Birdy by Karen Cushman. Age 12 and up. (Clarion)

Multicultural/Contemporary

Molly's Pilgrim by Barbara Cohen. Ages 5–8. (Lothrop)

Hamster Chase by Anastasia Suen (Peter's Neighborhood series). Ages 6–9. (Viking EASY-TO-READ series, Level 2)

Do You Know Me by Nancy Farmer. Ages 8–12. (Puffin)

Shabanu: Daughter of the Wind by Suzanne Fisher Staples. Ages 10–14. (Random House)

Grab Hands and Run by Frances Temple. Age 10 and up. (HarperTrophy)

Mystery

The High-Rise Private Eyes: The Case of the Missing Monkey by Cynthia Rylant. Ages 6–9. (Greenwillow)

The Case of the Cat's Meow by Crosby Bonsall. Ages 6–9. (Harper I CAN READ series, Level 2)

The Mystery of the Pirate Ghost by Geoffrey Hayes. Ages 7–9. (Random House STEP INTO READING series, Step 3)

Culpepper Adventures series (*The Case of the Dirty Bird, Dunc's Doll, Culpepper's Cannon, Dunc Gets Tweaked,* etc.) by Gary Paulsen. Ages 8–12. (Yearling)

Deep Doo-Doo and the Mysterious E-Mail by Michael Delaney. Ages 9–12. (Dutton)

AMERICAN GIRL HISTORY MYSTERIES series (*Hoofbeats of Danger, Secrets on 26th Street, Voices at Whisper Bend, The Smuggler's Treasure,* etc.) Various authors. Ages 9–12. (Pleasant Company)

The Westing Game by Ellen Raskin. Age 10 and up. (Dutton)

Sammy Keyes and the Hotel Thief by Wendelin Van Draanen. Ages 10–13. (Random House)

Poetry

Days Like These: A Collection of Small Poems, edited by Simon James. Ages 4–9. (Candlewick Press)

It's Raining Pigs and Noodles: Poems by Jack Prelutsky. Ages 5–9. (Greenwillow)

Falling Up by Shel Silverstein. Age 7 and up. (HarperCollins)

Popcorn by James Stevenson. Ages 7–11. (Morrow)

Insectlopedia: Poems and Paintings by Douglas Florian. Ages 7–12. (Harcourt Brace)

If You're Not Here, Please Raise Your Hand: Poems About School by Kalli Dakos. Ages 8–12. (Aladdin)

The Dream Keeper and Other Poems by Langston Hughes. Age 9 and up. (Knopf)

Science Fiction/Fantasy

Alien for Rent by Betsy Duffy. Ages 7–10. (Delacorte)

MY FATHER'S DRAGON series (*My Father's Dragon, Elmer and the Dragon, The Dragons of Blueland*) by Ruth Stiles Gannett. Ages 7–10. (Random House)

THE INDIAN IN THE CUPBOARD series (*The Indian in the Cupboard, The Return of the Indian, The Secret of the Indian, The Mystery of the Cupboard, The Key to the Indian*) by Lynn Reid Banks. Ages 8–12. (Doubleday)

The Wizard's Hall by Jane Yolen. Ages 9–12. (Scholastic)

REDWALL series (*Redwall, Mossflower, Mattimeo, Marlfox*) by Brian Jacques. Ages 9–13. (Philomel)

HIS DARK MATERIALS series (*The Golden Compass, The Subtle Knife, The Amber Spyglass*) by Philip Pullman. Age 10 and up. (Knopf)

NONFICTION

Activity Books

The Kid's Garden: The Anytime, Anyplace Guide to Sowing & Growing Fun by Avery Hart and Paul Mantell. Ages 7–11. (Williamson Publishing Company)

The Everything Kids' Baseball Book: Star Players, Great Teams, Baseball Legends, and Tips on Playing Like a Pro by Rich Mintzer. Ages 7–12. (Adams Media Corporation)

The Everything Kids' Nature Book by Kathiann M. Kowalski. Ages 7–12. (Adams Media Corporation)

Shocking, Slimy, Stinky, Shiny Science Experiments by Steve Parker. Ages 7–12. (Sterling Publishing Company)

Cooking on a Stick: Campfire Recipes for Kids and *Sleeping in a Sack: Camping Activities for Kids* by Linda White. Ages 8–12. (Gibbs Smith Jr.)

The Kids' Karate Book by Michael J. Dunphy, Ph.D. Ages 8–12. Comes with regulation-size karate belt. (Workman Publishing)

Cobi Jones Soccer Games by Cobi Jones and Andrew Gutelle. Ages 8–12. Comes with size 4 practice ball. (Workman Publishing)

101 Nature Experiments: A Step-by-Step Guide by David Burnie. Ages 8–13. (Dorling Kindersley)

Books-Plus

(These books are packaged with merchandise to facilitate hands-on learning.)

The Book of Cards for Kids by Gail MacColl. Clear instruction booklet and deck of oversize cards for playing four traditional card games. Ages 6–10. (Workman Publishing)

Marbles: A Player's Guide by Shar Levine and Vicki Scudmore. Includes 24 marbles, a drawstring bag, plastic playing mat, and booklet with rules to 35 games, techniques, and marble lore. Age 6 and up. (Sterling Publishing Company)

The Best Ever Paper Airplanes Book & Kit. Includes book, paper, pens, and stencils to create over 100 different paper airplanes. Age 8 and up. (Sterling Publishing Company)

The Dinosaur Hunter's Kit. Includes a handbook, fossil replica, and excavation tools. Age 8 and up. (Running Press)

Boston's Museum of Science Inventor's Workshop. Includes handbook and materials to build five inventions. Age 9 and up (younger with supervision). (Running Press)

History

It Happened in the White House: Extraordinary Tales from America's Most Famous Home by Kathleen Karr, illustrated by Paul Meisel. Ages 7–10. (Hyperion)

Mary on Horseback: Three Mountain Stories by Rosemary Wells. Ages 8–12. (Dial Books)

Ghost Liners: Exploring the World's Greatest Lost Ships by Robert Ballard. Ages 8–12. (Little, Brown)

The Amazing Pop-Up Pull-Out Mummy Book by David Hawcock. Ages 9 and up. (Dorling Kindersley)

From Hand to Mouth, Or, How We Invented Knives, Forks, Spoons, and Chopsticks and the Manners to Go with Them by James Giblin. Ages 9–12. (HarperCollins)

Through My Eyes by Ruby Bridges (autobiography of the first African American child to integrate an elementary school in Louisiana). Ages 9–13. (Scholastic)

Life: Our Century in Pictures for Young People, edited by Richard B. Stolley. Age 10 and up. (Little, Brown)

Kinderlager: An Oral History of Young Holocaust Survivors by Milton J. Nieuwsma. Age 12 and up. (Holiday House)

Science/Nature

You Can't Smell a Flower with Your Ear! All About Your 5 Senses by Joanna Cole. Ages 6–9. (Grosset ALL ABOARD READING series, Level 2)

Volcanoes: Mountains That Blow Their Tops by Nicholas Nirgiotis. Ages 6–9. (Grosset ALL ABOARD READING series, Level 2)

Terror Below! True Shark Stories by Dana del Prado. Ages 7–9. (Grosset ALL ABOARD READING series, Level 3)

Looking into My Body. Ages 6–10. (Reader's Digest Children's Books)

Weather at Your Fingertips by Judy Nayer, illustrated by Terri and Joe Chicko. Ages 2–8. (McClanahan Book Company)

The Big Book of Bugs! by Matthew Roberton, consulting editor. Age 7 and up. Comes with 3-D glasses. (Welcome Enterprises)

The Humongous Book of Dinosaurs. Age 7 and up. Comes with 3-D glasses. (Stewart, Tabori & Chang)

Sports

Inline Skating by Dawn Irwin. Ages 8–12. (Dorling Kindersley SUPERGUIDES series)

Gymnastics: The Trials, the Triumphs, the Truth by Dan Gutman. Ages 9–13. (Puffin Books)

Triumph on Everest: A Photobiography of Sir Edmund Hillary by Broughton Coburn. Age 10 and up. (National Geographic Society)

Nonfiction Series

These series are grouped together in a bookstore or shelved under the appropriate topic in the library.

DISCOVERY KIDS (Discovery Communication). Pocket-size paperbacks full of facts on topics such as Spies & Detectives, Terror Under the Sea, and Bloodthirsty Pirates. Ages 7–12.

EYEWITNESS BOOKS (Dorling Kindersley). Over 100 titles on a variety of subjects, including animals, science, and sports. Age 9 and up.

KLUTZ BOOKS (Klutz). These books come with all the materials necessary to do the activities described in the simple instructions. Topics include sewing, beads, yo-yos, card games, cooking, and jump ropes. Age 7 and up, depending on activity.

Resources for Parents

INTERNET RESOURCES

Barnes & Noble.com (www.bn.com). This is the Web site of Barnes & Noble, the bookselling giant. At the home page, click on "Kids" to take you to the children's book section. There, you can search for books by age-group, subject, or key word. Scroll down to the bottom of the page and click on "The Reader's Catalog Bookshelf" to read reviews of best-selling books listed by age-group.

ALA Resources for Parents, Teens and Kids (www.ala.org/parents/index .html). This section of the American Library Association Web site lists recommended Web sites for kids, book suggestions, software for kids and teens, and articles for parents on reading and books.

New York Public Library's "On-Lion" for Kids (www.nypl .org/branch/kids). Contains recommended reading lists with holiday themes, information on authors and favorite book characters, links to science and technology sites for kids, and a section for parents and teachers.

Helping Your Child Learn to Read (www.ed.gov/pubs/parents/ Reading /index.html). This guide for parent,s from the U.S. Department of Education, aims to encourage their children to read. Includes articles, activities, and a recommended reading list.

Reviews from Parent Council www.parentcouncil.com). The Parent Council organization's reviews of outstanding children's reading material is provided by parents, teachers, and librarians. You can search the site by topic or age-group.

BOOKS

Games for Reading: Playful Ways to Help Your Child Read by Peggy Kaye (Pantheon Books)

Honey for a Child's Heart: The Imaginative Use of Books in Family Life by Gladys Hunt (Zondervan Publishing House)

Starting Out Right: A Guide to Promoting Children's Reading Success, edited by M. Susan Burns, Catherine E. Snow, and Peg Griffin (National Academy Press)

Preventing Reading Difficulties in Young Children, edited by Peg Griffin, Catherine E. Snow, and M. Susan Burns (National Academy Press)

Nonfiction Matters: Reading, Writing and Research in Grades 3–8 by Stephanie Harvey (Stenhouse Publishers)

Dumbing Down Our Kids: Why American Children Feel Good About Themselves but Can't Read, Write or Add by Charles J. Sykes (St. Martin's Press)

Guided Reading: Making It Work. Two Teachers Share Their Insights, Strategies, and Lessons for Helping Every Child Become a Successful Reader by Carleen Dacruz Payne and Mary Schulman Browning (Scholastic)

Books to Build On: A Grade-by-Grade Resource Guide for Parents and Teachers, edited by John Holdren and E. D. Hirsch (Dell Publishing)

Why Our Children Can't Read and What We Can Do About It: A Scientific Revolution in Reading by Dianne McGuiness (Simon & Schuster)

Credits and Permissions

THE AUTHOR GRATEFULLY acknowledges the following authors and publishers who granted permission to reprint the copyrighted text excerpts and cover art that appear in this book:

Bantam Doubleday Dell Books for Young Readers: *Lily's Crossing* text copyright © 1997 by Patricia Reilly Giff, cover copyright © 1997 by Kamil Vojnar; *Purple Climbing Days* text copyright © 1985 by Patricia Reilly Giff, cover copyright © 1985 by Blanche Sims; *The Smugglers* text copyright © 1999 by Iain Lawrence, cover copyright © 1999 by Patrick Whelan; *Chinese Cinderella: The True Story of an Unwanted Daughter* text copyright © 1999 by Adeline Yen Mah, cover photograph courtesy of Adeline Yen Mah; *The Boys Start the War* text copyright © 1993 by Phyllis Reynolds Naylor, cover copyright © 1993 by Joe Csatari; *Nate the Great and Me* text copyright © 1998 by Marjorie Weinman Sharmat, cover copyright © 1998 by Marc Simont

Carolrhoda Books: *Little Wolf's Book of Badness* text copyright © 1995 by Ian Whybrow, cover copyright © 1995 by Tony Ross

Charlesbridge: *Steam, Smoke, and Steel: Back in Time with Trains* text and cover copyright © 2000 by Patrick O'Brien

DK Ink: *Minnie and Moo Go to the Moon* text and cover copyright © 1998 by Denys Cazet; *No More Strangers Now: Young Voices from a New South Africa* text copyright © 1998 by Tim McKee, cover copyright © 1998 by Anne Cecelia Blackshaw

Dorling Kindersley: *Amazing Snakes* text and cover copyright © 1990 by Dorling Kindersley Ltd., London; *Pirates!* text and cover copyright © 1998 by Dorling Kindersley Ltd., London; *Pond Life: A Close-Up Look at the Natural*

World text and cover copyright © 1992 by Dorling Kindersley Ltd., London; *My Pony Book* text and cover copyright © 1998 by Dorling Kindersley, Ltd., London

Farrar, Straus & Giroux: *Tuck Everlasting* text and cover copyright © 1975 by Natalie Babbitt; *The Goats* text and cover copyright © 1987 by Brock Cole; *The Trolls* text copyright © 1999 by Polly Horvath, cover copyright © 1999 by Wendy Anderson Halperin; *Gus and Grandpa* text copyright © 1997 by Claudia Mills, cover copyright © 1997 by Catherine Stock; *Not My Dog* text copyright © 1999 by Colby Rodowsky, cover copyright © 1999 by Thomas F. Yezerski; *Holes* text copyright © 1998 by Louis Sachar, cover copyright © 1998 by Vladimir Radunsky

Filter Press: *Little Fox's Secret: The Mystery of Bent's Fort* text copyright © 1999 by Mary Peace Finley, cover copyright © 1999 by Filter Press

Front Street: *Math Rashes* text copyright © 2000 by Douglas Evans, cover copyright © 2000 by Larry Di Fiori

Front Street/Cricket Books: *Oh No, It's Robert!* text copyright © 1999 by Barbara Seuling, cover copyright © 1999 by Paul Brewer

Fulcrum Publishing: *The Deep Time Diaries* text and cover copyright © 2000 by Gary Raham

Girl Press: *Cool Women: The Thinking Girl's Guide to the Hippest Women in History* text and cover copyright © 1998 by Girl Press

Grosset & Dunlap: *Dragon Breath* text copyright © 1997 by Jane O'Connor, cover copyright © 1997 by Jeff Spackman

Harcourt Brace: *Parachuting Hamsters and Andy Russell* text copyright © 2000 by David A. Adler, cover copyright © 2000 by Wil Hillenbrand; *Lives of the Presidents: Fame, Shame (and What the Neighbors Thought)* text copyright © 1999 by Kathleen Krull, cover copyright © 1998 by Kathryn Hewitt; *Smart Dog* text copyright © 1998 by Vivian Vande Velde, cover copyright © 1998 by Brad Weinman

HarperCollins: *Abigail Takes the Wheel* text copyright © 1990 by Avi, cover copyright © 1990 by Don Bolognese; *A is for AARRGH!* text copyright © 1999 by William J. Brooke, cover copyright © 1999 by Bill Cigliano; *Flat Stanley* text copyright © 1964, 1992 by Jeff Brown, cover copyright © 1996 by Steve Bjorkman; *Bloomability* text copyright © 1998 by Sharon Creech, cover copyright © 1998 by HarperCollins; *Athletic Shorts: 6 Short Stories* text copyright © 1991 by Chris Crutcher, cover copyright © 1991 by Bryce Lee; *The Whipping Boy* text copyright © 1986 by Sid Fleischman, cover copyright © 1986 by Peter Sis; *Albertina the Practically Perfect* text copyright © 1998 by Susi Gregg Fowler, cover copyright © 1998 by Jim Fowler; *How to Talk to Your Dog* text copyright © 1985 by Jean Craighead George, cover copyright © 2000 by Sue Truesdell; *Julie of the Wolves* text copyright © 1972 by Jean Craighead George, cover copyright © 1985 by Wendell Minor; *Go for the Goal* text copyright © 1999 by Mia Hamm, Aaron Heifetz, cover copyright © 1999 by HarperCollins; *Here Comes the Strikeout* text and cover copyright © 1965, 1992 by Leonard Kessler; *Who Eats What? Food Chains and Food Webs* text copyright © 1995 by Patricia Lauber, cover copyright © 1995 by Holly Keller; *Ella Enchanted* text copyright © 1997 by Gail Carson Levine, cover copyright © 1997 by Mark Elliott; *The Lion, the Witch and the Wardrobe* text copyright © 1950, 1978 by C. S. Lewis Pte Ltd, cover copyright © 1994 by Leo and Diane Dillon; *Emma's Magic Winter* text copyright © 1998 by Jean Little, cover copyright © 1998 by Jennifer Plecas; *No Pretty Pictures* text copyright © 1998 by Anita Lobel, cover photograph courtesy of Anita Lobel; *Arthur, For the Very First Time* text copyright © 1980 by Patricia MacLachlan, cover copyright © 1989 by Ruth Sanderson; *Sarah, Plain and Tall* text copyright © 1985 by Patricia MacLachlan, cover copyright © 1985 by Marcia Sewall; *The Drinking Gourd: A Story of the Underground* Railroad text copyright © 1970 by F. N. Monjo, cover copyright © 1970 by Fred Brenner; *Amelia Bedelia* text copyright © 1963 by Margaret Parish, renewed 1991 by the Estate of Margaret Parish, cover copyright © 1963, 1991 by Fritz Siebel; *The Great Gilly Hopkins* text copyright © 1978 by Katherine Paterson, cover copyright © 1978 by Fred Marcellino; *Sideways Stories from Wayside School* text copyright © 1978 by Louis Sachar, cover copyright © 1985 by Avon Books; *Greg's Microscope* text copyright © 1963 by Millicent E. Selsam, cover copyright © 1963 by Arnold Lobel; *The Adventures of Snail at School* text and cover copyright © 1993 by John Stadler; *Charlotte's Web* text copyright © 1952, 1980 by E. B. White, cover copyright © 1952, 1980 by Garth Williams; *Little House on the Prairie* text copyright © 1935 by Laura Ingalls Wilder, copyright © renewed 1963 by Roger L. MacBride, cover copyright © 1953, 1981 by Garth Williams

Houghton Mifflin Company: *On My Honor* text copyright © 1986 by Marion Dane Bauer, cover copyright © 1986 by Troy Howell; *Kids at Work: Lewis Hine and the Crusade Against Child Labor* text copyright © 1994 by Russell Freedman, cover photographs by Lewis Hine; *The Top of the World: Climbing Mount Everest* text and cover copyright © 1999 by Steve Jenkins; *Owl in Love* text copyright © 1993 by Patrice Kindl, cover copyright © 1993 by Wil Hillenbrand; *Anastasia Krupnik* text copyright © 1979 by Lois Lowry, cover copyright © 1979 by Diane DeGroat; *The Giver* text copyright © 1993 by Lois Lowry, cover photographs copyright © 1993 by Lois Lowry; *The New Way Things Work* text copy-right © 1988, 1998 by David Macaulay, Neil Ardley, cover copyright © 1988, 1998 by David Macaulay; *The Boys' War* text copyright

© 1990 by Jim Murphy, cover photograph courtesy of the Library of Congress; *Find the Constellations* text and cover copyright © 1954, 1962, 1966, 1976 by H. A. Rey, © renewed 1982 by Margaret Rey. Revised and updated in 1988 by Jay M. Pasachoff.

Hyperion: *The Doll People* text copyright © 2000 by Ann M. Martin and Laura Godwin, cover copyright © 2000 by Brian Selznick; *Cockroach Cooties* text copyright © 2000 by Laurence Yep, cover copyright © 2000 by Kam Mak

Kingfisher: *Dig and Sow! How Do Plants Grow?* text and cover copyright © 2000 by Snapdragon Publishing Ltd.; *I Wonder Why I Blink and Other Questions about My Body* text and cover copyright © 1992 by Grisewood & Dempsey. Reproduced by permission of Kingfisher Publications, Inc.

Little, Brown: *In the Huddle With . . . John Elway* text copyright © 1999 by the Estate of Matthew F. Christopher, cover copyright © Time, Inc.; *The Kid Who Only Hit Homers* text copyright © 1972 by Matt Christopher, cover copyright © 1986 by Glenn Harrington; *Maniac Magee* text copyright © 1990 by Jerry Spinelli, cover copyright © 1990 by Carol Palmer; *Revenge of the Snob Squad* text copyright © 1998 by Julie Anne Peters, cover copyright XXXXXXXXXXXXXXX ***BRENDA: I ONLY HAVE THE COVER

McGraw-Hill: *Dr. Fred's Weather Watch: Create and Run Your Own Weather Station* text copyright © 2000 by Alfred B. Bortz, cover copyright © 2000 by McGraw-Hill

McIntosh & Otis: *Fat Men from Space* text copyright © 1977 Daniel Manus Pinkwater

The Millbrook Press: *Martian Fossils on Earth?* text copyright © 1997 by Alfred B. Bortz, cover copyright © 1997 by Millbrook Press; *Brain Surgery for Beginners and Other Operations for Minors* text copyright © 1993 by Steve Parker, cover copyright © 1993 by David West

Rolf Myller for *How Big Is a Foot?* text and cover copyright © 1962 by Rolf Myller, published by Dell Yearling

National Geographic Society: *Light Shining Through the Mist: A Photobiography of Dian Fossey* text copyright © 1998 by Tom L. Matthews, cover copyright © 1998 by National Geographic Society

Orchard Books: *Nothing But the Truth* text copyright © 1991 by Avi, cover copyright © 1991 by Peter Catalanotto

The Penguin Group: *Cam Jansen and the Mystery of the Stolen Corn Popper* text copyright © 1986 by David A. Adler, cover copyright © 1986 by Susanna Natti; *Amber Brown Is Not a Crayon* text copyright © 1994 by Paula Danziger, cover copyright © 1994 by Tony Ross; *Buggy Riddles* text copyright © 1986 by Katy Hall and Lisa Eisenberg, cover copyright © 1986 by Simms Taback; *Horrible Harry in Room 2B* text copyright © 1988 by Suzy Kline, cover copyright © 1988 by Frank Remkiewicz; *What's the Matter with Herbie Jones?* text copyright © 1986 by Suzy Kline, cover copyright © 1986 by Richard Williams; *I Am Rosa Parks* text copyright © 1997 by Rosa Parks, cover copyright © 1997 by Wil Clay; *A Long Way from Chicago* text copyright © 1998 by Richard Peck, cover copyright © 1998 by Steve Cieslawski; *Your Mother Was a Neanderthal* text copyright © 1993 by Jon Scieszka, cover copyright © 1993 by Lane Smith

Random House: *Abe Lincoln's Hat* text copyright © 1994 by Martha Brenner, cover copyright © 1994 by Donald Cook; *The Chalk Box Kid* text copyright © 1987 by Clyde Robert Bulla, cover copyright © 1987 by Thomas B. Allen; *Dinosaur Days* text copyright © 1985 by Joy Cowley, cover copyright © 1985 by Richard Roe; *Moonwalk: The First Trip to the Moon* text copyright © 1989 by Judy Donnelly, cover copyright © 1989 by Dennis Davidson; *The Titanic: Lost . . . and Found* text copyright © 1987 by Judy Donnelly, cover copyright © 1987 by Keith Kohler; *Barry: The Bravest Saint Bernard* text copyright © 1973 by Lynn Hall, cover copyright © 1992 by Antonio Castro; *Baseball's Greatest Hitters* text copyright © 1995, 2000 by S. A. Kramer, cover copyright © 1995 by Jim Campbell; *Dinosaurs Before Dark* text copyright © 1992 by Mary Pope Osborne, cover copyright © 1992 by Sal Murdocca; *Junie B. Jones and the Stupid Smelly Bus* text copyright © 1992 by Barbara Park, cover copyright © 1992 by Denise Brunkus; *Marvin Redpost: Alone in His Teacher's House* text copyright © 1994 by Louis Sachar, cover copyright © 1994 by Barbara Sullivan; *It Is a Good Day to Die* text copyright © 1998 by Herman J. Viola

Scholastic, Inc.: *The Invasion* text copyright © 1996 by Katherine Applegate, cover copyright © 1996 by Scholastic; Animorphs is a registered trademark of Scholastic, Inc.; *The Magic School Bus Inside the Earth* text copyright © 1987 by Joanna Cole, cover copyright © 1997 by Bruce Degen; The Magic School Bus is a registered trademark of Scholastic, Inc.; *Monster Manners* text copyright © 1985 by Joanna Cole, cover copyright © 1985 by Jared Lee; *Red-Eyed Tree Frog* text copyright © 1999 by Joy Cowley, cover copyright © 1999 by Nic Bishop; *Questions and Answers About Weather* text copyright © 1969 by M. Jean Craig, cover copyright © 1996 by Scholastic, Inc.; *Fire!* text copyright © 1998 by Joy Masoff, published by Scholastic Reference, an imprint of Scholastic, Inc.; *. . . If You Lived at the Time of the American Revolution* text copyright © 1997 by Kay Moore, cover copyright © 1997 by Scholastic; *At Her Majesty's Request* text copyright © 1999 by Walter Dean Myers; *The*

Adventures of Captain Underpants text and cover copyright © 1997 by Dav Pilkey, published by Blue Sky Press, an imprint of Scholastic, Inc.; *For YOUR Eyes Only!* text copyright © 1997 by Joanne Rocklin, cover copyright © 1996 by Scholastic, Inc.; *if you only knew* text copyright © 1998 by Rachel Vail, cover illustration copyright © 1998 by Lisa Desimini; *Harry Potter and the Sorcerer's Stone* cover, characters, names and all related indicia are trademarks of Warner Bros. copyright © 2001; *The Journal of Wong Ming-Chung: A Chinese Miner, California, 1852* text copyright © 2000 by Laurence Yep

Simon & Schuster: *The One in the Middle is the Green Kangaroo* text copyright © 1981 by Judy Blume, cover copyright © 1991 by Irene Trivas; *Charlie and the Chocolate Factory* text copyright © 1964 by Roald Dahl, illustration copyright © 1988 by Viking Penguin Inc.; *My Teacher is an Alien* text and cover copyright © 1989 by General Licensing Company; *Bunnicula: A Rabbit-Tale of Mystery* text copyright © 1979 by Deborah and James Howe, cover copyright © 1996 by Alan Daniel; *Tornadoes!* text and cover copyright © 1999 by The Weather Channel, Inc.; *From the Mixed-Up Files of Mrs. Basil E. Frankweiler* text and cover copyright © 1967 by E. L. Konigsburg; *Hatchet* text copyright © 1987 by Gary Paulsen, cover copyright © 1987 by Neil Waldman; *It's Disgusting and We Ate It! True Food Facts from Around the World and Throughout History* text copyright © 1998 by James Solheim, cover copyright © 1998 by Eric Brace; *Peppermints in the Parlor* text copyright © 1980 by Barbara Brooks Wallace, cover copyright © 1996 by Richard Williams

Walker Publishing Company: *Dear Mrs. Ryan, You're Ruining My Life* text copyright © 2000 by Jennifer B. Jones, cover copyright © 2000 by James Bernardin

Watts Publishing Group: *Weirdo's War* text copyright © 1996 by Michael Coleman, cover copyright © 1998 by Walter Lyon Krudop

General Index

NOTE: The 125 featured books are listed alphabetically in a separate Index of Book Titles. The authors of those books appear in the Authors Index.

A

Action. *See* Fast-Paced Plot
Activities, 16, 17–18
Adolescents, 14
Adventure
  Hatchet, 288–289
  Julie of the Wolves, 285–287
  Smugglers, The, 304–305
  Tuck Everlasting, 201–202
  Weirdo's War, 271–273
  Whipping Boy, The, 166–167
Age groups, 2–3, 19. *See also* Reading
    levels; *specific age groups*
Ages 3–8, picture books for, 20–21
Ages 4–8, 52–53
Ages 4–9, 145–146
Ages 5–8, 5, 34–35
Ages 5–9
  easy reader books for, 21–24
  I Wonder Why I Blink, 87–88
  Who Eats What?, 85–86

Age 5 and up, 95–96
Ages 6–8
  Abe Lincoln's Hat, 56–57
  Adventures of Snail at School, The,
    48–49
  Amelia Bedelia, 46–47
  Cat in the Hat, The, 44–45
  Dinosaur Days, 54–55
  Dragon Breath, 71–72
  Emma's Magic Winter, 50–51
  Here Comes the Strikeout, 42–43
  Minnie and Moo Go to the Moon,
    40–41
  Monster Manners, 36–37
  Nate the Great and Me, 75–76
Ages 6–9
  Albertina the Practically Perfect,
    81–82
  Dinosaurs Before Dark, 77–78
  Gus and Grandpa, 38–39
  I Am Rosa Parks, 89–90
  Junie B. Jones and the Stupid Smelly
    Bus, 79–80
  Magic School Bus Inside the Earth,
    The, 142–144
  Marvin Redpost: Alone in His
    Teacher's House, 83–84

Ages 6–9, *continued*
  One in the Middle Is the Green
    Kangaroo, The, 63–64
  Purple Climbing Days, 65–66
Ages 6–10, 149–150
Ages 7–8, 91–92
Ages 7–9
  Amazing Snakes, 140–141
  Barry: The Bravest Saint Bernard,
    153–154
  Baseball's Greatest Hitters, 97–98
  Buggy Riddles, 61–62
  Drinking Gourd, The, 73–74
  Greg's Microscope, 67–68
  Moonwalk, 93–94
  Pirates!, 151–152
Ages 7–10
  chapter books for, 24–25
  Adventures of Captain Underpants,
    The, 114–116
  Amber Brown Is Not a Crayon,
    111–113
  Cam Jansen and the Mystery
    of the Stolen Corn Popper,
    108–110
  Chalk Box Kid, The, 103–105
  Flat Stanley, 106–107
  Horrible Harry in Room 2B,
    101–102
  Little Wolf's Book of Badness,
    137–139
  Not My Dog, 128–129
  Oh No, It's Robert, 135–136
  Parachuting Hamsters and Andy
    Russell, 117–119
  Questions and Answers About
    Weather, 157–158
  Sarah, Plain and Tall, 123–125
  Tornadoes!, 161–162
  Your Mother Was a Neanderthal,
    130–132

Ages 7–11
  Fire!, 155–156
  How to Talk to Your Dog,
    159–160
  . . . If You Lived at the Time of the
    American Revolution, 250–252
Ages 7–12, 244–245
Ages 8–9, 69–70
Ages 8–10, 133–134
Ages 8–11
  Arthur, for the Very First Time,
    176–177
  Math Rashes, 172–173
  Top of the World, The, 147–148
Ages 8–12
  humor of, 5
  All Day Nightmare, 168–169
  Boys Start the War, The, 203–205
  Brain Surgery for Beginners and
    Other Major Operations for
    Minors, 253–254
  Bunnicula, 174–175
  Charlie and the Chocolate
    Factory, 184–185
  Charlotte's Web, 206–208
  Cockroach Cooties, 180–181
  Dear Mrs. Ryan, You're Ruining
    My Life, 195–196
  Doll People, The, 209–211
  Fat Men from Space, 126–127
  Lily's Crossing, 221–223
  Lion, the Witch and the Wardrobe,
    The, 230–232
  Little House on the Prairie,
    192–194
  My Pony Book, 246–247
  My Teacher Is an Alien, 178–179
  Peppermints in the Parlor,
    197–198
  Phantom Tollbooth, The,
    277–278

Sideways Stories from Wayside School, 170–171
Smart Dog, 182–183
Trolls, The, 199–200
Tuck Everlasting, 201–202
What's the Matter with Herbie Jones?, 120–122
Whipping Boy, The, 166–167
Ages 8–13, 241–243, 329–330
Ages 8 and up, 238–240
Ages 9–12
    Anastasia Krupnik, 265–267
    Deep Time Diaries, The., 312–314
    Find the Constellations, 248–249
    For YOUR Eyes Only!, 224–226
    From the Mixed-Up Files of Mrs. Basil E. Frankweiler, 212–214
    Goats, The, 301–303
    Invasion, The, 235–237
    Journal of Wong Ming-Chung, The, 215–217
    Kid Who Only Hit Homers, The, 189–191
    Lives of the Presidents, 255–257
    Long Way from Chicago, A, 218–220
    Maniac Magee, 233–234
    On My Honor, 186–188
    Revenge of the Snob Squad, 227–229
Ages 9–13
    Bloomability, 268–270
    Dr. Fred's Weather Watch, 260–262
    If You Only Knew, 274–276
    In the Huddle with . . . John Elway, 258–259
    Weirdo's War, 271–273
Ages 10–14, 304–305, 334–336

Age 10 and up
    A Is for AARRGH!, 279–281
    Boys' War, The, 320–322
    Cool Women, 309–311
    Go for the Goal, 337–338
    Great Gilly Hopkins, The, 292–294
    Holes, 282–284
    It Is a Good Day to Die, 331–333
    Julie of the Wolves, 285–287
    Kids at Work, 339–341
    Light Shining Through the Mist, 315–316
    No Pretty Pictures, 317–319
    Owl in Love, 290–291
Age 11 and up, 295–297, 323–325
Age 12 and up
    Athletic Shorts, 306–308
    Chinese Cinderella, 342–344
    Giver, The, 298–300
    Hatchet, 288–289
ALL ABOARD READING series, 23, 57, 88
All ages, 326–328
AMERICAN GIRL series, 125
American History, 250–252
Anatomy, 87–88
ANDY RUSSELL series, 119
Animal Behavior, 159–160
Animal Characters, 174–175, 206–208
ANIMORPHS series, 237
Appeal. *See* Reluctant Reader Appeal
Astronomy, 248–249
AT HOME WITH SCIENCE series, 96
Autobiography, 337–338

B

Baseball, 97–98
BEGINNER BOOKS series, 23, 37, 62

Beginning readers. *See* Easy readers

Bentley, Nancy, 2, 3, 27

Best Books for Kids Who (Think They) Hate to Read, The

  using, v, 29–31

  Web site for, vi

Biography

  Abe Lincoln's Hat, 56–57

  At Her Majesty's Request, 334–336

  I Am Rosa Parks, 89–90

  Kids at Work, 339–341

  Light Shining Through the Mist, 315–316

  Lives of the Presidents, 255–257

  Sports Biography, 258–259

Brain Function, 253–254

C

CAM JANSEN MYSTERY series, 110, 118

CAPTAIN UNDERPANTS series, 116

Carter, Betty, 9, 14

Categories. *See* Fiction; Genres; Nonfiction; Reading levels

Center for Reading and Writing (Rider University), 3, 12, 16

Chapter books

  about, 24–25, 31

  reading recommendations, 99–162

CHRONICLE OF AMERICA series, 155–156

CHRONICLES OF NARNIA series, 232

Civil War, 320–322

Comprehension

  reading comfort level vs., 7, 13, 14–15

  reading difficulties and, 1–2

Concise Chapters

  about, 6–7

  Abigail Takes the Wheel, 69–70

Adventures of Captain Underpants, The, 114–116

Adventures of Snail at School, The, 48–49

Albertina the Practically Perfect, 81–82

All Day Nightmare, 168–169

Amazing Snakes, 140–141

Amber Brown Is Not a Crayon, 111–113

Arthur, for the Very First Time, 176–177

At Her Majesty's Request, 334–336

Athletic Shorts, 306–308

Baseball's Greatest Hitters, 97–98

Bloomability, 268–270

Boys Start the War, The, 203–205

Boys' War, The, 320–322

Bunnicula, 174–175

Cam Jansen and the Mystery of the Stolen Corn Popper, 108–110

Chalk Box Kid, The, 103–105

Charlie and the Chocolate Factory, 184–185

Charlotte's Web, 206–208

Chinese Cinderella, 342–344

Cockroach Cooties, 180–181

Cool Women, 309–311

Dear Mrs. Ryan, You're Ruining My Life, 195–196

Deep Time Diaries, The, 312–314

Dig and Sow!, 95–96

Dinosaurs Before Dark, 77–78

Doll People, The, 209–211

Dr. Fred's Weather Watch, 260–262

Drinking Gourd, The, 73–74

Emma's Magic Winter, 50–51

Find the Constellations, 248–249

Fire!, 155–156

Flat Stanley, 106–107

For YOUR Eyes Only!, 224–226

Giver, The, 298–300

Go for the Goal, 337–338

Gus and Grandpa, 38–39

Hatchet, 288–289

Holes, 282–284

Horrible Harry in Room 2B, 101–102

I Am Rosa Parks, 89–90

. . . If You Lived at the Time of the American Revolution, 250–252

If You Only Knew, 274–276

In the Huddle with . . . John Elway, 258–259

Invasion, The, 235–237

It Is a Good Day to Die, 331–333

It's Disgusting and We Ate It!, 244–245

Journal of Wong Ming-Chung, The, 215–217

Junie B. Jones and the Stupid Smelly Bus, 79–80

Kids at Work, 339–341

Kid Who Only Hit Homers, The, 189–191

Lily's Crossing, 221–223

Lion, the Witch and the Wardrobe, The, 230–232

Little Fox's Secret, 133–134

Little House on the Prairie, 192–194

Lives of the Presidents, 255–257

Long Way from Chicago, A, 218–220

Martian Fossils on Earth?, 329–330

Marvin Redpost: Alone in His Teacher's House, 83–84

Math Rashes, 172–173

Minnie and Moo Go to the Moon, 40–41

My Pony Book, 246–247

My Teacher Is an Alien, 178–179

Nate the Great and Me, 75–76

New Way Things Work, The, 326–328

No More Strangers Now, 323–325

Nothing but the Truth, 295–297

Not My Dog, 128–129

Oh No, It's Robert, 135–136

One in the Middle Is the Green Kangaroo, The, 63–64

On My Honor, 186–188

Parachuting Hamsters and Andy Russell, 117–119

Peppermints in the Parlor, 197–198

Pirates!, 151–152

Pond Life, 149–150

Questions and Answers About Weather, 157–158

Sarah, Plain and Tall, 123–125

Sideways Stories from Wayside School, 170–171

Smart Dog, 182–183

Smugglers, The, 304–305

Titanic, The, 91–92

Tornadoes!, 161–162

Trolls, The, 199–200

Tuck Everlasting, 201–202

Weirdo's War, 271–273

What's the Matter with Herbie Jones?, 120–122

Whipping Boy, The, 166–167

Your Mother Was a Neanderthal, 130–132

Contemporary Fiction

Albertina the Practically Perfect, 81–82

Contemporary Fiction, *continued*
   Amber Brown Is Not a Crayon,
     111–113
   Anastasia Krupnik, 265–267
   Arthur, for the Very First Time,
     176–177
   Athletic Shorts, 306–308
   Bloomability, 268–270
   Boys Start the War, The, 203–205
   Chalk Box Kid, The, 103–105
   Cockroach Cooties, 180–181
   Dear Mrs. Ryan, You're Ruining
     My Life, 195–196
   Emma's Magic Winter, 50–51
   For YOUR Eyes Only!, 224–226
   From the Mixed-Up Files of Mrs.
     Basil E. Frankweiler, 212–214
   Goats, The, 301–303
   Great Gilly Hopkins, The, 292–294
   Greg's Microscope, 67–68
   Gus and Grandpa, 38–39
   If You Only Knew, 274–276
   Julie of the Wolves, 285–287
   Junie B. Jones and the Stupid
     Smelly Bus, 79–80
   Maniac Magee, 233–234
   Marvin Redpost: Alone in His
     Teacher's House, 83–84
   My Teacher Is an Alien, 178–179
   Nothing but the Truth, 295–297
   Not My Dog, 128–129
   Oh No, It's Robert, 135–136
   One in the Middle Is the Green
     Kangaroo, The, 63–64
   On My Honor, 186–188
   Purple Climbing Days, 65–66
   Revenge of the Snob Squad,
     227–229
   Weirdo's War, 271–273
   What's the Matter with Herbie
     Jones?, 120–122

D

DEAR AMERICA series, 217
DELL YEARLING FIRST CHOICE
   CHAPTER BOOKS series, 107
Dinosaurs, 54–55
DINOTOPIA series, 314
Dolls, 209–211
DORLING KINDERSLEY series, 24, 146

E

Easy readers
   about, 21–24
   reading recommendations, 23–24,
     33–57, 59–98
Ecology, 85–86
EEK! STORIES TO MAKE YOU SHRIEK
   series, 71–72
Extracurricular activities, 16, 17–18
EYEWITNESS JUNIORS series, 141
EYEWITNESS READERS series, 152

F

Fable, 34–35
Fantasy
   Ella Enchanted, 238–240
   Harry Potter and the Sorcerer's
     Stone, 241–243
   Lion, the Witch and the Wardrobe,
     The, 230–232
   Phantom Tollbooth, The,
     277–278
   Tuck Everlasting, 201–202
Fast-Paced Plot
   about, 6
   Abe Lincoln's Hat, 56–57
   Abigail Takes the Wheel, 69–70
   Adventures of Captain Underpants,
     The, 114–116
   A Is for AARRGH!, 279–281

Albertina the Practically Perfect, 81–82

All Day Nightmare, 168–169

Amber Brown Is Not a Crayon, 111–113

Amelia Bedelia, 46–47

Anastasia Krupnik, 265–267

Athletic Shorts, 306–308

Barry: The Bravest Saint Bernard, 153–154

Boys Start the War, The, 203–205

Bunnicula, 174–175

Cam Jansen and the Mystery of the Stolen Corn Popper, 108–110

Cat in the Hat, The, 44–45

Charlie and the Chocolate Factory, 184–185

Dear Mrs. Ryan, You're Ruining My Life, 195–196

Deep Time Diaries, The, 312–314

Dinosaurs Before Dark, 77–78

Doll People, The, 209–211

Dragon Breath, 71–72

Drinking Gourd, The, 73–74

Ella Enchanted, 238–240

Emma's Magic Winter, 50–51

Fat Men from Space, 126–127

Flat Stanley, 106–107

From the Mixed-Up Files of Mrs. Basil E. Frankweiler, 212–214

Giver, The, 298–300

Goats, The, 301–303

Go for the Goal, 337–338

Great Gilly Hopkins, The, 292–294

Greg's Microscope, 67–68

Harry Potter and the Sorcerer's Stone, 241–243

Hatchet, 288–289

Here Comes the Strikeout, 42–43

Holes, 282–284

Horrible Harry in Room 2B, 101–102

How Big Is a Foot?, 34–35

In the Huddle with . . . John Elway, 258–259

Invasion, The, 235–237

Julie of the Wolves, 285–287

Junie B. Jones and the Stupid Smelly Bus, 79–80

Kid Who Only Hit Homers, The, 189–191

Lily's Crossing, 221–223

Lion, the Witch and the Wardrobe, The, 230–232

Little Fox's Secret, 133–134

Little Wolf's Book of Badness, 137–139

Long Way from Chicago, A, 218–220

Magic School Bus Inside the Earth, The, 142–144

Maniac Magee, 233–234

Marvin Redpost: Alone in His Teacher's House, 83–84

Math Rashes, 172–173

Minnie and Moo Go to the Moon, 40–41

Monster Manners, 36–37

Moonwalk, 93–94

My Teacher Is an Alien, 178–179

Nate the Great and Me, 75–76

No Pretty Pictures, 317–319

Nothing but the Truth, 295–297

Oh No, It's Robert, 135–136

One in the Middle Is the Green Kangaroo, The, 63–64

On My Honor, 186–188

Owl in Love, 290–291

Parachuting Hamsters and Andy Russell, 117–119

Fast-Paced Plot, *continued*
　Peppermints in the Parlor, 197–198
　Phantom Tollbooth, The,
　　277–278
　Purple Climbing Days, 65–66
　Red-Eyed Tree Frog, 52–53
　Revenge of the Snob Squad,
　　227–229
　*Sideways Stories from Wayside
　　School,* 170–171
　Smart Dog, 182–183
　Smugglers, The, 304–305
　Steam, Smoke, and Steel, 145–146
　Titanic, The, 91–92
　Trolls, The, 199–200
　Tuck Everlasting, 201–202
　Weirdo's War, 271–273
　*What's the Matter with Herbie
　　Jones?,* 120–122
　Whipping Boy, The, 166–167
　Your Mother Was a Neanderthal,
　　130–132
FEAR STREET series, 169
Fiction, about, 25, 27–28
Field trips, 16
Fifth grade, lap time for, 12–13
Fire Fighting, 155–156
FIRST GRADE FRIENDS series, 23
First grade reading difficulties, 2
Food, 244–245
"Formula for Failure," 9, 14
Fourth grade
　lap time, 12–13
　reading difficulties, 1–2
FREAKY FACTS TRIVIA series, 8
FRIENDSHIP RING series, 276

G

Genres, 29, 30. *See also specific genres*
Geology, 142–144, 312–314

GIVE YOURSELF GOOSEBUMPS
　series, 169
Glazer, Susan Mandel, 3, 12, 16
GOOSEBUMPS series, 169
Grade levels. *See also* Reading levels;
　specific grade levels
　lap time and, 12–13
　middle grades, 26–27,
　　31, 163
　reading difficulties for, 1–2
Greene, Graham, 1
GROSSET ALL ABOARD READING
　series, 23, 57, 88

H

HANDS-ON SCIENCE series, 96
HARPER I CAN READ series, 23, 47,
　49, 55
HARRY POTTER series, 6, 243
HELLO MATH READER!
　series, 23, 35
HELLO READER! series, 23, 53, 90,
　92, 154
HERBIE JONES series, 122
Historical Fiction
　Abigail Takes the Wheel, 69–70
　Drinking Gourd, The, 73–74
　Journal of Wong Ming-Chung, The,
　　215–217
　Lily's Crossing, 221–223
　Little Fox's Secret, 133–134
　Little House on the Prairie,
　　192–194
　Long Way from Chicago, A,
　　218–220
　Sarah, Plain and Tall, 123–125
　Smugglers, The, 304–305
Historical Mystery, 197–198
Horror, 168–169
HOW THINGS WORK series, 146

Humor

about, 5, 22–23

Adventures of Captain Underpants, The, 114–116

Adventures of Snail at School, The, 48–49

A Is for AARRGH!, 279–281

Amber Brown Is Not a Crayon, 111–113

Amelia Bedelia, 46–47

Anastasia Krupnik, 265–267

Arthur, for the Very First Time, 176–177

Athletic Shorts, 306–308

Bloomability, 268–270

Boys Start the War, The, 203–205

Brain Surgery for Beginners and Other Major Operations for Minors, 253–254

Buggy Riddles, 61–62

Bunnicula, 174–175

Cat in the Hat, The, 44–45

Charlie and the Chocolate Factory, 184–185

Charlotte's Web, 206–208

Cockroach Cooties, 180–181

Cool Women, 309–311

Dear Mrs. Ryan, You're Ruining My Life, 195–196

Deep Time Diaries, The, 312–314

Dig and Sow!, 95–96

Dinosaurs Before Dark, 77–78

Doll People, The, 209–211

Ella Enchanted, 238–240

Fat Men From Space, 126–127

Flat Stanley, 106–107

For YOUR Eyes Only!, 224–226

From the Mixed-Up Files of Mrs. Basil E. Frankweiler, 212–214

Great Gilly Hopkins, The, 292–294

Gus and Grandpa, 38–39

Harry Potter and the Sorcerer's Stone, 241–243

Holes, 282–284

Horrible Harry in Room 2B, 101–102

How Big Is a Foot?, 34–35

How to Talk to Your Dog, 159–160

If You Only Knew, 274–276

It's Disgusting and We Ate It!, 244–245

Junie B. Jones and the Stupid Smelly Bus, 79–80

Little Wolf's Book of Badness, 137–139

Long Way from Chicago, A, 218–220

Magic School Bus Inside the Earth, The, 142–144

Maniac Magee, 233–234

Marvin Redpost: Alone in His Teacher's House, 83–84

Math Rashes, 172–173

Minnie and Moo Go to the Moon, 40–41

Monster Manners, 36–37

My Teacher Is an Alien, 178–179

Nate the Great and Me, 75–76

Not My Dog, 128–129

Oh No, It's Robert, 135–136

One in the Middle Is the Green Kangaroo, The, 63–64

Owl in Love, 290–291

Parachuting Hamsters and Andy Russell, 117–119

Phantom Tollbooth, The, 277–278

Purple Climbing Days, 65–66

Revenge of the Snob Squad, 227–229

Humor, *continued*
  Sideways Stories from Wayside School, 170–171
  Smart Dog, 182–183
  Trolls, The, 199–200
  What's the Matter with Herbie Jones?, 120–122
  Whipping Boy, The, 166–167
  Your Mother Was a Neanderthal, 130–132
Humorous Contemporary Fiction
  Math Rashes, 172–173
  Sideways Stories from Wayside School, 170–171
  Smart Dog, 182–183
  Trolls, The, 199–200
Humorous Fantasy, 36–37, 184–185
Humorous Fiction
  Adventures of Captain Underpants, The, 114–116
  A Is for AARRGH!, 279–281
  Amelia Bedelia, 46–47
  Cat in the Hat, The, 44–45
  Flat Stanley, 106–107
  Holes, 282–284
  Horrible Harry in Room 2B, 101–102
  Little Wolf's Book of Badness, 137–139
  Whipping Boy, The, 166–167
  Your Mother Was a Neanderthal, 130–132
Humorous Science, 126–127

I

I CAN READ series, 23, 47, 49, 55
Illustrations. *See* Visual Appeal
Inside the Mind of a Child, 22, 26
Instructional reading level, 3

Internet. *See* Web sites
I WONDER WHY . . . series, 88

J

JUNIE B. JONES series, 79–80

K

Kid Relevance
  about, 7
  A Is for AARRGH!, 279–281
  Albertina the Practically Perfect, 81–82
  Amazing Snakes, 140–141
  Amber Brown Is Not a Crayon, 111–113
  Anastasia Krupnik, 265–267
  Arthur, for the Very First Time, 176–177
  Athletic Shorts, 306–308
  Baseball's Greatest Hitters, 97–98
  Bloomability, 268–270
  Boys Start the War, The, 203–205
  Boys' War, The, 320–322
  Brain Surgery for Beginners and Other Major Operations for Minors, 253–254
  Buggy Riddles, 61–62
  Chalk Box Kid, The, 103–105
  Charlie and the Chocolate Factory, 184–185
  Charlotte's Web, 206–208
  Chinese Cinderella, 342–344
  Cockroach Cooties, 180–181
  Cool Women, 309–311
  Dear Mrs. Ryan, You're Ruining My Life, 195–196
  Dig and Sow!, 95–96
  Dinosaur Days, 54–55

Doll People, The, 209–211

Dr. Fred's Weather Watch, 260–262

Ella Enchanted, 238–240

Emma's Magic Winter, 50–51

Fire!, 155–156

For YOUR Eyes Only!, 224–226

From the Mixed-Up Files of Mrs. Basil E. Frankweiler, 212–214

Giver, The, 298–300

Goats, The, 301–303

Go for the Goal, 337–338

Great Gilly Hopkins, The, 292–294

Greg's Microscope, 67–68

Gus and Grandpa, 38–39

Harry Potter and the Sorcerer's Stone, 241–243

Here Comes the Strikeout, 42–43

Holes, 282–284

Horrible Harry in Room 2B, 101–102

How to Talk to Your Dog, 159–160

I Am Rosa Parks, 89–90

. . . If You Lived at the Time of the American Revolution, 250–252

If You Only Knew, 274–276

In the Huddle with . . . John Elway, 258–259

It's Disgusting and We Ate It!, 244–245

I Wonder Why I Blink, 87–88

Julie of the Wolves, 285–287

Junie B. Jones and the Stupid Smelly Bus, 79–80

Kids at Work, 339–341

Kid Who Only Hit Homers, The, 189–191

Lily's Crossing, 221–223

Lion, the Witch and the Wardrobe, The, 230–232

Little Wolf's Book of Badness, 137–139

Maniac Magee, 233–234

Marvin Redpost: Alone in His Teacher's House, 83–84

My Pony Book, 246–247

New Way Things Work, The, 326–328

No More Strangers Now, 323–325

No Pretty Pictures, 317–319

Nothing but the Truth, 295–297

Not My Dog, 128–129

Oh No, It's Robert, 135–136

One in the Middle Is the Green Kangaroo, The, 63–64

On My Honor, 186–188

Owl in Love, 290–291

Purple Climbing Days, 65–66

Questions and Answers About Weather, 157–158

Revenge of the Snob Squad, 227–229

Sarah, Plain and Tall, 123–125

Smart Dog, 182–183

Tornadoes!, 161–162

Tuck Everlasting, 201–202

Weirdo's War, 271–273

What's the Matter with Herbie Jones?, 120–122

KIDS OF THE POLK STREET SCHOOL series, 66

KINGFISHER BACKYARD BOOKS series, 24

L

Language skills, oral, 16–17

Lap time, 12–13

Learning to love reading, 9–18
    discussing books and, 13–14
    easy readers for, 22
    lap time for, 12–13
    oral language needed for, 16–17
    personal interests and, iv, 10–11
    reading levels and, 14–15
    self-selecting books for, 3, 11–12
    through activities, 16
    through life experiences, 15
    through parents' example, 10
    time available for, 17–18
LET'S-READ-AND-FIND-OUT
        SCIENCE series, 86
LITTLE HOUSE series, 194
LOOK CLOSER series, 150
Love of reading. See Learning to love
    reading

M

Magazines, 11
MAGIC SCHOOL BUS SCIENCE
        CHAPTER BOOK series, 144
Magic School Bus series, 144
Magic Tree House series, 77–78
Mann Middle School (Colorado),
        2, 27
MARVIN REDPOST series, 83–84
Memoirs, 317–319, 342–344
Meteorites, 329–330
Meteorology, 260–262
Middle grades
    about, 26–27, 31, 163
    reading recommendations, 163–262
Middle school, reading difficulties
        during, 1–2
Monitoring your child's reading, 12
Mountaineering, 147–148
Movies, novelizations of, 4
MY NAME IS AMERICA series, 217

Mystery. See also Suspense
    All Day Nightmare, 168–169
    Bunnicula, 174–175
    Cam Jansen and the Mystery of the
        Stolen Corn Popper, 108–110
    From the Mixed-Up Files of Mrs.
        Basil E. Frankweiler, 212–214
    Historical Mystery, 197–198
    Nate the Great and Me, 75–76
    Parachuting Hamsters and Andy
        Russell, 117–119

N

NARNIA series, 232
NATE THE GREAT series, 75–76
Native American History, 331–333
Nonfiction, about, 24, 25, 28

O

Oral language skills, 16–17

P

Paleontology, 312–314
Photographs. See Visual Appeal
Picture books, 20–21
Pirates, 151–152
Plants, 95–96
Pond Flora and Fauna, 149–150
Ponies, 246–247

Q

QUESTIONS & ANSWERS series, 249

R

Race Relations, 323–325
RANDOM HOUSE BEGINNER BOOKS
    series, 23, 37, 62

RANDOM HOUSE STEP INTO READING series, 23, 24, 57, 92, 94, 98, 152
Reading aloud, 12–13, 20
Reading difficulties, 1–2
Reading Is Fundamental (RIF) organization, 11, 17
Reading levels. *See also specific age groups*
  chapter books, 24–25, 31, 99–162
  comfort vs. comprehension, 7, 13, 14–15
  easy readers, 21–24, 33–57, 59–98
  middle grades, 26–27, 31, 163, 163–262
  overview, 2–4, 29, 30–31
  picture books, 20–22
  recreational vs. instructional, 3
  variety in, 14–15
  young adult, 27–28, 31, 263–344
Reluctant reader, described, 1–2
Reluctant Reader Appeal, 5–8. *See also specific categories*
  Concise Chapters, 6–7
  Fast-Paced Plot, 6
  Humor, 5
  Kid Relevance, 7
  Suitable Text, 7
  Unique Presentation, 8
  Visual Appeal, 8
  Well-Defined Characters, 5–6
Rescue Dogs, 153–154
Riddles, 61–62
RIF (Reading Is Fundamental) organization, 11, 17

S

SCHOLASTIC CHRONICLE OF AMERICA series, 155–156

SCHOLASTIC HELLO MATH READER! series, 23, 35
SCHOLASTIC HELLO READER! series, 23, 53, 90, 92, 154
SCHOLASTIC QUESTIONS & ANSWERS series, 249
SCHOLASTIC'S MAGIC SCHOOL BUS series, 144
School Library Journal, 9
Science Fiction
  Giver, The, 298–300
  Invasion, The, 235–237
  My Teacher Is an Alien, 178–179
SCIENCE FUNDAMENTALS series, 262
Self-help books, 26
Series books
  about, 22
  ALL ABOARD READING, 23, 57, 88
  AMERICAN GIRL, 125
  ANDY RUSSELL, 119
  ANIMORPHS, 237
  AT HOME WITH SCIENCE, 96
  CAM JANSEN, 110, 118
  CAPTAIN UNDERPANTS, 116
  CHRONICLES OF NARNIA, 232
  DEAR AMERICA, 217
  DELL YEARLING FIRST CHOICE CHAPTER BOOKS, 107
  DINOTOPIA, 314
  DORLING KINDERSLEY, 24, 146
  EEK! STORIES TO MAKE YOU SHRIEK, 71–72
  EYEWITNESS JUNIORS, 141
  EYEWITNESS READERS, 152
  FEAR STREET, 169
  FIRST GRADE FRIENDS, 23
  FREAKY FACTS TRIVIA, 8
  FRIENDSHIP RING, 276
  GIVE YOURSELF GOOSEBUMPS, 169
  GOOSEBUMPS, 169
  HANDS-ON SCIENCE, 96

Series Books, *continued*
   HARPER I CAN READ, 23, 47,
     49, 55
   HARRY POTTER, 6, 243
   HERBIE JONES, 122
   HOW THINGS WORK, 146
   I WONDER WHY . . . , 88
   JUNIE B. JONES, 79–80
   KIDS OF THE POLK STREET
     SCHOOL, 66
   KINGFISHER BACKYARD BOOKS, 24
   LET'S-READ-AND-FIND-OUT
     SCIENCE, 86
   LITTLE HOUSE, 194
   LOOK CLOSER, 150
   MAGIC SCHOOL BUS, 144
   MAGIC SCHOOL BUS SCIENCE
     CHAPTER BOOK, 144
   MAGIC TREE HOUSE, 77–78
   MARVIN REDPOST, 83–84
   MY NAME IS AMERICA, 217
   NATE THE GREAT, 75–76
   RANDOM HOUSE BEGINNER
     BOOKS, 23, 37, 62
   RANDOM HOUSE STEP INTO
     READING, 23, 24, 57, 92, 94,
     98, 152
   SCHOLASTIC CHRONICLE OF
     AMERICA, 155–156
   SCHOLASTIC HELLO MATH
     READER!, 23, 35
   SCHOLASTIC HELLO READER!, 23,
     53, 90, 92, 154
   SCHOLASTIC QUESTIONS &
     ANSWERS, 249
   SCIENCE FUNDAMENTALS, 262
   SNOB SQUAD, 227–229
   TIME WARP TRIO, 131–132
   WEATHER CHANNEL
     PRESENTS, 162
   A WORLD OF DIFFERENCE, 245

Shipwrecks, 91–92
Snakes, 140–141
SNOB SQUAD series, 227–229
Soccer Techniques, 337–338
Social Reform, 339–341
South Africa, 323–325
Space Travel, 93–94
Spooky Fiction, 71–72
Sports, 42–43, 306–308
Sports Biography, 258–259
Sports Fiction, 189–191
STEP INTO READING series, 23, 24,
   57, 92, 94, 98, 152
Supernatural, 290–291
Suspense, 197–198

T

Talking Animals, 48–49, 137–139
Technology, 326–328
Teenagers, discussing books with, 14
Television, 4, 15, 17
Tests, 2, 3
Texas Women's University's School
   of Library and Information
   Studies, 9
Third grade reading difficulties, 1–2
Time Travel, 77–78, 130–132
TIME WARP TRIO series, 131–132
Trains, 145–146
Transition books. *See* Chapter books
Tree Frogs, 52–53

U

Unique Presentation
   about, 8
   Abe Lincoln's Hat, 56–57
   All Day Nightmare, 168–169
   Amazing Snakes, 140–141
   At Her Majesty's Request, 334–336

Barry: The Bravest Saint Bernard,
    153–154
Boys' War, The, 320–322
*Brain Surgery for Beginners and
    Other Major Operations for
    Minors,* 253–254
Chinese Cinderella, 342–344
Cool Women, 309–311
Deep Time Diaries, The, 312–314
Dig and Sow!, 95–96
Dinosaur Days, 54–55
Dr. Fred's Weather Watch, 260–262
Find the Constellations, 248–249
Fire!, 155–156
Go for the Goal, 337–338
How Big Is a Foot?, 34–35
How to Talk to Your Dog, 159–160
*. . . If You Lived at the Time of the
    American Revolution,* 250–252
It Is a Good Day to Die, 331–333
It's Disgusting and We Ate It!,
    244–245
I Wonder Why I Blink, 87–88
Journal of Wong Ming-Chung, The,
    215–217
Kids at Work, 339–341
Light Shining Through the Mist,
    315–316
Little House on the Prairie,
    192–194
Lives of the Presidents, 255–257
*Magic School Bus Inside the Earth,
    The,* 142–144
Martian Fossils on Earth?, 329–330
My Pony Book, 246–247
New Way Things Work, The,
    326–328
No More Strangers Now, 323–325
No Pretty Pictures, 317–319
Nothing but the Truth, 295–297
Phantom Tollbooth, The, 277–278

Pirates!, 151–152
Pond Life, 149–150
*Questions and Answers About
    Weather,* 157–158
Red-Eyed Tree Frog, 52–53
Steam, Smoke, and Steel, 145–146
Top of the World, The, 147–148
Tornadoes!, 161–162
Who Eats What?, 85–86
Using this book, 29–31

V

Visual Appeal
    about, 8
    *Adventures of Captain Underpants,
        The,* 114–116
    Amazing Snakes, 140–141
    Baseball's Greatest Hitters, 97–98
    Boys' War, The, 320–322
    *Brain Surgery for Beginners and
        Other Major Operations for
        Minors,* 253–254
    Buggy Riddles, 61–62
    Cool Women, 309–311
    Deep Time Diaries, The, 312–314
    Dig and Sow!, 95–96
    Dinosaur Days, 54–55
    Find the Constellations, 248–249
    Fire!, 155–156
    Greg's Microscope, 67–68
    *. . . If You Lived at the Time of the
        American Revolution,* 250–252
    It's Disgusting and We Ate It!,
        244–245
    I Wonder Why I Blink, 87–88
    Kids at Work, 339–341
    Light Shining Through the Mist,
        315–316
    *Magic School Bus Inside the Earth,
        The,* 142–144

Visual Appeal, *continued*
  Martian Fossils on Earth?,
    329–330
  Moonwalk, 93–94
  My Pony Book, 246–247
  New Way Things Work, The,
    326–328
  No More Strangers Now,
    323–325
  Pirates!, 151–152
  Pond Life, 149–150
  Red-Eyed Tree Frog, 52–53
  Steam, Smoke, and Steel, 145–146
  Titanic, The, 91–92
  Top of the World, The, 147–148
  Tornadoes!, 161–162
  Who Eats What?, 85–86
Vocabulary, oral, 16–17

W

Weather, 157–158, 161–162
WEATHER CHANNEL PRESENTS
  series, 162
Web sites
  for *Best Books for Kids . . .* , vi
  Reading Is Fundamental organi-
    zation, 11
  role of reading for, 10
Well-Defined Characters
  about, 5–6
  Abe Lincoln's Hat, 56–57
  *Adventures of Captain Underpants,
    The*, 114–116
  A Is for AARRGH!, 279–281
  Albertina the Practically Perfect,
    81–82
  Amber Brown Is Not a Crayon,
    111–113
  Amelia Bedelia, 46–47

Anastasia Krupnik, 265–267
Arthur, for the Very First Time,
  176–177
At Her Majesty's Request,
  334–336
Athletic Shorts, 306–308
Bloomability, 268–270
Boys Start the War, The, 203–205
Bunnicula, 174–175
*Cam Jansen and the Mystery
  of the Stolen Corn Popper*,
  108–110
Cat in the Hat, The, 44–45
Chalk Box Kid, The, 103–105
Charlie and the Chocolate Factory,
  184–185
Charlotte's Web, 206–208
Chinese Cinderella, 342–344
Cockroach Cooties, 180–181
*Dear Mrs. Ryan, You're Ruining
  My Life*, 195–196
Dinosaurs Before Dark, 77–78
Doll People, The, 209–211
Dragon Breath, 71–72
Drinking Gourd, The, 73–74
Ella Enchanted, 238–240
Emma's Magic Winter, 50–51
Fat Men from Space, 126–127
For YOUR Eyes Only!, 224–226
*From the Mixed-Up Files of Mrs.
  Basil E. Frankweiler*, 212–214
Giver, The, 298–300
Goats, The, 301–303
Go for the Goal, 337–338
Great Gilly Hopkins, The,
  292–294
Gus and Grandpa, 38–39
*Harry Potter and the Sorcerer's
  Stone*, 241–243
Hatchet, 288–289

Here Comes the Strikeout, 42–43

Holes, 282–284

Horrible Harry in Room 2B, 101–102

If You Only Knew, 274–276

Invasion, The, 235–237

It Is a Good Day to Die, 331–333

Journal of Wong Ming-Chung, The, 215–217

Julie of the Wolves, 285–287

Junie B. Jones and the Stupid Smelly Bus, 79–80

Light Shining Through the Mist, 315–316

Lily's Crossing, 221–223

Lion, the Witch and the Wardrobe, The, 230–232

Little Fox's Secret, 133–134

Little House on the Prairie, 192–194

Little Wolf's Book of Badness, 137–139

Lives of the Presidents, 255–257

Long Way from Chicago, A, 218–220

Magic School Bus Inside the Earth, The, 142–144

Maniac Magee, 233–234

Marvin Redpost: Alone in His Teacher's House, 83–84

Math Rashes, 172–173

Minnie and Moo Go to the Moon, 40–41

Monster Manners, 36–37

My Teacher Is an Alien, 178–179

Nate the Great and Me, 75–76

No More Strangers Now, 323–325

No Pretty Pictures, 317–319

Not My Dog, 128–129

Oh No, It's Robert, 135–136

One in the Middle Is the Green Kangaroo, The, 63–64

Owl in Love, 290–291

Parachuting Hamsters and Andy Russell, 117–119

Peppermints in the Parlor, 197–198

Phantom Tollbooth, The, 277–278

Pirates!, 151–152

Purple Climbing Days, 65–66

Revenge of the Snob Squad, 227–229

Sarah, Plain and Tall, 123–125

Sideways Stories from Wayside School, 170–171

Smart Dog, 182–183

Smugglers, The, 304–305

Trolls, The, 199–200

Tuck Everlasting, 201–202

Weirdo's War, 271–273

Whipping Boy, The, 166–167

Your Mother Was a Neanderthal, 130–132

Women's Studies, 309–311

World History, 244–245

A WORLD OF DIFFERENCE series, 245

Y

Young adult

about, 27–28, 31

reading recommendations, 263–344

Author Index

A

Adler, David, 108–110, 117–119
Applegate, K. A., 235–237
Avi, 69, 295–297
Avison, Brigid, 87–88

B

Babbitt, Natalie, 201–202
Bauer, Marion Dane, 186–188
Blume, Judy, 63–64
Bortz, Fred, 260–262, 329–330
Brenner, Martha, 56
Brooke, William, 279–281
Brown, Jeff, 106–107
Bulla, Clyde Robert, 103–105

C

Cazet, Denys, 40–41
Chipman, Dawn, 309–311
Christopher, Matt, 189–191,
    258–259
Cole, Brock, 301–303
Cole, Joanna, 36–37, 142–144

Coleman, Michael, 271–273
Coville, Bruce, 178–179
Cowley, Joy, 52–53
Craig, M. Jean, 157–158
Creech, Sharon, 268–270
Crutcher, Chris, 306–308

D

Dahl, Roald, 184–185
Danziger, Paula, 111–113
Donnelly, Judy, 91–94

E

Eisenberg, Lisa, 61–62
Evans, Douglas, 172–173

F

Finley, Mary Peace, 133–134
Fleischman, Sid, 166–167
Florence, Mari, 309–311
Fowler, Susi Gregg, 81–82
Freedman, Russell, 339–341

G

George, Jean Craighead, 159–160, 285–287
Giff, Patricia Reilly, 65–66, 221–223
Godwin, Laura, 209–211

H

Hall, Katy, 61–62
Hall, Lynn, 153–154
Hamm, Mia, 337–338
Haskins, Jim, 89–90
Heifetz, Aaron, 337–338
Horvath, Polly, 199–200
Howe, Deborah, 174–175
Howe, James, 174–175

J

Jenkins, Steve, 147–148
Jones, Jennifer, 195–196
Juster, Norton, 277–278

K

Kessler, Leonard, 42–43
Kindl, Patrice, 290–291
Kline, Suzy, 101–102, 120–122
Konigsburg, E. L., 212–214
Kramer, S. A., 97–98
Krull, Kathleen, 255–257

L

Lauber, Patricia, 85–86
Lawrence, Iain, 304–305
Levine, Gail Carson, 238–240
Lewis, C. S., 230–232
Little, Jean, 50–51
Lobb, Janice, 95–96

Lobel, Anita, 317–319
Lowry, Lois, 265–267, 298–300

M

Macaulay, David, 326–328
MacLachlan, Patricia, 123–125, 176–177
Mah, Adeline Yen, 342–344
Martin, Ann, 209–211
Masoff, Joy, 155–156
Matthews, Tom, 315–316
Maynard, Christopher, 151–152
McKee, Tim, 323–325
Meyers, Walter Dean, 334–336
Mills, Claudia, 38–39
Milton, Joyce, 54–55
Monjo, F. N., 73–74
Moore, Kay, 250–252
Murphy, Jim, 320–322
Myller, Rolf, 34–35

N

Naylor, Phyllis Reynolds, 203–205
Nelson, Pam, 309–311

O

O'Brien, Patrick, 145–146
O'Connor, Jane, 71–72
Osborne, Mary Pope, 77–78

P

Parish, Peggy, 46–47
Park, Barbara, 79–80
Parker, Steve, 253–254
Parks, Rosa, 89–90
Parsons, Alexandra, 140–141

Paterson, Katherine, 292–294
Paulsen, Gary, 288–289
Peck, Richard, 218–220
Peters, Julie Anne, 227–229
Pilkey, Dav, 114–116
Pinkwater, Daniel Manus, 126–127
Pritchard, Louise, 246–247

R

Raham, Gary, 312–314
Rey, H. A., 248–249
Rocklin, Joanne, 22, 26, 224–226
Rodowsky, Colby, 128–129
Rose, Sally, 161–162
Rowling, J. K., 241–243

S

Sachar, Louis, 83–84, 170–171,
    279–281, 282–284
Scieszka, Jon, 130–132
Selsam, Millicent, 67–68
Seuling, Barbara, 8, 135–136
Seuss, Dr., 1, 44–45
Sharmat, Marjorie Weinman, 75–76
Shepherd, J. Marshall, 260–262

Solheim, James, 244–245
Spinelli, Jerry, 233–234
Stadler, John, 48–49
Stine, R. L., 168–169

T

Taylor, Barbara, 149–150

V

Vail, Rachel, 274–276
Velde, Vivian Vande, 182–183
Viola, Herman, 331–333

W

Wallace, Barbara Brooks, 197–198
Wax, Naomi, 309–311
White, E. B., 206–208
Whybrow, Ian, 137–139
Wilder, Laura Ingalls, 192–194

Y

Yep, Laurence, 180–181, 215–217

Index of Book Titles

A

Abe Lincoln's Hat, 56–57

Abigail Takes the Wheel, 69–70

Adventures of Captain Underpants, The, 114–116

Adventures of Snail at School, The, 48–49

A Is for AARRGH!, 279–281

Albertina the Practically Perfect, 81–82

All Day Nightmare, 168–169

Amazing Snakes, 140–141

Amber Brown Is Not a Crayon, 111–113

Amelia Bedelia, 46–47

Anastasia Krupnik, 265–267

Arthur, for the Very First Time, 176–177

At Her Majesty's Request: An African Princess in Victorian England, 334–336

Athletic Shorts: 6 Short Stories, 306–308

B

Barry: The Bravest Saint Bernard, 153–154

Baseball's Greatest Hitters, 97–98

Bloomability, 268–270

Boys Start the War, The, 203–205

Boys' War: Confederate and Union Soldiers Talk About the Civil War, The, 320–322

Brain Surgery for Beginners and Other Major Operations for Minors: A Scalpel-Free Guide to Your Insides, 253–254

Buggy Riddles, 61–62

Bunnicula: A Rabbit-Tale of Mystery, 174–175

C

Cam Jansen and the Mystery of the Stolen Corn Popper, 108–110

Cat in the Hat, The, 44–45

Chalk Box Kid, The, 103–105

Charlie and the Chocolate Factory, 184–185

Charlotte's Web, 206–208

Chinese Cinderella: The True Story of an Unwanted Daughter, 342–344

Cockroach Cooties, 180–181

Cool Women: The Thinking Girl's Guide to the Hippest Women in History, 309–311

D

Dear Mrs. Ryan, You're Ruining My Life, 195–196
Deep Time Diaries, The, 312–314
Dig and Sow! How Do Plants Grow?, 95–96
Dinosaur Days, 54–55
Dinosaurs Before Dark, 77–78
Doll People, The, 209–211
Dragon Breath, 71–72
Dr. Fred's Weather Watch: Create and Run Your Own Weather Station, 260–262
Drinking Gourd: A Story of the Underground Railroad, The, 73–74

E

Ella Enchanted, 238–240
Emma's Magic Winter, 50–51

F

Fat Men from Space, 126–127
Find the Constellations, 248–249
Fire!, 155–156
Flat Stanley, 106–107
For YOUR Eyes Only!, 224–226
From the Mixed-Up Files of Mrs. Basil E. Frankweiler, 212–214

G

Giver, The, 298–300
Goats, The, 301–303

Go for the Goal: A Champion's Guide to Winning in Soccer, 337–338
Great Gilly Hopkins, The, 292–294
Greg's Microscope, 67–68
Gus and Grandpa, 38–39

H

Harry Potter and the Sorcerer's Stone, 241–243
Hatchet, 288–289
Here Comes the Strikeout, 42–43
Holes, 282–284
Horrible Harry in Room 2B, 101–102
How Big Is a Foot?, 34–35
How to Talk to Your Dog, 159–160

I

I Am Rosa Parks, 89–90
. . . If You Lived at the Time of the American Revolution, 250–252
If You Only Knew, 274–276
In the Huddle with . . . John Elway, 258–259
Invasion, The, 235–237
It Is a Good Day to Die: Indian Eyewitnesses Tell the Story of the Battle of Little Bighorn, 331–333
It's Disgusting and We Ate It! True Food Facts from Around the World, 244–245
I Wonder Why I Blink and Other Questions About My Body, 87–88

J

Journal of Wong Ming-Chung: A
Chinese Miner, California,
1852, The, 215–217
Julie of the Wolves, 285–287
Junie B. Jones and the Stupid Smelly
Bus, 79–80

K

Kids at Work: Lewis Hine and the
Crusade Against Child Labor,
339–341
Kid Who Only Hit Homers, The,
189–191

L

Light Shining Through the Mist: A
Photobiography of Dian Fossey,
315–316
Lily's Crossing, 221–223
Lion, the Witch and the Wardrobe,
The, 230–232
Little Fox's Secret: The Mystery of
Bent's Fort, 133–134
Little House on the Prairie,
192–194
Little Wolf's Book of Badness,
137–139
Lives of the Presidents: Fame, Shame
(and What the Neighbors
Thought), 255–257
Long Way from Chicago, A,
218–220

M

Magic School Bus Inside the Earth,
The, 142–144
Maniac Magee, 233–234

Martian Fossils on Earth?: The Story
of Meteorite ALH 84001,
329–330
Marvin Redpost: Alone in His
Teacher's House, 83–84
Math Rashes, 172–173
Minnie and Moo Go to the Moon,
40–41
Monster Manners, 36–37
Moonwalk: The First Trip to the
Moon, 93–94
My Pony Book, 246–247
My Teacher Is an Alien, 178–179

N

Nate the Great and Me, 75–76
New Way Things Work, The,
326–328
No More Strangers Now: Young Voices
from a New South Africa,
323–325
No Pretty Pictures: A Child of War,
317–319
Nothing but the Truth: A Documentary Novel, 295–297
Not My Dog, 128–129

O

Oh No, It's Robert, 135–136
One in the Middle Is the Green Kan-
garoo, The, 63–64
On My Honor, 186–188
Owl in Love, 290–291

P

Parachuting Hamsters and Andy Russell, 117–119
Peppermints in the Parlor, 197–198

Phantom Tollbooth, The,
    277–278
Pirates!, 151–152
*Pond Life: A Close-Up Look at the
    Natural World,* 149–150
Purple Climbing Days, 65–66

Q

Questions and Answers About Weather,
    157–158

R

Red-Eyed Tree Frog, 52–53
Revenge of the Snob Squad,
    227–229

S

Sarah, Plain and Tall, 123–125
Sideways Stories from Wayside School,
    170–171
Smart Dog, 182–183
Smugglers, The, 304–305

*Steam, Smoke, and Steel: Back in
    Time with Trains,* 145–146

T

Titanic: Lost . . . and Found, The,
    91–92
*Top of the World: Climbing Mount
    Everest, The,* 147–148
Tornadoes!, 161–162
Trolls, The, 199–200
Tuck Everlasting, 201–202

W

Weirdo's War, 271–273
What's the Matter with Herbie Jones?,
    120–122
Whipping Boy, The, 166–167
*Who Eats What? Food Chains and
    Food Webs,* 85–86

Y

Your Mother Was a Neanderthal,
    130–132

About the Author

LAURA BACKES was lucky enough to grow up in a house bursting with reading material because her father was book editor of the *Chicago Tribune* and the *Denver Post* newspapers. Laura has worked in the publishing industry since 1986 as an editor, as a literary agent, and as the publisher of *Children's Book Insider, The Newsletter for Children's Writers.* Laura and her husband, Jon Bard, currently publish The CBI Collection, a variety of how-to books and tools for children's book writers. They also dispense information and advice for children's writers through their Web site Write4Kids at www.write4kids.com. Laura teaches children's book writing workshops and speaks at writer's conferences and parenting groups around the country on creating and choosing books for children. She lives in Fort Collins, Colorado, with her husband, one son, two dogs, and hundreds of books.